Assessing Comment Quality in Object-Oriented Languages

Inauguraldissertation
der Philosophisch-naturwissenschaftlichen Fakultät
der Universität Bern

written by
Pooja Rani
from Panipat, India

Supervisors:
Prof. Dr. O. Nierstrasz
Dr. Sebastiano Panichella

Examiner:
Dr. Alberto Bacchelli

Bern, 31.01.2022   Dean: Prof. Dr. Zoltan Balogh

This dissertation can be downloaded from `scg.unibe.ch`.

Copyright ©2022 by Pooja Rani
`https://poojaruhal.github.io/`

This work is licensed under the terms of the *Creative Commons Attribution– ShareAlike 3.0 Switzerland* license. The license is available at `http://creativecommons.org/licenses/by-sa/3.0/ch/`

Attribution–ShareAlike

First edition, January 2022

A seed, through support, patience, and persistency, becomes a tree.

Abstract

Previous studies have shown that high-quality code comments support developers in software maintenance and program comprehension tasks. However, the semi-structured nature of comments, several conventions to write comments, and the lack of quality assessment tools for all aspects of comments make comment evaluation and maintenance a non-trivial problem. To understand the specification of high-quality comments to build effective assessment tools, our thesis emphasizes *acquiring a multi-perspective view of the comments, which can be approached by analyzing (1) the academic support for comment quality assessment, (2) developer commenting practices across languages, and (3) developer concerns about comments.*

Our findings regarding the *academic support* for assessing comment quality showed that researchers primarily focus on Java in the last decade even though the trend of using polyglot environments in software projects is increasing. Similarly, the trend of analyzing specific types of code comments (method comments, or inline comments) is increasing, but the studies rarely analyze class comments. We found 21 quality attributes that researchers consider to assess comment quality, and manual assessment is still the most commonly used technique to assess various quality attributes. Our analysis of *developer commenting practices* showed that developers embed a mixed level of details in class comments, ranging from high-level class overviews to low-level implementation details across programming languages. They follow style guidelines regarding what information to write in class comments but violate the structure and syntax guidelines. They primarily face problems locating relevant guidelines to write consistent and informative comments, verifying the adherence of their comments to the guidelines, and evaluating the overall state of comment quality.

To help researchers and developers in building comment quality assessment tools, we contribute: (i) a systematic literature review (SLR) of ten years (2010–2020) of research on assessing comment quality, (ii) a taxonomy of quality attributes used to assess comment quality, (iii) an empirically validated taxonomy of class comment information types from three programming languages, (iv) a multi-programming-language approach to automatically identify the comment information types, (v) an empirically validated taxonomy of comment convention-related questions and recommendation from various Q&A forums, and (vi) a tool to gather discussions from multiple developer sources, such as Stack Overflow, and mailing lists.

Our contributions provide various kinds of empirical evidence of the developer's interest in reducing efforts in the software documentation process, of the limited support developers get in automatically assessing comment quality, and of the challenges they face in writing high-quality comments. This work lays the foundation for future effective comment quality assessment tools and techniques.

Acknowledgment

Back in 2017, while working in the software industry, I could have never imagined a Ph.D., until my sudden curiosity about research brought it. For me, the Ph.D. was not about getting a degree or a title, but an adventurous journey to learn about various scientific aspects. I am glad I joined it.

I would like to express my sincere gratitude to a wonderful advisor, Oscar for giving me an opportunity to be part of the Software Composition Group. Your continuous trust, patience, and support made this journey possible and enjoyable. I am very grateful for having another amazing co-advisor, Sebastiano. Your positive attitude and constant belief in me (when I did not) always lifted my spirit. A big thank you to both of you for encouraging my research and helping me grow as a researcher and as a person.

I am thankful to Alberto Bacchelli for accepting to be the external examiner in my Ph.D. committee. I would also like to thank Timo Kehrer for chairing the examination.

As no scientific work is lone work, I want to thank all my collaborators who gave me different perspectives: Andrea for his sincerity, Alexander for his enthusiasm, Mohammad for being critical, Nataliia for her veracity, and Arianna for her calmness during the tight deadlines. A big thanks to the SCG family, who listened, appreciated, and criticized me when necessary. Thank you for all the wonderful SCG trips we could make before the pandemic. I thank Manuel for being my office mate and his insightful discussions, Pascal for inventing "Pooja thingy/proof", and reviewing my thesis in detail, Reza for his funny stories, Nitish for cooking delicious food, Aliaksei for his persuasive Smalltalk discussions, Nevena for WoMentoring, Olie for his cool ideas, and Andrei for his witty jokes.

I am grateful to Bettina, for her immeasurable help and support in all areas, including administrative work. Furthermore, I am indebted to Jonas, Mathias, Lino, Michael, and Suada for their thesis work. I want to thank Pascal, Marcel, Julius, and Silas to ease my life in teaching the P2 course.

I want to thank all of my friends from India and Switzerland for being there for me: Amit for motivating me to pursue a Ph.D. and sustain it, Magdalena and Jyoti for their inspiring science discussions, and Sanjeet for her goodwill. Big thank you to Shailja, Eti, Vaishali, Vishakha, Vishal, Digvijay, Naveen, Lavina, Pallavi, Abhimanyu, and Manish for fun calls.

Above all, I would like to thank my family for their trust in me. I can not express how grateful I am to my mother and father who always supported my education despite all stereotypes and taboos behind girls' education in their society. Your everlasting positivity and prayers have helped me achieve it. I am thankful to Vikram, Mohit, and Sanjeet for challenging my thoughts, but still having faith in me. I hope I can make you all proud.

Contents

Contents   vi

List of Figures   ix

List of Tables   xi

1 Introduction   1
    1.1 Thesis Statement 4
    1.2 Contributions 5
    1.3 Outline 7
    1.4 Study Replicability 9

2 State of the Art   11
    2.1 Academic Support for Comment Quality Assessment 12
       2.1.1 Comment Quality Attributes 12
       2.1.2 Comment Quality Assessment Techniques 13
       2.1.3 Previous SLRs on Code Comments 13
    2.2 Developer Commenting Practices 14
       2.2.1 Comment Information Types 15
       2.2.2 Automation of Comment Information Types 16
       2.2.3 Comment Adherence to Conventions 18
    2.3 Commenting Practice Concerns 19
    2.4 Summary and Conclusion 20

3 Academic Support for Comment Quality Assessment   23
    3.1 Study Design 25
       3.1.1 Research Questions 25
       3.1.2 Data Collection 27
       3.1.3 Data Selection 29
       3.1.4 Data Evaluation 32
    3.2 Results 36

		3.2.1 Comment Types	36
		3.2.2 Comment Quality Attributes	38
		3.2.3 Comment Quality Assessment Techniques	39
		3.2.4 Study Contribution Types	41
		3.2.5 Study Evaluation	42
	3.3	Implications and Discussion	42
	3.4	Threats to Validity	43
	3.5	Summary and Conclusion	44

4 Comment Information Types (CITs)   47
    4.1 Motivation 49
    4.2 Study Design 51
        4.2.1 Research Questions 51
        4.2.2 Data Collection 52
        4.2.3 Analysis Method 56
    4.3 Results 61
        4.3.1 Mapping Taxonomies 62
        4.3.2 CCTM Taxonomy 63
    4.4 Implications and Discussion 67
    4.5 Threats to Validity 69
    4.6 Summary and Conclusion 70

5 Automated Identification of CITs   73
    5.1 Motivation 75
    5.2 Study Design 75
        5.2.1 Data Collection 75
        5.2.2 Analysis Method 76
    5.3 Results 79
    5.4 Implications and Discussion 86
    5.5 Threats to Validity 88
    5.6 Summary and Conclusion 89

6 Comment Adherence to Conventions   91
    6.1 Motivation 93
    6.2 Study Design 94
        6.2.1 Research Questions 94
        6.2.2 Data Collection 95
        6.2.3 Analysis Method 96
    6.3 Results 103
        6.3.1 Comment Conventions Suggested by the Guidelines . 103
        6.3.2 Adherence of Comments to Conventions 105
    6.4 Implications and Discussion 114
    6.5 Threats to Validity 117
    6.6 Summary and Conclusion 118

7 Commenting Practice Concerns — 119
- 7.1 Study Design 120
  - 7.1.1 Research Questions 120
  - 7.1.2 Data Collection 121
  - 7.1.3 Analysis Method 122
- 7.2 Results 127
  - 7.2.1 High-Level Topics 127
  - 7.2.2 Question Types 129
  - 7.2.3 Developer Information Needs 130
  - 7.2.4 Recommended Comment Convention 137
- 7.3 Implications and Discussion 138
- 7.4 Threats to Validity 140
- 7.5 Summary and Conclusion 141

8 Conclusion and Future Work — 143
- 8.1 Conclusion 143
- 8.2 Future Work 146
  - 8.2.1 Comment Quality Assessment Tools and Techniques 146
  - 8.2.2 Information Granularity in Comments 146
  - 8.2.3 Tool Support for Comments 148
  - 8.2.4 Documentation Sources 149
  - 8.2.5 Speculative Analysis of Comment Quality 150
- 8.3 Concluding Remarks 150

A Appendix — 151
- A.1 Makar: A Framework for Multi-source Studies based on Unstructured Data 151
  - A.1.1 Makar Architecture 152
  - A.1.2 Case Study 155
- A.2 Included Studies for SLR 156
- A.3 Pharo Template Models 161
- A.4 Developer Information Needs 162

Bibliography — 165

List of Figures

1.1	Thesis overview	4
3.1	Data collection method implemented in the literature review	26
3.2	Relevant papers by venue	31
3.3	Relevant papers by year	31
3.4	Types of comments per programming language	36
3.5	Frequency of analyzed QAs over year	37
3.6	Types of techniques used to analyze various QAs	40
3.7	Types of evaluation for each contribution type	41
4.1	A class comment in Java	49
4.2	A class comment in Python	49
4.3	A class comment in Smalltalk	50
4.4	Distribution of Java projects	54
4.5	Distribution of Python projects	54
4.6	Distribution of Smalltalk projects	55
4.7	Distribution of Pharo7 comments	55
4.8	Information types found in Smalltalk comments	57
4.9	Research methodology to answer SRQ_1 and SRQ_2	59
4.10	The Python class comment classified in various categories	61
4.11	Mapping of Smalltalk categories to Java and Python	62
4.12	The categories found in class comments ($CCTM$) of various projects of each programming language shown on the y-axis. The x-axis shows the categories inspired from existing work in black and the new categories in green	64
5.1	Research methodology to answer SRQ_1	75
5.2	Matrix representation of a classifier	76
5.3	Performance of the different classifiers based on the F-measure for the NLP + TA feature set	81
6.1	Class comment template in Pharo 7	94

List of Figures

6.2	Research methodology to answer SRQ_1 and SRQ_2	95
6.3	Comment conventions from PEP 257	99
6.4	Comment convention rules formulated from the Pharo 7 template	100
6.5	The trend of classes with and without comments in Pharo versions.	101
6.6	Convention types in Java and Python guidelines	104
6.7	Types of class comment conventions in Java, Python, and Smalltalk guidelines	106
6.8	Percentage of comments that follow the rules, do not follow them, or to which rules are not applicable.	107
6.9	Types of rules followed or not in Java, Python, and Smalltalk projects	108
6.10	The trend of information types in Pharo versions	110
6.11	Distribution of style adherence differences between Pharo versions	110
6.12	The trend of following content style rules across Pharo versions	110
6.13	Comments following formatting guidelines	112
6.14	Comments following subject-form guidelines	112
7.1	Research methodology to answer the SRQs	123
7.2	Types of questions identified on SO and Quora	129
7.3	Distribution of *question types* and *information needs* categories	131
7.4	Distribution of comments' syntax and format discussions	135
7.5	Distribution of the features developers are interested in	135
A.1	Architecture overview of Makar	153
A.2	Search interface of Makar	154
A.3	Dataset preparation interface of Makar	154
A.4	Preprocessing steps in Makar with the transformations	155
A.5	Writing style constraints formulated from the Pharo 1 template	161
A.6	Writing style constraints formulated from the templates of Pharo 2 and 3	161
A.7	Writing style constraints formulated from the Pharo 4 template	162
A.8	Writing style constraints formulated from the templates of Pharo 5, 6, and 7	162
A.9	Taxonomy of information needs on SO and Quora	163

List of Tables

1.1	Tool and datasets produced in our studies	9
2.1	Comparison of related works on comment information categorization	16
3.1	Included journals, conferences, and workshops	28
3.2	Included studies	32
3.3	QAs mentioned by Zhi *et al.* and other works	34
3.4	Type of contributions the study makes	35
4.1	Comments found in Java projects	53
4.2	Comments found in Python projects	54
4.3	Comments found in Pharo 7 core	55
4.4	Comments found in Smalltalk projects	56
4.5	23 information types	58
5.1	Top frequent comment categories with at least 40 comments . . .	78
5.2	Results for Java, Python, and Smalltalk obtained through different ML models and features	80
5.3	Results for Java using the Random Forest classification model . .	82
5.4	Results for Python using the Random Forest classification model	84
5.5	Results for Smalltalk using the Random Forest classification model	84
5.6	Assessment of the information types based on QAs (identified in chapter 3)	88
6.1	Overview of the selected projects and their style guidelines. . . .	97
6.2	Types of comment conventions or rules	98
6.3	The information types from the CCTM suggested or not by the guidelines	113
6.4	Various QAs emerged from the style guidelines	116
7.1	Posts or questions extracted from SO and Quora	124

LIST OF TABLES

7.2	Categories of *question types*	125
7.3	Ten topics generated by LDA considering the most important topic words	128
7.4	Types of Information developers seek on SO and Quora	132
7.5	Comment conventions recommended by developers on SO and Quora	139

1

Introduction

You are only entitled to the action, never to its fruits.

Gita

Software documentation is an essential component of software systems. It exists in various forms, such as software architecture documents, requirement documents, wikis, code comments *etc.* Among others, developers consider code comments one of the most trustworthy forms of documentation as it assists them in code comprehension and maintenance tasks. However, achieving high-quality comments is difficult due to loose natural language syntax conventions, developers adopting different conventions, and the lack of tools to assess comment quality. Given the increasing usage of multi-programming language environments, it is essential to understand the specification of high-quality code comments across programming languages and how to assess them.

In this thesis, we study code comments from various aspects, such as developer commenting practices, their concerns related to comments, and quality attributes, in order to understand the specification of high-quality comments to build effective assessment tools. We first conduct a systematic literature review to gather the overview of comment quality assessment attributes and techniques. Next, we analyze what type of information developers usually write in comments and how they write them across languages. Then, we further analyze to what extent developers follow the style guidelines in writing various types of information. Finally, we analyze various community platforms to understand developer concerns about commenting practices.

1. Introduction

SOFTWARE systems are often written in several programming languages [1], and interact with many hardware devices and software components [86, 166]. To deal with such software complexity, and to ease maintenance tasks, developers tend to document their software with various artifacts, such as design documents and code comments [38]. They document various levels of detail about code in various types of documentation, such as software architecture information in the architecture documents, design components in design documents, functional and non-functional software requirements in requirement documents, and code entities in code comments. Moreover, well-documented code facilitates various software development and maintenance activities [38, 34]. Recent studies show that developers consider code comments to be more trustworthy than other forms of software documentation and use them for implementing new features, selecting suitable APIs [184, 98], and detecting bugs [161, 162]. Code comments are written using a mix of code and natural language sentences, and their syntax and semantics are neither enforced by a programming language nor checked by the compiler. Consequently, developers are free to use any convention for writing comments [111], thus making comment quality assessment a non-trivial problem.

Researchers have proposed numerous comment quality evaluation models based on a number of metrics [81, 111] and classification approaches [159]. Zhi *et al.* conducted a systematic mapping of software documentation studies (from 1971 to 2011) and proposed a meta-model for documentation quality [183]. They considered various types of documentation, such as requirement and architecture documentation in addition to code comments, but not all attributes to assess documentation fit exactly to code comments. For instance, the *consistency* quality attribute for software documentation indicates that the documentation is consistent with other documents. In contrast, for code comments, it is also used to express that the comment is consistent with the associated code. Additionally, only 10% of the studies considered by Zhi *et al.* concern code comments. Since the number of studies targeting comments has been increasing in the past decade, it is important to have a unifying model of quality attributes researchers use to assess comment quality, and tools and techniques they use to measure these quality attributes.

Although the unifying model presents the notion of high comment quality according to the researchers' perspective, it lacks the developers' perspective regarding comments, such as what they write inside comments, how they write them, what comment conventions they follow in writing comments, what concerns them about commenting practices, and what are their information needs. To gain an insight into the developer perspective, we need to characterize developer commenting practices and their concerns.

Previous studies have characterized developer commenting practices in OOP languages by classifying comments based on the information that comments contain [70, 159, 115, 182]. Given the variety of comment types (class, method, or inline) not all comment types describe the source code at the same levels of abstraction. Therefore, the quality assessment tools need to be tailored accordingly. For example, class comments in Java should present high-level information about a class, whereas method comments should present implementation-level details [109]. These commenting conventions vary across programming languages. For instance, in comparison to Java, class comments in Smalltalk are expected to contain both high-level design details and low-level implementation details. However, what information developers actually embed in class comments across languages is not well studied. Given the increasing use of multi-language software systems [165] and persistent concerns about maintaining high documentation quality, it is critical to understand what developers write in a particular comment type, and to build tools to check the embedded information across languages.

Code conventions to write good comments vary across programming languages. To support developers in writing consistent and informative comments, programming language communities, such as those for Java and Python, and large organizations such as Google, and Oracle provide coding style guidelines [76, 121, 65]. However, to what extent these guidelines cover commenting conventions, such as conventions to write content, style, and syntax of comments is unknown. It is essential to identify which aspects they cover and study the extent to which developers follow these aspects while writing comments. This can help in building tools and approaches to support developers adhere to the style guidelines to have high-quality comments.

As the guidelines provide brief conventions to write comments, and these conventions are often scattered across the guidelines, developers find it hard to locate the required commenting conventions and comply with them [48]. Additionally, the availability of several guidelines for a language makes developers unsure about which comment conventions to use for what kinds of comments. Previous works have highlighted that developers ask questions on various platforms, such as Stack Overflow (SO), and mailing lists, to satisfy their information needs about software documentation [17, 4]. However, which specific concerns developers raise about commenting practices are unclear. For example, do developers seek best practices for comments, or verify if their comments follow the guidelines? Understanding this aspect can help other developers and the scientific community to know where developers need support to ensure high-quality comments.

Even when a comment adheres to its coding style guidelines from all aspects, such as content, syntax, and style, it is still possible that the comment is incomplete or inconsistent with the code, and thus lacks the desired high quality [150, 85, 46]. Therefore, numerous quality attributes that can affect comment quality need to be considered in the overall assessment of comments. To bridge the gap between the notion of high comment quality researchers propose and the concrete commenting practices developers follow, we need a deeper understanding of both researcher and developer perspectives.

To gain the required understanding, we analyze comments from both perspectives, of researchers in terms of what they use and propose to measure comment quality, and of developers in terms of what they ask and what they write in comments. Figure 1.1 illustrates the exploration of these perspectives (*e.g.*, P1, P2) with respect to each chapter and research question.

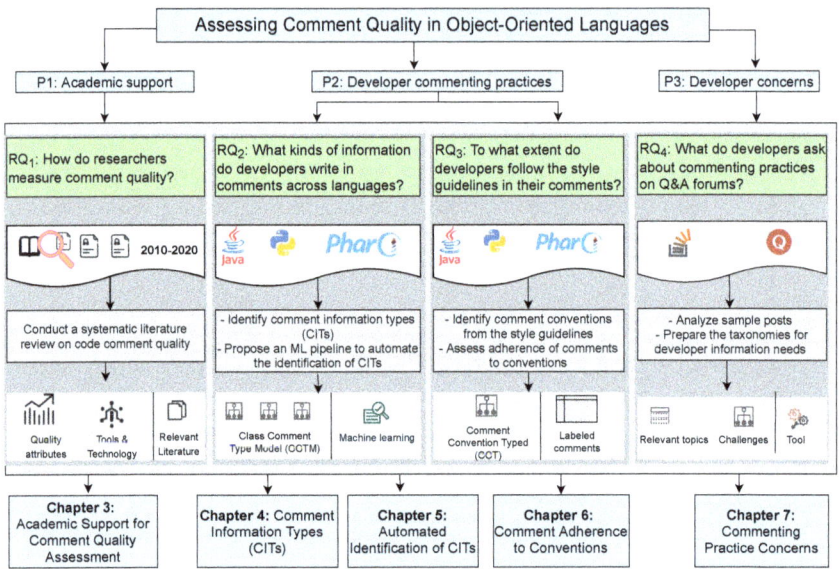

Figure 1.1: Thesis overview

1.1 Thesis Statement

The goal of this thesis is to investigate practices in writing and evaluation of code comments in a stepwise manner to ultimately improve comment quality assessment techniques. We state our thesis as follows:

> *Understanding the specification of high-quality comments to build effective assessment tools requires a multi-perspective view of the comments. The view can be approached by analyzing (P1) the academic support for comment quality assessment, (P2) developer commenting practices across languages, and (P3) their concerns about comments.*

To explore each perspective, we conduct various studies, such as systematic mapping and empirical studies focusing on four main research questions:

*P*1 : Identifying the quality attributes, tools, and techniques that researchers propose to assess comment quality.

RQ_1: How do researchers measure comment quality?

*P*2 : Understanding the commenting practices developers follow in writing comments in various programming languages, such as Java, Python, and Smalltalk with the research questions:

RQ_2: What kinds of information do developers write in comments across languages?

RQ_3: To what extent do developers follow the style guidelines in their comments?

*P*3 : Identifying the key concerns developers post on Q&A forums related to comments with the research question:

RQ_4: What do developers ask about commenting practices on Q&A forums?

Exploring each perspective provides various insights into developer practices, concerns, and support that can be leveraged to improve the current understanding about the code comments. It can also help in establishing advanced approaches to assess comments automatically, thus, laying the foundation of a novel comment quality assessment system in this field.

1.2 Contributions

The contribution of this research is presented with respect to each perspective. We use the 📄 icon for published papers, 🗋 for submitted papers, 🗂 for taxonomies, and 🔧 for the proposed tools.

*P*1 : We present for the first perspective:

- Chapter 3 → 🗂 a list of relevant quality attributes to assess comments, and a review of existing tools and techniques that assess these quality attributes.
  🗋 Pooja Rani, Arianna Blasi, Nataliia Stulova, Sebastiano Panichella, Alessandra Gorla, and Oscar Nierstrasz. A decade of code comment quality assessment: A systematic literature review. *Journal of Systems and Software*, 2021

*P*2 : We present for the second perspective:

5

- Chapter 4 → ⛃ an overview of the Smalltalk class commenting trends over seven major releases from 2008 till 2019, an empirically validated taxonomy, called CCTM (Class Comment Types Model), characterizing the information types found in class comments of Smalltalk, and mapping of the CCTM taxonomy to the taxonomies available in Java and Python.
  📄 Pooja Rani, Sebastiano Panichella, Manuel Leuenberger, Mohammad Ghafari, and Oscar Nierstrasz. What do class comments tell us? An investigation of comment evolution and practices in Pharo Smalltalk. *Empirical Software Engineering*, 26(6):1–49, 2021

- Chapter 5 →, an automated approach that is able to classify class comments according to CCTM with high accuracy in a language independent manner.
  📄 Pooja Rani, Sebastiano Panichella, Manuel Leuenberger, Andrea Di Sorbo, and Oscar Nierstrasz. How to identify class comment types? A multi-language approach for class comment classification. *Journal of Systems and Software*, 181:111047, 2021

- Chapter 6 → ⛃ an empirically validated taxonomy, called CCT, characterizing the convention types found in various coding style guidelines of Java, Python, and Smalltalk, and an assessment of the extent to which developers follow these conventions in writing class comments.
  📄 Pooja Rani, Suada Abukar, Nataliia Stulova, Alexander Bergel, and Oscar Nierstrasz. Do comments follow commenting conventions? A case study in Java and Python. In *2021 IEEE 21st International Working Conference on Source Code Analysis and Manipulation (SCAM)*, 2021

$P3$: We present for the third perspective:

- Chapter 7 → ⛃ an empirically validated taxonomy of commenting practices related questions from various Q&A forums, and recommendations given by experts on Q&A forums about commenting practices.
  📄 Pooja Rani, Mathias Birrer, Sebastiano Panichella, Mohammad Ghafari, and Oscar Nierstrasz. What do developers discuss about code comments? In *2021 IEEE 21st International Working Conference on Source Code Analysis and Manipulation (SCAM)*, 2021

- Appendix A → ⚙ a tool to conduct a mining study on multiple sources or forums.

📄 Mathias Birrer, Pooja Rani, Sebastiano Panichella, and Oscar Nierstrasz. Makar: A framework for multi-source studies based on unstructured data. In *2021 IEEE International Conference on Software Analysis, Evolution and Reengineering (SANER)*, pages 577–581, 2021

1.3 Outline

In this thesis, we explore each perspective with respect to the state of the art works, their motivation, methodology, results, and contributions.

Chapter 2 reviews the state of the art of comment analysis with respect to each perspective and their corresponding research questions. The chapter addresses various topics concerning this thesis and highlights the gaps that needs to be addressed.

Chapter 3 explores the notion of quality in the context of comments by conducting a systematic literature review (SLR). In the SLR, we review the proceedings of the past ten years *i.e.*, 2010 until 2020 from the relevant Software Engineering (SE) conferences and journals that assess comment quality. We gather which quality attributes the relevant papers assess, and which tools and techniques they propose or use to evaluate them. Our results suggest that consistency of comments with the code, readability of comments, and relevancy of the content are often analyzed, whereas conciseness, coherence, and accessibility are rarely analyzed. We find that manual assessment is still the most frequently used technique to measure various quality attributes. Most of the studies analyze code comments mainly in Java, especially method comments. However, they rarely analyze class comments even though class comments in object-oriented languages assist developers in comprehending a high-level overview of the class. We address many of these concerns in the following chapters, for instance, we analyze the content of class comments of three programming languages (chapter 4), establish a language-independent machine learning-based approach to identify relevant information from comments (chapter 5), compare developer commenting practices to the suggested guidelines (chapter 6), and gather their commenting concerns (chapter 7) to improve the overall quality aspect of comments. As chapter 3 provides insight into the researchers' perspective, the subsequent chapters provide insights into the developers' perspective on writing comments, following various guidelines to write them, and raising concerns about comments.

Chapter 4 shows how previous studies have investigated the commenting practices in various systems independently, but have not observed the commenting practices across languages and specific to a comment type. We also confirm these results in our previous study (chapter 3). To address this concern, we first analyze class comments in Smalltalk and formulate a taxonomy, called CCTM. We then map the CCTM taxonomy to the code comment taxonomies available in Java and Python specific to their class comments. Our results highlight that developers express different kinds of information (more than 15 information types) in class comments ranging from the high-level overview to low-level implementation details across programming languages. As these information types can help developers in accessing the relevant information for their tasks, it can help researchers in developing the approaches to identify them automatically and then assessing their quality. Chapter 5 establishes an approach to automatically identify the information types.

In **Chapter 5** we automate the identification of information types from class comments using CCTM across languages. The results from chapter 3 highlighted such a need for an automated approach to assess comments. We apply various machine learning algorithms with different feature sets to find the most suitable method for identifying the information types in comments. Our results suggested that the Random Forest algorithm fed by the combination of NLP+TF-IDF features achieved the best classification performance for the frequent categories over the investigated languages. It identified the top six most frequent categories with relatively high precision (ranging from 78% to 92% for the selected languages), recall (ranging from 86% to 92%), and F-measure (ranging from 77% to 92%). However, it achieved less stable results for Smalltalk compared to Python and Java. Though initial results seem promising, comment classification is still not perfect for evaluating all aspects of comments.

Chapter 6 shows what comment conventions various coding style guidelines suggest and to what extent developers follow them. Our results from chapter 4 highlighted that class comments contain various types of information. In this chapter, we found that not all of these information types are suggested by coding guidelines and vice versa, and this behavior is observed across all the selected languages. This analysis provides insight into supporting developers in following the commenting conventions to have consistent comments. As developers become confused in following the conventions, it is vital to understand which specific challenges they face related to code comments. We gather such challenges in the next chapter (chapter 7).

Chapter 7 attempts to identify developer discussions from the Q&A forums about commenting practices. In the first part, we identify the types of questions developers often ask about commenting practices on SO and Quora. Then we analyze what recommendations expert developers from these forums suggest to questioners to resolve their confusions. Our results indicate that developers ask questions about the best practices to write comments (15% of the questions), and generate comments automatically using various tools and technologies. We also observe that developers are interested in embedding various kinds of information, such as code examples and media *e.g.*, images in their code comments, but lack clear guidelines to write them. Additionally, the results show that developers are interested in automatically assessing their comments to ensure quality, but lack the tools and techniques to do so.

Chapter 8 revisits the research questions, presents the concluding remarks, and indicates potential future work in the direction of developing tools and techniques to improve code comments, software documentation, and code comprehension.

Appendix A presents the supplementary results and the tool named *Makar*.

1.4 Study Replicability

González *et al.* characterized the reproducibility of a study in empirical software engineering studies and showed that *Dataset Availability* is an essential dimension [64]. To provide replicability of our studies, and to promote the open-science movement, various tools and datasets produced along with the manuscripts are made publicly accessible.

Table 1.1: Tool and datasets produced in our studies

Dataset	Host
Comment quality assessment attributes and techniques	GitHub [126]
Comment information types in Smalltalk	Zenodo [130]
Comment information types in Java and Python	GitHub [129]
Automated identification of comment information types	GitHub [129]
Java and Python comment conventions	Zenodo [127]
Developer commenting concerns	Zenodo [128]
Makar tool	Zenodo [131]

2
State of the Art

DEVELOPERS document code in various types of software documentation [38]. Code comments are an important type of software documentation that has been proven to assist developers in various software engineering tasks [39, 98, 161]. As code comments are written in natural language form, and not checked by the compiler, developers are free to use various conventions to write them. Developers embed various kinds of information in comments to support other developers in understanding and maintaining code. Given the importance of code comments in software development, researchers put effort into various comment-related tasks, such as automatically generating and summarizing comments [69, 108], using comments to detect bugs [161], assessing comment quality [81, 159], detecting inconsistency between code and comments [137, 176], and examining co-evolution of code and comments [55, 75]. Their aim is to have high-quality comments to support developers in various software engineering-related tasks at different phases of the software development life cycle (SDLC). However, the lack of a standard definition, appropriate measures, and tools make comment quality assessment a non-trivial task.

Several empirical studies have targeted understanding code comments focusing on different aspects and aims. In the following sections, we describe the state of the art for each perspective and their corresponding research questions.

2.1 Academic Support for Comment Quality Assessment

Software quality is frequently represented as a contextual concept [?]. In a marketplace of highly cut-throat technologies, the significance of having quality software is currently not a benefit, but a vital factor for organizations to be successful [16]. Therefore, the identification and quantification of important characteristics is required as a first step to measure a high-quality piece of software [16]. The object-oriented paradigm has changed the code elements and metrics that we used to measure software, such as size, performance, and complexity to metrics based on inheritance, polymorphism, encapsulation, and abstraction [32]. However, SE (object-oriented) metrics vary in their applicability of what they measure, and how they measure. The metric and quality models developed for such systems are not restricted to code, but they can also be applied to code comments. Though there is no standard definition of a "good comment", there exist various assumptions about it. According to Wan et al., a good comment should be at least correct, fluent, and consistent [171]. On the other hand, according to Khamis et al. and Steidl et al. the comments that are long and textually similar to the code are considered high-quality [81, 159]. Another similar assumption is that if a comment helps the developer understand the code, it is considered to be a high-quality comment. However, beyond the various assumptions, there is currently no study to present all quality attributes (QAs) important for code comments. Additionally, an overall picture of how these different QAs are evaluated in an automatic or semi-automatic manner is also missing for comments.

2.1.1 Comment Quality Attributes

Arthur et al. identified the desirable QAs as a first step to measure software quality, especially the main QAs of good documentation [13]. Various researchers conducted surveys with developers from the industry to find important QAs of good software documentation. Forward and Lethbridge surveyed 48 developers and highlighted developer concerns about outdated documentation and thus documentation being untrustworthy [56]. Chen and Huang surveyed 137 project managers and software engineers [30]. Their study highlighted the typical quality problems developers face in maintaining software documentation, such as adequacy, completeness, traceability, consistency, and trustworthiness. Robillard et al. conducted personal interviews with 80 practitioners and presented the important attributes for good documentation, such as including examples and usage information, complete, organized, and better design [138]. Similarly, Plosch et al. surveyed 88 practitioners and identified consistency, clarity, accuracy, readability, organization, and understandability as the most important QAs for documentation [118]. They also indicated that developers do not consider documentation standards important (*e.g.*, ISO 26514:2008, IEEE Std.1063:2001). Sohan et *al.* in their survey study highlighted the importance of examples in documentation [153]. The majority of the highlighted documentation QAs apply to code comments as well (as a type of software documentation). However, which specific QAs (*e.g.*, outdated, complete, consistent, traceable) researchers consider important to assess code comment quality and how these QAs are measured is yet to be studied.

2.1.2 Comment Quality Assessment Techniques

Researchers have focused on evaluating comment quality based on various aspects, such as assessing the adequacy of comments [13], their content quality [81, 159], analyzing co-evolution of comments and code [55], or detecting inconsistent comments [137, 176]. For instance, Ying *et al.* and Storey *et al.* assessed task comment quality [180, 160]. They highlighted the need to automatically assess comment quality. Several works have proposed tools and techniques to automatically assess the comments using specific QAs and metrics [81, 159, 185, 137, 89, 176]. Specifically, Khamis *et al.* assessed the inline comment quality based on the two quality attributes: consistency and language quality [81]. They used a heuristic-based approach to measure these quality attributes. Steidl *et al.* evaluated documentation comment quality based on four QAs, such as consistency, coherence, completeness, and usefulness of comments using a machine learning-based model [159]. Zhou *et al.* proposed a heuristic and natural language processing-based technique to detect incomplete and incorrect comments [185]. These works have proposed various new QAs to assess comment quality, such as completeness, coherence, and language quality, that are not included in previous quality models. Therefore, a unifying overview of comment QAs and their assessment approaches is still missing. In this regard, we complement these previous works by investigating comment QAs discussed in the last decade of research by conducting an SLR.

2.1.3 Previous SLRs on Code Comments

Previous literature reviews have provided the quality models for software documentation [45, 183, 154, 106]. Specifically, Ding *et al.* conducted an SLR to explore the usage of knowledge-based approaches in software documentation [45]. They identified twelve QAs. They also highlighted the need to improve QAs, especially conciseness, credibility, and ambiguity. Zhi *et al.* have explored various types of software documentation to see which QAs impact it [183]. Both of the studies considered the timeline until 2011. Additionally, only 10% of their studies focused on code comments, and they have not studied how the proposed quality assessment approaches are computed in practice for comments. Inspired by these related studies, we focus specifically on the code comment aspect. Song *et al.* conducted a literature review on code comment generation techniques, and indicated the need to design an objective comment quality assessment model [154]. Complementarily, Nazar et al. [106] presented a literature review in the field of summarizing software artifacts, which included source code comment generation as well as bug reports, mailing lists, and developer discussion artifacts. We complement these previous studies since we mainly focus on quality assessment of manually-written comments.

With the increasing amount of literature in the field of assessing comment quality, and still persistent need to improve comment quality assessment approaches, we conduct an SLR. With this work, we identify various QAs that are either not included in previous quality models, or used with different terminology. We gather various techniques that are used to measure the identified QAs to see which of them are more frequently used than others in assessing comment quality.

Our results show that researchers focus on various kinds of comments, such as method comments, inline comments, and todo comments. However, none of them analyze specifically class comments. Though the trend of analyzing comments of more than one programming language is increasing, 90% of the studies primarily focus on the Java programming language and only 15% of them focus on Python. Thus, the empirical evidence for these languages is restricted to one language and generalizing it to other languages requires more analysis and effort.

Understanding the QAs and techniques researchers propose to assess comments is important, but it is incomplete without understanding how developers write comments, *i.e.*, what information they write, what conventions they follow, and what their concerns are regarding comments. In the next sections, we characterize developer commenting practices and their related concerns about comments.

2.2 Developer Commenting Practices

To characterize developer commenting practices, we analyzed comments based on their evolution, specific comment types, classification, and adherence to the guidelines.

Considering the importance of code comments, several researchers analyzed comments quantitatively and qualitatively. Woodfield *et al.* studied the usefulness of comments quantitatively, and measured the effects of comments on program comprehension [178]. They found that the groups of programmers who were given a program with comments were better able to answer more questions about a program in a quiz than the programmers who were given the program without comments.

A few studies focused on the evolution of comments. Schreck *et al.* qualitatively analyzed the evolution of comments over time in the Eclipse project [144], whereas Jiang *et al.* [77] quantitatively examined the evolution of source code comments in PostgreSQL. Fluri *et al.* analyzed the co-evolution of code and comments in Java and discovered that changes in comments are triggered by a change in source code [54]. They found that newly-added code is rarely commented. Interestingly, in contrast to their results, we find that the commenting behavior of Smalltalk developers is different. Developers comment newly-added code, as well as commenting old classes. In another study, Fluri *et al.* claimed that the investigation of commenting behavior of a software system is independent of the object-oriented language under the assumption that common object-oriented languages follow similar language constructs to add comments [55]. We investigate the assumption with another object-oriented programming language and discover that Smalltalk follows different comment conventions for class comments. Smalltalk separates the class comment from the source code and supports different kinds of information like warnings, pre-conditions, and examples in class comments. Thus, it indicates that programming languages use different conventions for writing comments. However, what information developers actually embed in class comments and how these practices vary across languages requires further investigation.

2.2.1 Comment Information Types

Previous studies indicated that code comments contain various types of information that can help developers in various activities and tasks [180, 111, 159, 115, 185, 72]. We summarize these related works based on the development systems, programming language, and comment entity (*e.g.*, source code comments, class comments, inline comments) as shown in Table 2.1.

Ying *et al.* [180] inspected specific types of comments, namely the Eclipse task comments, and categorized them on the basis of the different uses of such comments made by developers, for example, for communication purposes, or to bookmark current and future tasks. Padioleau *et al.* proposed comment categories based on the actual meaning of comments [111]. They use "W questions", such as *What is in a comment?*, *Who can benefit?*, *Where is the comment located?*, *When was the comment written?* Hata *et al.* have categorized only the links found in comments [72]. Similar to these studies, our work is aimed at supporting developers in discovering important types of information from class comments. Specifically, we rely on the question: *What is in a comment?*, and classify the comments accordingly.

Our results from the SLR highlight that researchers focus on various kinds of comments, such as method comments, inline comments, or TODO comments, however, none of them specifically analyze class comments. The results also show that although the trend of analyzing comments of more than one programming language is increasing, 90% of the studies focus on Java and only 15% of them focus on Python. Therefore, we focus specifically on class commenting practices of various programming languages. We specifically classify class comments of three languages, Java, Python, and

2. State of the Art

Table 2.1: Comparison of related works on comment information categorization

Study	Comment types	System analyzed	Proposed categories
Ying et al. (2005) [180]	Task	[**Java**]: Eclipse Architect's Workbench (AWB) project	communication, pointer to a change request, bookmark, current task, future task, location marker, concern tag (**7 categories**)
Padioleau et al. (2009) [111]	Source code	[**C**]: Linux, FreeBSD, OpenSolaris [**Java**]: Eclipse, [**C/C++**]: MySQL and Firefox	type, interface, code relationship, past future, meta, explanation (**6 categories**)
Haouari et al. (2011) [70]	Source code	[**Java**]: DrJava, SHome3D, jPlayMan	explanation comments, working comments, commented code, other (**3 categories**)
Steidl et al. (2013) [159]	Source code	[**Java**]: CSLessons, EMF, Jung, ConQAT, jBoss, voTUM, mylyn, pdfsam, jMol, jEdit, Eclipse, jabref, C++	copyright comments, header comments, member comments, inline comments, section comments, code comments (commented code), task comments (**7 categories**)
Pascarella et al. (2017) [115]	Source code	[**Java**]: Apache (Spark, Hadoop), Google (Guava, Guice), Vaadin, Eclipse	summary, expand, rational (intent), deprecation (warning), usage, exception, TODO, incomplete, commented code, directive, formatter, license, pointer, auto-generated, noise (**16 categories**)
Zhang et al. (2018) [182]	Source code	[**Python**]: Pandas, Django, Pipenv, Pytorch, Ipython, Mailpile, Requests	metadata, summary, usage, parameters, expand, version, development notes, todo, exception, links, noise (**11 categories**)
Shinyama et al. (2018) [148]	Local (inside methods)	[**Java**]: 1 000 projects [**Python**]: 990 projects	preconditions, post conditions, value description, instructions, guide, interface, meta information, comment out, directive, visual cue, uncategorized (**11 categories**)
Hata et al. (2019) [72]	Links in comments	[**C, C++, Java, JavaScript, Python, PHP, Ruby**]: Projects from GitHub	links (**1 category**)

Smalltalk, and develop an approach to identify comment types in a language independent manner.

2.2.2 Automation of Comment Information Types

Steidl et al. classified the comments in Java and C/C++ programs based on the position and syntax of the comments, e.g., inline comments, block comments, header comments, *etc.* [159]. Differently from Steidl *et al.*, our work focuses on analyzing and identifying semantic information found in class comments in Java, Python, and Smalltalk. We classify class comments by mapping them to their "header comments" category. In the case of Smalltalk, their four other categories of comments (task comments, copyright comments, member comments, and section comments) are available inside the class comment but are not annotated with any specific tags as in Java and C/C++. Pascarella *et al.* identified the information types from Java code comments and presented a taxonomy [115]. Similarly, Zhang *et al.* identified information types from Python code comments[182]. In the case of Java, we use the taxonomy from Pascarella *et al.* to build our Java CCTM categories and the taxonomy from Zhang *et al.* to build Python CCTM categories.

Compared to the Java code comment taxonomy of Pascarella *et al.*, we rarely find *formatter*, *commented code*, *todo*, *directive*, or *license* categories in class comments. Similarly, compared to the Python comment taxonomy of Zhang *et al.*, we rarely observe the *version*, *todo*, or *noise* categories in our Python class comment taxonomy. More importantly, we find other types of information in Java and Python class comments that developers embed in the class comments but were not included in their taxonomies, such as the *warning*, *observation*, *recommendation*, and *precondition* categories. More in general, our work complements and extends the studies of Pascarella *et al.* and Zhang *et al.* by focusing on class comments in three different languages, which makes our work broader in terms of studied languages as well as the types of code comments reported and automatically classified.

Forward and Lethbridge surveyed 48 developers and highlighted developers' interest in automating the documentation process [56]. Specifically, they indicated that documentation tools should extract knowledge from core resources. Automatically identifying various information types embedded in comments and extracting them can help developers find relevant information easily. To achieve this goal, several studies explored numerous approaches based on heuristics or textual features [47, 181, 148, 60]. For instance, Dragan *et al.* used a rule-based approach to identify the stereotype of a class based on the class signature [47]. Their work is aimed at recognizing the class type (*e.g.*, data class, controller class) rather than the type of information available within class comments, which is the focus of our work. Steidl *et al.* classified the comments in Java and C/C++ programs automatically using machine learning approaches. They used the position and syntax of the comments as features to classify comments. Shinyama *et al.* [148] focused on discovering specific types of local comments (*i.e.*, explanatory comments) that explain how the code works at a microscopic level inside the functions. Similar to our work, Shinyama *et al.* and Geist *et al.* considered recurrent patterns, but crafted them manually as extra features to train the classifier. Thus, our approach is different, as it is able to *automatically* extract different natural language patterns (heuristics), combining them with other textual features, to classify class comment types of different languages.

In contrast to these previous approaches, we extract the natural language patterns (heuristics) automatically using a tool, NEON, combine them with other textual features, and test our approach across languages. We found that our natural language-based approach combined with TF-IDF classifies class comments with high accuracy for the investigated languages.

2.2.3 Comment Adherence to Conventions

Comment conventions. Coding style guidelines or standards suggest various conventions to write comments [65, 121, 76]. Kernighan and Pike highlighted the need to follow commenting standards, and proposed various guidelines [80]. Nevertheless, to what extent developers follow commenting standards in writing comments is not well explored. Therefore, after characterizing developer commenting practices in terms of what they write in comments, we move to understand commenting conventions various guidelines provide, whether developers follow these guidelines in writing their comments, and what specific conventions they follow.

Numerous studies have measured the impact of different coding styles on program comprehension [23, 178] and on open source collaboration [174]. The studies suggested researchers to put effort into improving the stylistic consistency of the projects. However, quantifying the coding style and measuring the stylistic inconsistency of projects is not a trivial task. Oman *et al.* justified the need for a programming (coding) style taxonomy and designed the taxonomy for comprehending and identifying the specific style factors [110]. Taking inspiration from their work, Mi *et al.* attempted to characterize the programming style quantitatively and measured the stylistic inconsistency in C++ [99]. However, the metrics to measure comment style are restricted to the ratio of the number of comment lines (inline comments or multiline comments) to the code. In this context, we study diverse coding style guidelines of Java, Python, and Smalltalk and identify the type of conventions they provide for comments. We develop a taxonomy of comment conventions types (*i.e.*, CCT) to specify which aspect (syntax, style, content, or format) is covered in the style guidelines and to what extent.

Adherence of comments to the conventions. Jiang *et al.* studied the source code comments in the PostgreSQL application. They focused on function comments *i.e.*, comments before the declaration of a function (header comments) and comments within the function body and trailing the functions (non-header comments). They observed an initial fluctuation in the ratio of header and non-header comments due to the introduction of a new commenting style, but they did not investigate further the commenting style [77]. Marin investigated the psychological factors that drive developers to comment [94]. The study concluded that developers use different comment styles in their code depending on the programming language they have used earlier. We also partially confirm this result as we found Java style block comments within Smalltalk class comments.

Nurvitadhi *et al.* studied the impact of class comments and method comments on program comprehension in Java, and created a template for class comments in Java [109]. They suggested to include the purpose of the class, what the class does, and the collaboration between classes. The Smalltalk class comment template covers similar aspects with a CRC style for the class comment. The CRC style emphasizes mentioning the intent, responsibilities, and collaborations of the class. However, whether developers follow these aspects or not in their comments is unstudied. Previous works, including Bafatakis *et al.* and Simmons *et al.*, evaluated the compliance of Python code to Python style guidelines [15, 149]. However, they included only a few comment conventions and missed many other content and writing style conventions. To the best of our knowledge, we are the first to conduct a study to characterize the commenting conventions of the guidelines, the commenting styles of developers, and to measure the extent of their adherence to the standard guidelines across languages.

In our study, we find various comment conventions, such as grammar rules, the syntax of writing different types of information that developers often follow, or violate. We measure the adherence of Smalltalk class comments to the default comment template and find that developers follow the writing and content conventions of the template. Java and Python do not provide any default template to write comments, but support multiple style guidelines for each project, thus collecting and verifying their comment conventions against comments is more tricky. We study diverse projects in Java and Python and find that developers follow writing and content conventions more than other types, confirming the prior results of Smalltalk.

2.3 Commenting Practice Concerns

Happel *et al.*, in their survey on some popular recommender systems, discussed that getting useful documentation is not a trivial task, and requires many challenges to be addressed [71]. To understand the challenges developers face, and their information needs, researchers mine various crowd-sourced knowledge-based platforms.

Examining developer engagements and activities from different sources and understanding them in a topic context can guide the improvement of tools and practices within the topic [18, 4]. It also helps researchers and other developers in gathering developer information needs regarding a topic and understanding where they face challenges. Developers frequently use web resources to satisfy their information needs. Recently, researchers have started leveraging these resources, such as version control systems [31], archived communications [146, 147], execution logs [61], newsgroups [74], Q&A forums [7, 17, 141, 179, 84, 4], and mailing lists [4] to comprehend developer information needs.

Stack Overflow (SO) is one of the most popular platforms that researchers have studied to capture developers' questions about trends and technologies [7], security-related issues [179], documentation issues, *etc.* [4]. Recently researchers have started investigating Quora to get more insight into developer communities [84], *e.g.*, finding and predicting the popularity of the topics [172, 84], finding answerability of the questions [92], detecting the experts on specific topics [116, 107, 59], or analyzing anonymous answers [96]. According to our knowledge, our study is the first to investigate the Quora platform for code comments.

In the context of software documentation, Aghajani *et al.* studied documentation issues on SO, GitHub, and mailing lists [4], and formulated a taxonomy of these issues. However, they focused on the issues related to project documentation, such as wikis, user manuals, and code documentation, and did not focus on the style issues of the code comments. Our study focuses on all aspects of code comments including the content and style aspect of code comments. Barua *et al.* found questions concerning coding style and practice to be amongst those most frequently appearing on SO [17], but did not investigate further. They considered the topic amongst common English language topics instead of a software technical category due to the usage of generic words in this topic. As their focus was on technical categories, they did not explore the coding style questions further. Our study complements their work by exploring the specific aspects of coding styles, and focusing on comment conventions.

2.4 Summary and Conclusion

In this chapter, we reviewed the state of the art with respect to commenting practices and challenges, which focus mainly on (i) identifying various QAs for comment quality and approaches to measure the attributes, (ii) characterizing developer commenting practices across languages, and (iii) various sources utilized to understand developer information needs. The state of the art shows various approaches and aspects to characterize comments and assess their quality. They list various QAs that are important to measure software documentation quality and propose various approaches to measure these attributes. However, there is currently no study to present all quality attributes important for code comments. Additionally, an overall picture of how these different QAs are evaluated in an automatic or manual manner is also missing for comments. We address this limitation by providing a unifying view of the QAs used to assess comment quality and various techniques to measure these QAs.

The approaches to assess comment quality generally vary in the scope of the comments, the content inside comments, the software system comments belong to, and the techniques used to analyze comments. The majority of the analyses focus on Java comments, and do not investigate if developers' commenting practices vary across languages despite the increasing trend of using polyglot environments in software projects. Additionally, they only focus on limited metrics to assess comments automatically and do not consider information embedded inside comments. Thus, the efforts to automatically assess comment quality require a deeper understanding of the nature of developer commenting practices in terms of what information they embed inside comments, how they embed, and how they adhere to the coding guidelines to establish the QAs required for comment assessment. Our results highlighted the need to establish the QAs for comments, such as, completeness, coherence, consistency of an overall comment with respect to code and of a specific comment type. For instance, to decide whether the summary embedded in class comment is coherent or not, we must identify summary information from a class comment and then measure its coherence based on the definition of coherence quality attribute for comments. The first step in this direction is to automatically identify the information available in the comments. This is required to get useful documentation for novice or expert developers for various software development and maintenance tasks. We address these limitations by identifying various information types across languages, and by automatically classifying class comments from three programming languages, Java, Python, and Smalltalk. To further characterize developer commenting practices, we analyze various coding style guidelines that provide conventions to write comments.

To understand the challenges developers face, and their information needs, researchers mine various crowd-sourced knowledge-based platforms. However, what specific challenges developers face related to code comments have not yet been investigated. We fill this gap by analyzing popular Q&A forums and gathering the questions related to commenting practices. Identifying the developer challenges with comments can help us to establish the knowledge about what kinds of comments they consider as good, and what features developers seek in the future documentation tools. Therefore, we collect various comment conventions that developers recommend on these Q&A forums.

In the following chapters, we explore each perspective mentioned in the thesis statement and conduct various studies to fill the knowledge gaps.

3

Academic Support for Comment Quality Assessment

While it is widely accepted that high-quality matters in code comments just as it matters in source code, assessing comment quality in practice is still an open problem. There is no unique definition of quality when it comes to assessing code comments. Previous studies have investigated documentation quality from various aspects and measured it using various QAs and metrics. However, none of them provide a unifying model for comment quality assessment.

In this chapter, we present a systematic literature review (SLR) on the last decade of research in SE to identify the comment quality QAs and assessment approaches.

Our evaluation, based on the analysis of 2 353 papers which led to 48 relevant ones, shows that (i) most studies and techniques focus on comments in Java code, thus may not be generalizable to other languages, and (ii) the analyzed studies focus on four main QAs out of 21 QAs identified in the literature, with a clear predominance of checking the consistency between comments and the code.

This chapter is based on the journal article:

"P. Rani, A. Blasi, N. Stulova, S. Panichella, A. Gorla, and O. Nierstrasz. A Decade of comment quality assessment: A systematic literature review, JSS'21" [134]

WELL-Documented code facilitates various software development and maintenance activities [38, 34]. Developers document their code in various software documentation forms, code comments being one of the important forms where developers document various details, such as the rationale behind their code, an overview of the code, and algorithmic details [155]. Several studies have demonstrated that *high-quality* code comments can support developers in software comprehension, bug detection, and program maintenance activities [39, 98, 161].

Maintaining high-quality code comments is vital for software evolution activities, however, *assessing the overall quality of comments is not a trivial problem*. Developers use various programming languages, adopt project-specific conventions to write comments, and embed different kinds of information in a semi-structured or unstructured form [111, 115]. Additionally, the lack of quality assessment tools for comments makes ensuring comment quality in practice a complex task. Therefore, writing high-quality comments and maintaining them in projects is a responsibility mostly left to developers [6, 80].

The problem of *assessing the quality of code comments* has gained a lot of attention from researchers during the last decade [81, 159, 137, 115, 176]. Despite the interest of the research community in this topic, there is no clear agreement yet on what quality means when referring to code comments. Existing work on assessing comment quality rather mentions specific attributes of quality that can be easily quantified and evaluated, *e.g.*, by reporting *spelling* mistakes, or computing *completeness* by counting how many code elements have no comments. Having a general definition of quality when referring to code comments is challenging, as comments are diverse in their purpose and scope.

Even though specific comments follow all language-specific guidelines in terms of syntax, it is still difficult to automatically determine whether they satisfy other quality aspects, such as whether they are consistent or complete with respect to the code or not [185]. There exist various such aspects, *e.g.*, *readability, content relevance,* and *correctness* that should be considered when assessing comments, but tools do not support all of them. Therefore, a comprehensive study of the specific attributes that influence code comment quality and techniques proposed to assess them is essential for advancing the commenting tools.

Previous mapping and literature review studies have collected numerous QAs that are used to assess the quality of software documentation based on their importance and effect on the documentation quality. Ding *et al.* [45] focused specifically on software architecture and requirement documents, while Zhi *et al.* [183] analyzed code comments along with other types of documentation, such as requirement and design documents. They identified 16 QAs (shown in Table 3.3 later on) that influence the quality of software documentation. However, the identified QAs are extracted from a body of literature concerning rather old studies (*i.e.*, studies conducted prior to the year 2011) and are limited in the context of code comments. For instance, only 10% of the studies considered by Zhi *et al.* concerned code comments. It is still unknown which tools and techniques researchers propose to assess comment quality.

To achieve these objectives, we conduct an SLR to answer our main research question, RQ_1: *How do researchers measure comment quality?* We formulate various subsidiary research questions (SRQs), described in 3.1.1. We believe that mapping such studies to gather the overview of quality aspects and techniques can (i) help developers to adopt assessment techniques to have high-quality comments, and (ii) assist researchers in the field to identify comment QAs with tool support.

In particular, we review 2 353 studies and find 48 relevant to assessing comment quality from which we extract the programming language, the types of analyzed comments, QAs for comments, techniques to measure them, and the preferred evaluation type to validate their results. We observe that (i) most studies and techniques focus on comments in Java code, (ii) many techniques that are used to assess QAs are based on heuristics and thus may not be generalizable to other languages, (iii) a total of 21 QAs are used across studies, with a clear dominance of *consistency*, *completeness*, *accuracy*, and *readability*, and (iv) several QAs are often assessed manually rather than with the automated approaches. We find that the studies are rather evaluated by measuring performance metrics and surveying students than by performing validations with practitioners.

3.1 Study Design

3.1.1 Research Questions

Our *goal* is to foster research that aims at building better code comment assessment tools. To achieve this goal, it is essential to identify all QAs that influence comment quality and the tools and techniques which have been proposed in recent research to assess their quality. We formulate the following SRQs to answer RQ_1:

- SRQ_1: *What types of comments do researchers focus on when assessing comment quality?*
  Rationale: Comments are typically placed at the beginning of a file, to report licensing or author's information, or placed preceding a class or function to describe the overview of a class or function and their implementation details. Depending on the specific type of comment used in source code and the specific programming language, researchers may use different techniques to assess them. These techniques may not be generalizable to other languages. For example, studies analyzing class comments in object-oriented programming languages may need extra

effort to generalize the comment assessment approach to functional programming languages.

- SRQ$_2$: What QAs do researchers consider in assessing comment quality?
  Rationale: QAs may solely concern the syntactic aspects (*e.g.*, syntax of comments), writing style (*e.g.*, grammar), or content aspects (*e.g.*, consistency with the code) of the comments. Researchers may use different terminology for the same QA and thus these terms must be mapped across studies to have a unifying view of them [183], for instance, whether the *accuracy* QA is defined consistently across studies or not. Future studies that aim to improve specific attributes of comment quality evaluation may find this information useful.

- SRQ$_3$: Which techniques do researchers use to assess comment QAs?
  Rationale: Researchers may resort to simple heuristics-based techniques, or may use complex supervised or unsupervised machine learning (ML) techniques to automatically assess QAs. We aim to assess if there are clear winning techniques for this domain.

- SRQ$_4$: What kinds of contributions do studies often make?
  Rationale: Researchers may contribute various types of solutions, such as a metric, method, or tool to improve the comment quality field, however, it is unknown if there are specific kinds of solutions that are often proposed.

- SRQ$_5$: How do researchers evaluate their comment quality assessment studies?
  Rationale: Researchers may evaluate their comment assessment approaches, *e.g.*, by surveying developers, or by using a dataset of case studies. However, how often they involve professional developers and industries in such studies is unknown.

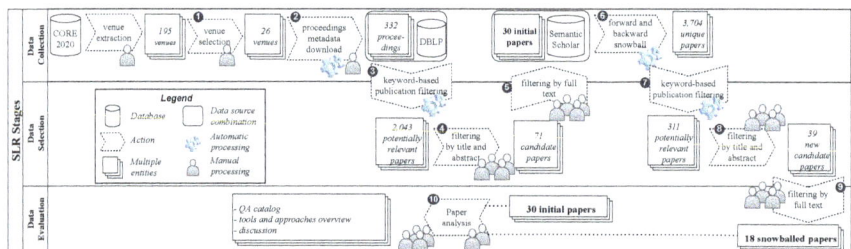

Figure 3.1: Data collection method implemented in the literature review

We perform an SLR which is an auditable and rigorous research method for "Evidence-Based Software Engineering (EBSE)." This method provides a way to collect, evaluate, and interpret relevant studies to a topic of interest (comment quality assessment). We carry out the SLR by following the widely accepted guidelines of Kitchenham *et al.* [82] and Keele [79]. Concretely, our SLR approach comprises three main steps, *i.e.*, data collection, data selection, and data evaluation, as shown in Figure 3.1.

3.1.2 Data Collection

Venue selection. We use the CORE ranking portal as a primary data source to identify all the potentially relevant conference and journal venues.[1] The portal provides assessments of major conferences and journals in the computing disciplines, and it is a well-established and regularly-validated registry maintained by the academic community. We extract all ranked journals in SE (search code 803 on the CORE portal) from the CORE portal[2] and all top conferences and workshops in the SE field (search code 4612).[3] This process provides us with an initial list of 85 journals and 110 conference venues.

We select in step ❶ 26 SE conferences and journals from 195 candidate venues based on the likelihood of finding relevant papers in the proceedings. We consider the proceedings from 2011 to 2020 since Zhi *et al.* investigated the works on software documentation quality — including code comments — from 1971 to 2011 [183]. We focus on A* and A conferences and journals, and add conferences of rank *B* or *C* if they are co-located with previously selected *A** and *A* conferences to have venues, such as the *IEEE/ACM International Conference on Program Comprehension* (ICPC) or the *IEEE International Workshop on Source Code Analysis and Manipulation* (SCAM) that focus on source code comprehension and manipulation. We prune venues that may not contain relevant contributions to source code comments. Specifically, we exclude a venue if its ten years of proceedings contain fewer than five occurrences of the words *documentation* or *comment*. This way, we exclude conferences, such as *IEEE International Conference on Engineering of Complex Computer Systems* (ICECCS), *Foundations of Software Science and Computational Structures* (FoSSaCS), and many others that primarily focus on other topics, such as verification or programming languages. Thus, we reduce our dataset to 20 conferences and six journals, as shown in 3.1.

In Table 3.1, we present the included venues: the column *Abbreviation* denotes the abbreviation used for the venue given in the *Venue* column, the column *R* denotes the corresponding CORE rank of the venue as of April

---

[1]https://www.core.edu.au/conference-portal
[2]http://portal.core.edu.au/jnl-ranks/?search=803&by=for&source=CORE2020&sort=arank&page=1
[3]http://portal.core.edu.au/conf-ranks/?search=4612&by=for&source=CORE2020&sort=arank&page=1

2021, and the column T specifies whether a venue is a conference (C) or a journal (J).

Table 3.1: Included journals, conferences, and workshops

Abbreviation	Venue	R	T
CSUR	ACM Computing Surveys	A*	J
TOSEM	ACM Transactions on Software Engineering and Methodology	A*	J
TSE	IEEE Transactions on Software Engineering	A*	J
EMSE	Empirical Software Engineering: an international journal	A	J
JSS	Journal of Systems and Software	A	J
IST	Information and Software Technology	A	J
ESEC/FSE	ACM SIGSOFT Symposium on the Foundations of Software Engineering	A*	C
ICSE	International Conference on Software Engineering	A*	C
ASPLOS	Architectural Support for Programming Languages and Operating Systems	A*	C
CAV	Computer Aided Verification	A*	C
ICFP	International Conference on Functional Programming	A*	C
OOPSLA	ACM Conference on Object Oriented Programming Systems Languages and Applications	A*	C
PLDI	ACM-SIGPLAN Conference on Programming Language Design and Implementation	A*	C
POPL	ACM-SIGACT Symposium on Principles of Programming Languages	A*	C
SIGMETRICS	Measurement and Modeling of Computer Systems	A*	C
ASE	Automated Software Engineering Conference	A	C
EASE	International Conference on Evaluation and Assessment in Software Engineering	A	C
ESEM	International Symposium on Empirical Software Engineering and Measurement	A	C
ICSME	IEEE International Conference on Software Maintenance and Evolution	A	C
MSR	IEEE International Working Conference on Mining Software Repositories	A	C
ISSRE	International Symposium on Software Reliability Engineering	A	C
VISSOFT	IEEE International Working Conference on Software Visualisation	B	C
ICGSE	IEEE International Conference on Global Software Engineering	C	C
ICPC	IEEE International Conference on Program Comprehension	C	C
MISE	International Workshop on Modelling in Software Engineering	C	C
SCAM	IEEE International Workshop on Source Code Analysis and Manipulation	C	C
WISA	International Conference on Web Information Systems and Applications	-	C
-	Software Quality Journal	C	J
SPE	Software: Practice and Experience	B	J
SAC	ACM Symposium on Applied Computing	B	C
MaLTeSQuE	IEEE Workshop on Machine Learning Techniques for Software Quality Evaluation	-	C
JSEP	Journal of Software: Evolution and Process	B	J
Internetware	Asia-Pacific Symposium on Internetware	-	C
IJCNN	IEEE International Joint Conference on Neural Networks	A	C
COMPSAC	International Computer Software and Applications Conference	B	C
APSEC	Asia-Pacific Software Engineering Conference	B	C
SEKE	International journal of software engineering and knowledge engineering	-	J

We consider only full papers (published in a technical track and longer than five pages) and retrieve in step ❷ the list of authors, the title of the paper, its abstract, and the number of pages of the publication for a total of 17 554 publications.

Keyword-based filtering. We apply in step ❸ a keyword-based filtering approach to select potentially relevant papers. To collect the relevant keywords for the keyword-based approach, we define three sets of keywords: K_1, K_2, and K_3. We examine the definition of *documentation* and *comment* in *IEEE Standard Glossary of Software Engineering Terminology* (IEEE Standard 610.12-1990) and add the identified keywords *comment*, *documentation*, and *specification* to the set K_1. We add further comment-related keywords to the set K_1 that are frequently mentioned in the context of code comments.

3.1. Study Design

Due to our specific interest in identifying the QAs that affect the comment quality, and the approaches to measure them, we formulate another keyword set K_2. To narrow down our search to the code comment-related studies, we formulate a third set of keywords K_3, to discard irrelevant studies in the initial phase. Based on the constructed keyword sets, we perform a three-step search on the conference proceedings using regular expressions. We account for possible upper- and lowercase letters in the keywords, and use word stems to select variations of keywords, *e.g.*, singular and plural forms. The script is publicly available in the replication package [126].

In the keyword-based filtering process, for every publication metadata record, we automatically check if the *title* and *abstract* fields:

1. **contain** at least one keyword from K_1: *comment, documentation, API, annotation, summar,* or *specification*

2. **and contain** at least one keyword from K_2: *quality, assess, metric, measure, score, analy, practice, structur, study,* or *studied*

3. but **do not contain** any of the keywords from K_3: *code review* (to exclude papers about code review comments) and *test*. We also extend K_3 with the words *keynote, invited,* and *poster* that sometimes appear in publications record titles, to exclude potential entries of non-technical papers that were not filtered out using the heuristics on the number of pages.

Such filtering will result in papers that explicitly mention concepts in which we are interested. For example, the paper *"A Human Study of Comprehension and Code Summarization"* from ICPC 2020 [158] contains the keywords *summar* from K_1 in the title and *quality* from K_2 in the abstract. However, the papers not sufficiently close to our research subject are excluded, *e.g.*, *"aComment: mining annotations from comments and code to detect interrupt related concurrency bugs"* from ICSE 2011 has two keywords *comment* and *annotation* from K_1 but none from K_2.

The final set of keywords (used for filtering) results from an iterative approach in which we manually scan the full venue proceedings metadata to make sure the set of keywords does not prune relevant papers, and refine the set of keywords during several iterative discussions. After applying the keyword-based filtering, we identify 2 043 studies as potentially relevant papers from a total of 17 554, which we review manually.

3.1.3 Data Selection

Four evaluators participate in assessing in step ❹ the 2 043 filtered papers to ensure that the papers indeed assess comment quality. Each paper is reviewed by three evaluators. The first evaluator independently decides the relevance of the paper, and then another evaluator reviews the paper. If they do not agree, the third evaluator reviews it, and the final decision is taken based on the majority-based voting mechanism. Evaluators decide by applying the inclusion and exclusion criteria to these papers.

Inclusion criteria

1. The topic of the paper is about code comment quality.

2. The study presents a model/technique/approach to assess code comments or software documentation including code comments.

Exclusion criteria

1. The paper is not in English.

2. It does not assess any form of quality aspects of comments *e.g.*, content, style, or language used.

3. It is not published in a technical track.

4. It is a survey paper.

5. It is not a peer-reviewed paper, or it is a pre-print.

6. It covers other documentation artifacts, *i.e.*, not comments.

7. It is shorter than five pages.

Thus, we reduce 2 043 papers to 71 candidate relevant papers with a fair agreement according to Cohen's Kappa (k=0.36). During this analysis process, some additional papers were found to be irrelevant. For example, the study by Aghajani *et al.* talks about the developer's perspective of software documentation. It seems relevant based on the title and abstract, but does not really assess code comment quality, and we thus discarded it [3]. We read in step ❺ their introduction, conclusion, and the study design (if needed) and discuss them amongst ourselves to ensure their relevance. After the discussion, we keep 30 papers.

To include other relevant papers that we might have missed with the venues-based approach, we perform in step ❻ a forward and backward snowballing approach for the 30 papers and retrieve 3 704 unique papers [177]. We apply in step ❼ the same keyword-based search and manual analysis in step ❽ to these 3 704 papers to find the candidate relevant papers, ending up with 39. After the discussion, we keep in step ❾ 18 papers.

In total, we find 48 relevant papers shown in Table 3.2 published in years shown in Figure 3.3 in the venues shown in Figure 3.2. In Table 3.2, the column *SID* indicates the study ID assigned to each paper (shown in A.2), and the column *Title* shows the title of the paper. In Figure 3.2, the color of a bar indicates the data collection phase in which the venue was first selected through the search process or snowball process.

3.1. Study Design

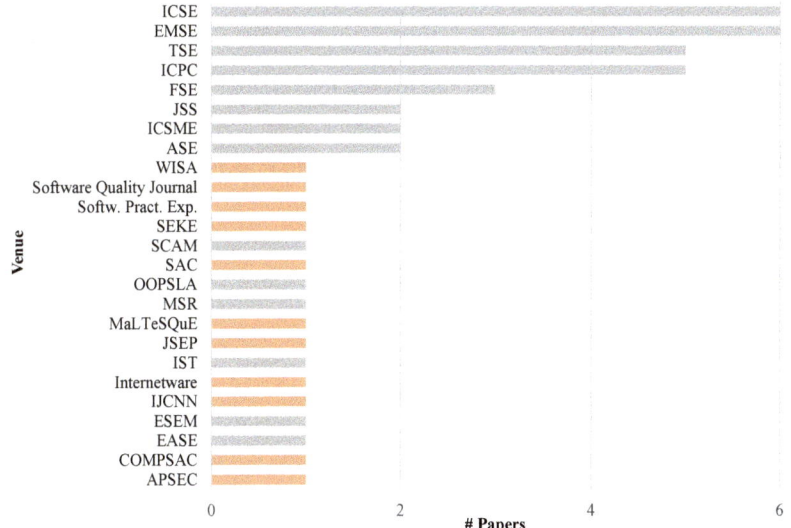

Figure 3.2: Relevant papers by venue

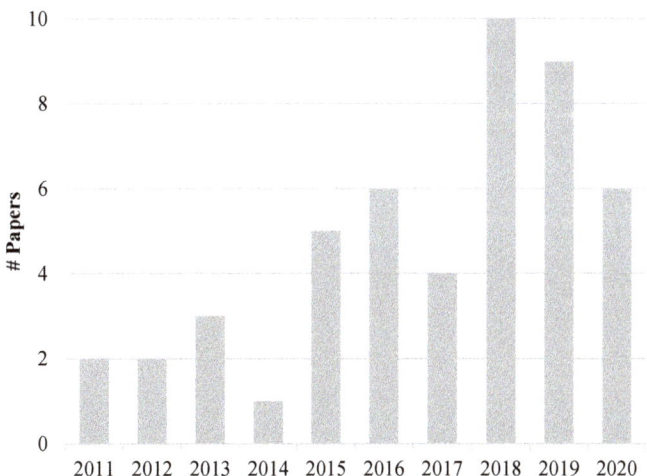

Figure 3.3: Relevant papers by year

Table 3.2: Included studies

SID	Title
[S1]	How Good is Your Comment? A Study of Comments in Java Programs.
[S2]	Quality analysis of source code comments.
[S3]	Evaluating usage and quality of technical software documentation: an empirical study.
[S4]	Inferring method specifications from natural language API descriptions.
[S5]	Using Traceability Links to Recommend Adaptive Changes for Documentation Evolution.
[S6]	On using machine learning to identify knowledge in API reference documentation.
[S7]	Detecting fragile comments.
[S8]	Automatically assessing code understandability: how far are we?
[S9]	Analyzing APIs documentation and code to detect directive defects.
[S10]	The effect of poor source code lexicon and readability on developers' cognitive load.
[S11]	A Large-Scale Empirical Study on Linguistic Antipatterns Affecting APIs.
[S12]	Improving API Caveats Accessibility by Mining API Caveats Knowledge Graph.
[S13]	A learning-based approach for automatic construction of domain glossary from source code and documentation.
[S14]	A framework for writing trigger-action todo comments in executable format.
[S15]	A large-scale empirical study on code-comment inconsistencies.
[S16]	Software documentation issues unveiled.
[S17]	The Secret Life of Commented-Out Source Code.
[S18]	Code Comment Quality Analysis and Improvement Recommendation: An Automated Approach
[S19]	A Human Study of Comprehension and Code Summarization.
[S20]	CPC: automatically classifying and propagating natural language comments via program analysis.
[S21]	Recommending insightful comments for source code using crowdsourced knowledge.
[S22]	Improving code readability models with textual features.
[S23]	Automatic Source Code Summarization of Context for Java Methods.
[S24]	Automatic Detection and Repair Recommendation of Directive Defects in Java API Documentation.
[S25]	Measuring Program Comprehension: A Large-Scale Field Study with Professionals.
[S26]	Usage and usefulness of technical software documentation: An industrial case study
[S27]	What should developers be aware of? An empirical study on the directives of API documentation.
[S28]	Analysis of license inconsistency in large collections of open source projects.
[S29]	Classifying code comments in Java software systems.
[S30]	Augmenting Java method comments generation with context information based on neural networks.
[S31]	Improving Source Code Lexicon via Traceability and Information Retrieval.
[S32]	Detecting API documentation errors.
[S33]	A Method to Detect License Inconsistencies in Large-Scale Open Source Projects.
[S34]	Recommending reference API documentation.
[S35]	Some structural measures of API usability.
[S36]	An empirical study of the textual similarity between source code and source code summaries.
[S37]	Linguistic antipatterns: what they are and how developers perceive them.
[S38]	Coherence of comments and method implementations: a dataset and an empirical investigation
[S39]	A comprehensive model for code readability
[S40]	Automatic Detection of Outdated Comments During Code Changes
[S41]	Classifying Python Code Comments Based on Supervised Learning
[S42]	Investigating type declaration mismatches in Python
[S43]	The exception handling riddle: An empirical study on the Android API.
[S45]	Migrating Deprecated API to Documented Replacement: Patterns and Tool
[S46]	A Topic Modeling Approach To Evaluate The Comments Consistency To Source Code
[S47]	Comparing identifiers and comments in engineered and non-engineered code: a large-scale empirical study
[S48]	Analyzing Code Comments to Boost Program Comprehension

3.1.4 Data Evaluation

We perform a final data evaluation on the 48 relevant publications identified in the data collection and selection phases. Then, we read in step ❿ each relevant study to identify various parameters to answer the research questions. For each paper, we extract common metadata, such as *publication year*, *venue*, *title*, *authors*, *authors' country*, and *authors' affiliation*. We then extract various fields (described in the following paragraphs) formulated to answer all research questions.

To answer SRQ$_1$: *What types of comments do researchers focus on when assessing comment quality?* we extract the *comment scope* and *language* fields, where the former describes what kinds of comments are under assessment, such as class, API, method (function), package, license, or inline comment, and the latter describes the programming language for which comments are assessed. In case a specific comment type is not mentioned, we consider it as "code comments."

To answer SRQ$_2$: *What QAs do researchers consider in assessing comment quality?* we gather various QAs that researchers mention to assess comments. Previous work by Zhi *et al.* listed various QAs that are considered important for software documentation quality, including code comments [183]. We adopt their QAs as an initial list and extend it if a study mentions any other QA. Their QAs are highlighted in bold in Table 3.3. As they considered various types of documentation, such as requirement and architecture documentation, not all their attributes fit exactly in our study. For instance, the category *format* indicates the format of the documentation (*e.g.*, UML, flow chart) in addition to the other aspects, such as the writing style of the document, use of diagrams, *etc.* As the format of the documentation is not applicable in our case due to our comment-specific interest, we keep only the applicable aspect of this QA. In the case a study uses different terminologies but has the same intent for the QAs in our list, we map them to our list and update the list of possible synonyms, or map them to the *other* category as shown in the column *Synonyms* in Table 3.3.

For the cases where the studies do not mention any specific QA and mention comment quality analysis in general, we map the study to the list of existing attributes or classify it as *other* based on their goal behind the quality analysis. For example, to support developers in easily finding relevant information for code comprehension tasks and to improve the comment quality assessment, Pascarella *et al.* identified various information types in comments [115]. They mentioned the study goal to improve comment quality and find relevant content, but did not mention any specific QA. Thus, we map their study to the *content relevance* attribute based on their study goal. Similarly, we map other comment classification studies, such as S06, S29, S41, and S48 to the *content relevance* attribute. At the same time, the studies on linguistic anti-patterns are mapped to the *consistency* attribute given that LAs are practices that lead to lexical inconsistencies among code elements, or between code and associated comments [12, 51, 2]. Negative attributes appearing in studies, such as *incompleteness* or *incorrectness* are mapped to their positive counterpart *completeness* or *correctness* to avoid duplication.

To answer SRQ$_3$: *Which techniques do researchers use to assess comment QAs?*, we collect the techniques (*technique type*) researchers propose or use to assess comment QAs. It describes if a technique, used to assess an QA, is based on natural language processing (NLP), heuristics, static

Table 3.3: QAs mentioned by Zhi *et al.* and other works

Quality Attribute	Synonyms	Description
Accessibility	availability, information hiding, easiness to find	if comment content can be accessed or retrieved by developers or not
Readability	clarity	the extent to which comments can be easily read by other readers
Spelling and grammar	natural language quality	grammatical aspect of the comment content
Trustworthiness		the extent to which developers perceive the comment as trustworthy
Author-related		identity of the author who wrote the comment
Correctness		the information in the comment is correct
Completeness	adequacy	how complete the comment content is to support development and maintenance tasks or whether there is missing information in comments
Similarity	uniqueness, duplication	how similar the comment is to other code documents or code
Consistency	uniformity, integrity	the extent to which the comment content is consistent with other documents or code
Traceability		the extent to which any modification in the comment can be traced, including who performed it
Up-to-date-ness		how the comment is kept up-to-date with software evolution
Accuracy	preciseness	accuracy or preciseness of the comment content, if the documentation is too abstract or vague and does not present concrete examples, then it can seem imprecise.
Information organization		how the information inside a comment is organized in comments
Format	including visual models, use of examples	quality of documents in terms of writing style, description perspective, use of diagram or examples, spatial arrangement, etc.
Coherence		how comment and code related to each other, *e.g.*, method comment should be related to the method name (S02, S38)
Conciseness		the extent to which comments are not verbose and do not contain unnecessary information (S23, S30, S47)
Content relevance		how relevant a comment or a part of a comment content is for a particular purpose (documentation, communication) (S01, S03, S29, S41, S47)
Maintainability		the extent to which comments are maintainable (S15-S17,S20-S21)
Understandability		the extent to which comments contribute in understanding the system (S19, S23)
Usability	usefulness	to which extent comments can be used by readers to achieve their objectives (S02, S16, S34, S35)
Documentation technology		whether the technology to write, generate, store documentation is the latest
Internationalization		the extent to which comments are correctly translated to other languages (S16)
Other		the study do not mention any QA and cannot be mapped to any of the above attributes

analysis, metrics, machine-learning (ML), or deep neural network (DNN) approaches. The intention behind it is to know which QAs are frequently assessed manually or using a particular automated approach. For example, if the study uses abstract syntax tree (AST)-based static analysis approaches then it is assigned to *static analysis*, if it uses machine-learning or deep-learning-based techniques then it is classified as *ML-based*, or *DNN-based*, respectively. A study using a mix of these techniques to assess an attribute can be assigned to each technique for the corresponding attribute. The studies do not always use automated techniques and can instead ask other developers to assess them manually; we assign such cases to the *manual assessment* category. In case the study uses a different technique than the mentioned ones, we extend the field values.

Table 3.4: Type of contributions the study makes

Category	Description
Method/technique	The study provides a novel or significant extension of an existing approach
Model	Provides a taxonomy to describe their observations or an automated model based on machine/deep learning
Metric	Provides a new metric to assess specific aspects of comments
Survey	Conducts survey to understand a specific problem and contribute insights from developers
Tool	Develops a tool to analyze comments

To answer SRQ_4: *What kinds of contributions do studies often make?* we capture the type of contribution researchers use or propose to assess comment quality. For instance, what kind of solutions the *solution proposal* research often proposes, such as a method, metric, model, or tool as described in Table 3.4.

SRQ_5: *How do researchers evaluate their comment quality assessment studies?* concerns how various kinds of contribution (*paper contribution* dimension) are evaluated in the studies. For example, it helps us to observe that if a study proposes a new method/technique to assess comments, then the authors also conduct an experiment on open-source projects to validate the contribution, or they consult the project developers, or both. We capture the type of evaluation in the *evaluation type* dimension. The dimension states the type of evaluation researchers conduct to validate their approaches, such as conducting an experiment on open-source projects, or surveying students, practitioners, or both. For automated approaches, we consider various performance metrics, also known as Information Retrieval (IR) metrics, that are used to assess the machine or deep learning-based models, such as Precision, Recall, F1-Measure, or accuracy under the *performance metrics*. In case the approach is validated by the authors of the work, we identify the evaluation type as *authors of the work*. The rationale

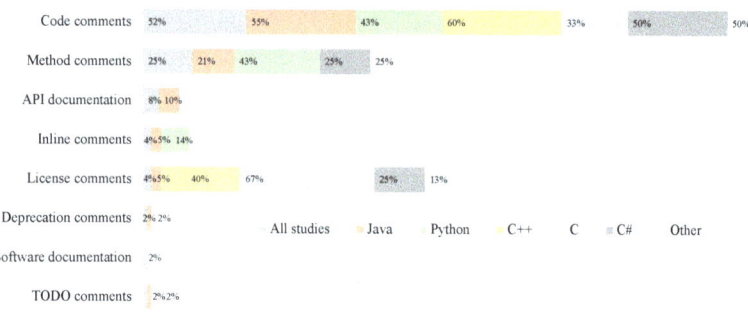

Figure 3.4: Types of comments per programming language

behind capturing this information is to identify the shortcomings in their evaluations, *e.g.*, how often the studies proposing a tool are validated with practitioners.

3.2 Results

3.2.1 Comment Types

Our results show that although researchers analyze comments from various programming languages, not all of these languages are equally popular. We find that Java is considered the most often in the comment quality assessment studies (in 88% of the studies), whereas, only 15% of the studies analyze comments of Python systems, and 10% of them analyze C++. The results are in contrast to the fact that various developer boards (GitHub, Stack Overflow[4], TIOBE [163]) show C/C++, Python, or JavaScript as equally or more commonly used programming languages. Only one study analyzes JavaScript comments (S44) despite JavaScript being reported to be the most popular language according to the Stack Overflow surveys of 2020 and 2021.[5] Given the emerging trend of studies leveraging natural-language information in JavaScript code [104, 93], more research on comment quality may be needed in the JavaScript environment.

As various types of source code comments exist in various programming languages to describe the code at various abstraction levels, half of the studies analyze all types of source code comments (*code comments*), whereas the remaining half focus on a specific type of comments, such as method or API, inline, or TODO comments as shown in Figure 3.4. The intent of various comment types varies, *e.g.*, Java class comments should present high-level information about the class, while method comments should present

---

[4]https://insights.stackoverflow.com/survey/2020
[5]https://insights.stackoverflow.com/survey/2021

implementation-level details [109]. By looking at the specific types of comments, we find that 25% of the studies focus exclusively on method and API comments. It shows the effort the research community puts into improving the API documentation. Other comment types are also analyzed to support developers with specific information types, such as license comments (S28, S33), TODOs (S14), inline (S17), or deprecation (S45) comments; we find no relevant paper that focuses specifically on the quality of *class* or *package* comments.

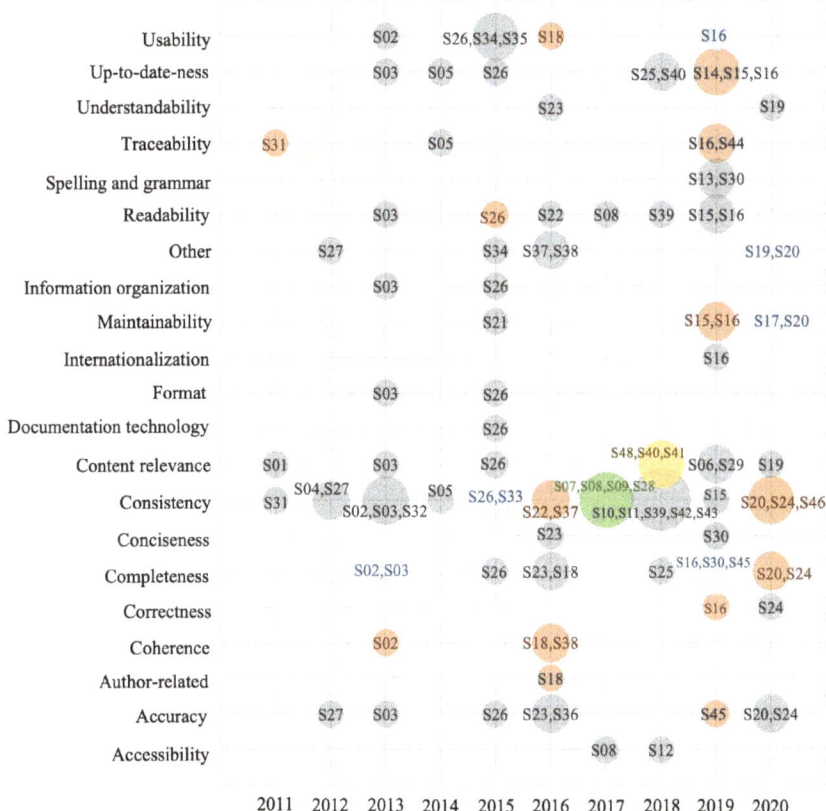

Figure 3.5: Frequency of analyzed QAs over year

> **Finding.** Even though 50% of the studies analyze all types of code comments, the rest focus on studying a specific type of comment, such as method comments, or inline comments, indicating research interest in leveraging a particular type of comment for specific development tasks. In terms of comment types, we observe class comments are not studied separately.

> **Finding.** 90% of the studies analyze comments from Java, while other languages have not yet received enough attention from the research community.

Zhi *et al.* showed that a majority of studies analyze just one type of system [183]. In contrast, our findings suggest that the trend of analyzing comments of multiple languages and systems is increasing. It also reflects the increasing use of polyglot environments in software development [165]. The "Other" label in Figure 3.4 comprises language-agnostic studies, *e.g.*, S16 or the studies considering less popular languages, *e.g.*, S33 focuses on COBOL. We find only one study (S44) that analyzes comments of six programming languages.

> **Finding.** The trend of analyzing multiple software systems of one or more programming languages, shows the increasing use of polyglot environments in software projects.

3.2.2 Comment Quality Attributes

Figure 3.5 shows all the attributes on the y-axis and the corresponding years on the x-axis. Each bubble in the plot highlights the quantity by the size of the bubble and IDs of the studies. In addition to the QAs found by Zhi *et al.*, highlighted in Table 3.3, we find 10 additional QAs that researchers use to assess comment quality, such as *usefulness, use of examples, usability, references, preciseness, natural language quality, maintainability, visual models, internationalization, documentation technology, content relevance, conciseness, coherence,* and *availability*. However, not all attributes reported by Zhi *et al.* for software documentation quality are used for comment quality. We find no mention of *trustworthiness* and *similarity* attributes even though several works highlighted their importance for high-quality documentation [169, 9, 37]. Similarly, Maalej *et al.* showed that developers trust code comments more than other types of software documentation [91]. This indicates the need to investigate the importance of trustworthy comments and develop approaches to assess them.

> **Finding.** Compared to the previous work by Zhi *et al.*, we find ten additional QAs researchers use to assess code comment quality.

We find that some attributes, such as *completeness, consistency, content relevance,* and *readability*, are often investigated, and *consistency* received constant and consistent attention across the years (S07, S08, S09, S29, S10, S11, S39, S42, S43) in contrast to *up-to-date-ness*, which received attention only in the last three years of the decade (S15, S16). We also find other attributes that are rarely investigated, such as *format, understandability, spelling and grammar, organization, internationalization, documentation technology, coherence, conciseness, author-related,* and *accessibility*.

More research is required to determine why these attributes draw intrinsically less attention than others for comments according to researchers or practitioners.

> **Finding.** While the QAs, such as *accuracy, consistency*, and *completeness* are frequently used to assess comment quality, other attributes, such as *coherence, conciseness*, and *understandability* are rarely investigated.

As each QA has its role and importance in overall comment quality, they are not measured in a mutually exclusive way. For instance, *accuracy* is measured by measuring the *correctness* and *completeness* of comment, such as *"the documentation is incorrect or incomplete and therefore no longer accurate documentation of an API"* (S24). Similarly, *up-to-date-ness* is measured through *consistency* of comments (S40) and *consistency* is evaluated and improved using *traceability* (S31). This indicates the need to clearly establish the dependency between various QAs and make developers and researchers aware of them to improve overall comment quality and build techniques accordingly. However, which techniques are currently used to measure various QAs is unknown. We explore this aspect in the following subsection.

> **Finding.** Many studies lack a clear definition of the QAs they use in their studies. This poses various challenges for developers and researchers, *e.g.*, understanding what a specific QA means, mapping the attribute to other similar attributes, and adapting the approaches to assess the attribute to a certain programming environment.

3.2.3 Comment Quality Assessment Techniques

We gather the types of techniques researchers use to measure the identified QAs. Figure 3.6 shows that the majority of the attributes are measured manually, *i.e.*, by asking developers to manually assess the QA (*manual assessment*) in comments. For instance, *coherence, format, organization, understandability*, and *usability* attributes are often measured manually. This indicates the need to investigate the challenges developers and researchers face in automating the measurement of such attributes. However, various studies did experiment with various automated approaches to speed up the comment quality assessment process. For instance, machine learning and heuristics-based approaches are often used to measure specific QAs, such as *consistency, content relevance*, and *up-to-date-ness* while ignoring other attributes. In machine learning-based approaches, researchers mostly use supervised machine learning techniques, which require human effort in labeling data. To avoid the longer training time and memory consumption of ML strategies, Kallis *et al.* used *fastText* to classify the issues reports on GitHub [78]. The *fastText* tool uses linear models and has achieved comparable results in classification to various deep-learning-based approaches.

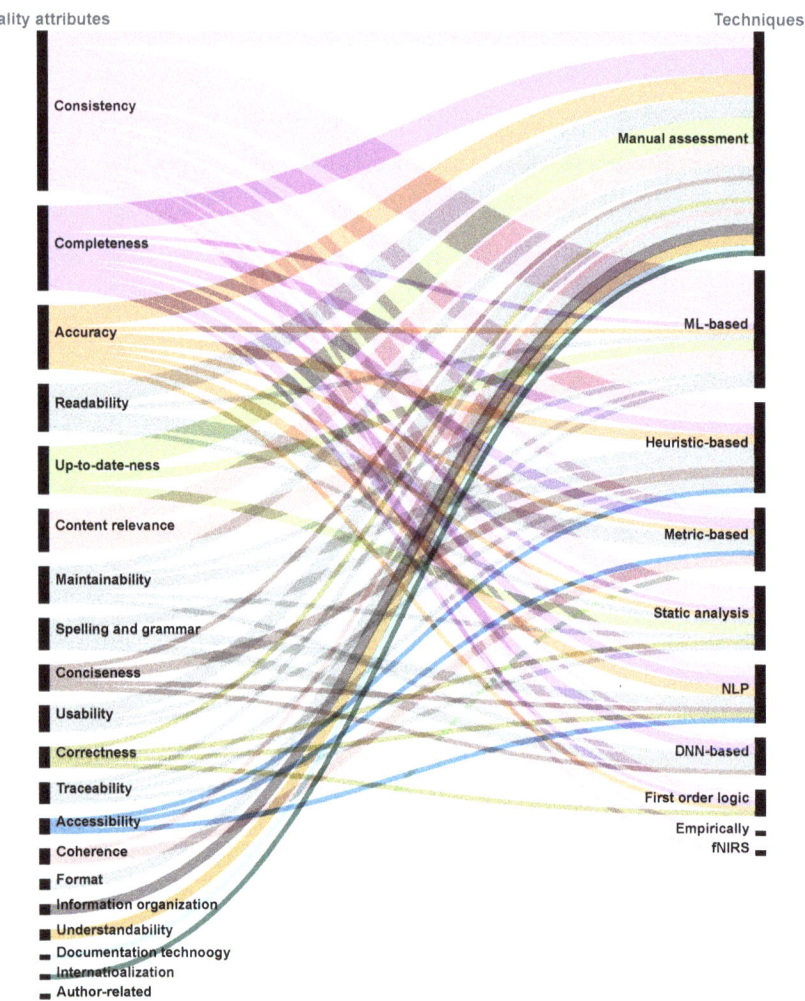

Figure 3.6: Types of techniques used to analyze various QAs

Minaee *et al.* showed that deep learning-based approaches surpassed common machine learning-based models in various text analysis areas, such as news categorization, and sentiment analysis [101]; It is worth exploring such approaches in the context of comments to reduce the effort in supervised machine learning techniques. In our study, we find studies, such as S06, S13, and S20 that use deep learning-based techniques partly along with machine learning-based techniques for specific attributes, such as *conciseness*, *spelling and grammar*, and *completeness*. However, there is still a huge number of attributes that are assessed manually and require heavy automation to support developers in automatically assessing comment quality.

> **Finding.** *Manual assessment* is still the most frequently-used technique to measure various QAs.

3.2.4 Study Contribution Types

Paper contribution	Evaluation type					
	Authors of the work	Experiment	Performance metrics	Survey practitioners	Survey practitioners and students	Survey students
Empirical results	S15 S16	S11		S26	S19	
Method/Technique	S30 S42 S44 S47	S07 S13 S28 S33 S45 S43 S46	S02 S04 S05 S07 S09 S13 S20 S41 S42	S02 S05 S21	S20 S23 S43	S10 S12
Metric	S36	S35			S18	
Model	S38 S27	S06 S27 S37 S38 S39	S06 S22 S29 S48 S40		S37	S40
Survey				S01 S03 S25	S08	
Tool		S32 S34	S17 S24		S14 S34	S24 S31

Figure 3.7: Types of evaluation for each contribution type

Contribution types. By categorizing the papers according to the *paper contribution* definition, Figure 3.7 shows that over 40% of papers propose an approach to assess code comments. A large part (75%) of them are heuristics-based approaches, *e.g.*, Zhou *et al.* and Wang *et al.* present such heuristics based on NLP (S9, S13). Models are the second contribution by frequency, which makes sense considering the increasing trend of leveraging machine learning during the considered decade: 60% of the relevant papers proposing models are based on such approaches.

Tool availability. Previous work indicated the developers' effort in seeking tools to assess documentation quality, and highlighted the lack of such tools [4]. Our study finds that 31% of the studies propose tools to assess specific QAs, mainly for detecting inconsistencies between comments and code. Of these studies proposing tools, 60% provide a link to them, indicating the potential hindrance in reproducibility of the remaining 40% of such studies.

Dataset availability. In terms of dataset availability, 50% of the studies provide a link to a replication package. Of the remaining papers, some provide a link to the case studies they analyze (typically open-source projects) [70], build on previously existing datasets [142], or mention the reasons why they could not provide a dataset. For instance, Garousi *et al.* indicated the company policy as a reason not to share the analyzed documentation in their case study [57].

> **Finding.** Nearly 50% of the studies still lack in the *replicability* dimension, as their respective dataset or tool is often not publicly accessible.

3.2.5 Study Evaluation

Figure 3.7 shows how authors evaluate their contributions. We see that code comment assessment studies generally lack a systematic evaluation, surveying only students, or conducting case studies on specific projects only. Most of the time, an experiment is conducted without assessing the results through any kind of external expertise judgment. Hence, only 30% of the relevant studies evaluate their approach with practitioners. This can lead to overfitting the approaches, and the approaches are unaware or not aligned exactly to industrial needs. Similarly, when a new *method/technique* or comment classification *model* is proposed, it is often assessed based on conventional performance metrics, such as Precision, Recall, or F1-Measure (S02, S04, S07, S29, S41, *etc.*), and rarely the results are verified in an industry setting or with practitioners.

3.3 Implications and Discussion

Comment Types and languages. The analysis of the comment quality assessment studies in the last decade shows that the trend of analyzing comments from multiple languages and systems is increasing compared to the previous decade, where a majority of the studies focus on one system [183]. It reflects the increasing use of polyglot environments in software development [165]. Additionally, while in the past researchers focused on the quality of code comments in general terms, there is a new trend of studies that narrow their research investigation to specific comment types (methods, TODOs, deprecation, inline comments), indicating the increasing interest of researchers in supporting developers in providing a particular type of information for program comprehension and maintenance tasks.

Emerging quality attributes. Our analysis shows that several new QAs are being studied by researchers, which were not identified in the previous work [183]. This change can be explained by the trend of analyzing specific types of comments. As a consequence of this shift of focus towards specific comment types, the same attributes used in prior studies can assume different definition nuances, depending on the kinds of comments considered. For example, the *up-to-date-ness* attribute, originally referred to as a cause of code-comment inconsistency, assumes a different interpretation in the context of TODO comments. A TODO comment that *becomes outdated* consists of a feature that will not be implemented, which means that such a comment should be addressed within some deadline, and then removed from the codebase (S14).

Mapping taxonomies. In recent years, several taxonomies concerning code comments have been proposed; however, all of them are characterized by a rather different focus, such as the scope of the comments (S02), the information embedded in the comment (S29, S41), the issues related to specific comment types (S06, S40, S48), as well as the programming language they belong to, thus missing an overall view of code comment taxonomy. Additionally, which taxonomy serves which purpose for developers, for example, accessing a certain kind of information, assessing a specific aspect of comment quality, or code, is not well explained. Thus, there is a need for a comprehensive code comment taxonomy or model that maps all these aspects and definitions in a more coherent manner to have a better overview of developer commenting practices across languages.

Investigation of less frequent quality attributes. While some QAs are frequently investigated, some are largely overlooked in the literature, such as *accessible*, *trustworthy*, and *understandable*. Additionally, there is not enough research into approaches and automated tools that ensure that comments are *accessible*, *trustworthy*, and *understandable*, despite numerous studies suggesting that having good code comments brings several benefits. As the techniques based on natural language processing and machine learning are increasingly used in assessing various aspects of comments, deep learning techniques do not yet seem to have gained a foothold within the community for assessing comment quality.

3.4 Threats to Validity

Threats to construct validity. This principally concerns the estimations used in the evaluation process. In this case, threats arise mainly because of (i) the imprecision in the automated selection and retrieval of relevant studies (*i.e.*, the three-step search on the conference proceedings based on regular expressions), and (ii) the subjectivity and error-proneness of the following manual classification and categorization of the papers.

We alleviated the first threat by manually classifying a sample of relevant papers from a set of conference proceedings, and comparing this classification with the one recommended by the automated approach based on regular expressions. This allowed us to gradually improve the initial set of regular expressions. To avoid any bias in the selection of the papers, we selected the regular expression in a deterministic way (as detailed in section 3.1): we first examined the definition of *documentation* and *comment* in *IEEE Standard Glossary of Software Engineering Terminology* (IEEE Standard 610.12-1990) and identified the relevant keywords. We further extended comment-related keywords that are frequently mentioned in the context of code comments. In addition, we formulated a set of keywords to discard irrelevant studies that presented similar keywords, e.g., code review comments. To verify the correctness of the final set of keywords, we manually scanned the full venue proceedings metadata to ensure the set of keywords did not prune relevant papers. This iterative approach allowed us to verify that our keyword-based filtering approach does not lead to false negatives for the selected venues.

We mitigated the second threat by applying a multi-stage manual classification of conference proceedings, involving multiple evaluators and reviewers, as discussed in section 3.1.

Threats to internal validity. This concerns confounding factors that could impact our outcomes. A potential source of bias might be related to the way we chose and analyzed the conference proceedings. To deal with potential threats regarding the actual regular expressions considered for the selection of relevant studies, we created regular expressions that tend to be inclusive, *i.e.*, that select papers that are at least marginally related to the topic of interest, and we took a final decision only after a manual assessment.

Threats to external validity. This concerns the generalization and completeness of results and findings. Although the number of analyzed papers is large, since it involves studies spanning the last ten years of research, there is still the possibility that we missed some relevant studies. We mitigated this threat by applying various selection criteria to select relevant conference proceedings, considering the well-established venues and communities related to code comment-related studies, as discussed in section 3.1. It is important to mention that we intentionally limit the scope in two ways, which poses threats to the completeness of the study results and findings. First, we mainly focus on research work investigating code comment quality, without integrating studies from industry tracks of conference venues (as done in previous studies close to ours [45, 183]). Second, we focus on the studies that involve manually written code comments in order to avoid auto-generated comments (already investigated in recent related work [154, 106]). To limit further potential threats concerning the completeness of our study, we use the snowball approach to reach potentially relevant studies that we could have missed with our venue selection. However, we support the argument of Garousi et al. [58], who report that a *multivocal* literature review, with further replications, is desirable to the overall interpretation of code comment QAs. It can be more complete by studying the *grey literature*, which can offer a more broad or practical perspective on the problem from industry and academic practitioners alike.

3.5 Summary and Conclusion

In this chapter, we studied the problem of *assessing the quality of code comments* by answering our RQ_1: *How do researchers measure comment*

3.5. Summary and Conclusion

quality?. To answer the research question, we conducted an SLR on source code comment quality evaluation practices in the decade of 2011 — 2020. We reviewed 2 353 studies and studied 48 relevant ones to understand the effort of SE researchers. We specifically explored the types of comments they focus on, the QAs they consider relevant, the techniques they use to assess their QAs, and finally, their contributions.

Our findings showed that most studies consider only comments in Java source files, and thus may not generalize to comments of other languages. Although the trend of analyzing specific types of comments has increased in the past decade, we highlighted that the studies rarely analyze class comments. We found 21 in total QAs to assess comments but the studies often focused on only a few QAs, with a clear dominance of *consistency*, *completeness*, *accuracy*, and *readability*. Some QAs, such as *conciseness*, *coherence*, *organization*, and *understandability* are rarely investigated. Compared to previous work by Zhi *et al.*, we found ten additional QAs researchers use to assess code comment quality. We also observed that the majority of the approaches to assess various QAs are based on manual evaluation or heuristics rather than automated approaches. Such approaches require validation on other languages and projects to generalize them.

We address some of these concerns in the next chapters. Specifically, in chapter 4, we analyze class comments of three languages, Java, Python, and Smalltalk, and map class commenting practices across languages. Additionally, in chapter 5, we address the concern of manual assessment rather than automated approaches, by establishing a language-independent approach to automatically identify specific information types from comments.

4

Comment Information Types (CITs)

The previous chapter discussed the notion of comment quality, the quality attributes, and tools and techniques researchers propose to assess comment quality. However, in order to understand the specification of high-quality comments, it is essential to comprehend the current developer commenting practices.

Previous studies have investigated code comments in various programming languages from different aspects, showing the importance of high-quality comments in program comprehension and maintenance activities, and the challenges in achieving high-quality code comments. However, very few studies have explored developer commenting practices, such as what types of information developers embed in comments, how they write such information types, and whether such practices vary across programming languages. Additionally, they have investigated source code comments as a whole unit, whereas different kinds of comments contain different types of information and can support developers in development tasks accordingly. In this chapter, we investigate class comments of various object-oriented programming languages to better understand developer commenting practices.

This chapter is based on the journal articles:
- "P. Rani, S. Panichella, M. Leuenberger, M. Ghafari, and O. Nierstrasz. What do class comments tell us? An investigation of comment evolution and practices in Pharo Smalltalk, EMSE'21" [136] and
- "P. Rani, S. Panichella, M. Leuenberger, A. Sorbo, and O. Nierstrasz. How to identify class comment types? A multi-language approach for class comment classification, JSS'21" [132]

4. COMMENT INFORMATION TYPES (CITs)

Given the relevance of code comments in program comprehension and maintenance tasks, previous works have analyzed code comments from various aspects, such as examining the co-evolution of comments and code [77, 54, 55, 75], assessing comment quality [81, 159, 88], identifying inconsistencies between code and comments [137, 176], or identifying bugs using comments [185]. Recently, few studies have focused on analyzing the information developers embed in comments with the aim to improve the quality of comments [111, 70, 159, 115, 182]. However, these works have focused on source code comments as a whole unit, and of a specific programming language, mainly Java. Thus, in this chapter, we aim to answer RQ_2: *What kinds of information do developers write in comments across languages?*

In object-oriented programming languages, various types of source code comments exist, such as inline comments, block comments, method comments, and class comments, but not all types are intended to contain the same information. For example, class comments in Java play an essential role in providing the high-level overview of a class [35], while method comments in providing the low-level implementation details [109]. We start our analysis by focusing on *class comments* as they help understand complex programs [109].

Class comments are written using different notations and guidelines in various languages [52]. Therefore, commenting practices of developers in terms of what they write in comments may vary across programming languages. For example, in Java (a statically-typed language), a class comment provides a high-level outline of a class *e.g.*, the purpose of the class, what the class does, and other classes of the system it interacts with [109]. In Python (a dynamically-typed language), the class comment guidelines suggest adding low-level details about public methods, instance variables, and subclasses, in addition to the high-level summary of the class [121, 120]. On the other hand, in Smalltalk (a dynamically-typed language), class comments contain high-level design details as well as low-level implementation details of the class, *e.g.*, the rationale behind the class, its instance variables, key methods, and important implementation-specific details. We argue that the extent to which class commenting practices vary across different languages is an aspect that has been only partially investigated in previous works.

Indeed, our results from the previous chapter confirm that class comments are rarely analyzed, while method comments and inline comments are often explored. With the recent development of complex frameworks and tools, multi-language software systems are increasingly common [165]. Therefore, investigating developer class commenting practices across languages is critical to assess and monitor the quality and evolution of comments. We examine developer class commenting practices (*e.g.*, comment content) in Java, Python, and Smalltalk. We describe the motivation that makes these languages ideal candidates for our analysis in section 4.1.

Our results highlight that developers embed 16 types of information in class comments, which vary from the high-level overview of the class to the low-level implementation details of the class across the investigated languages. Specifically, Python and Smalltalk class comments contain more low-level implementation details about the class compared to Java. Although various types of information are interweaved in class comments, we observed that developers use common natural language patterns to write similar types of information. Such patterns can be utilized to automatically identify these information types from comments and support developers in assessing them to have high-quality comments.

4.1 Motivation

Code commenting practices vary across programming languages depending on the language's paradigm, its involved communities, its purpose, and its usage in different domains.

For our investigation, we selected (i) Java and Python, two of the top programming languages according to the Google Trend popularity index [66] and the TIOBE index [163], and (ii) Pharo Smalltalk, as its class commenting practices emerged from Smalltalk-80 [117, 63]. Other criteria to select these languages are explained in the following paragraphs.

```java
/**
 * The server-side interface that controls Grid's selection state
 * SelectionModel should extend {@link AbstractGridExtension}.
 *
 * @author Vaadin Ltd
 * @since 8.0
 *
 * @param <T>
 *            the grid bean type
 * @see AbstractSelectionModel
 * @see SingleSelectionModel
 * @see MultiSelectionModel
 */
public interface GridSelectionModel<T> extends SelectionModel<T>, Extension {
    ...
}
```

Figure 4.1: A class comment in Java

```python
class OneHotCategorical(Distribution):
    r"""
    Creates a one-hot categorical distribution parameterized by :attr:`probs` or
    :attr:`logits`.

    Samples are one-hot coded vectors of size ``probs.size(-1)``.

    .. note:: The `probs` argument must be non-negative, finite and have a non-zero sum,
              and it will be normalized to sum to 1 along the last dimension. :attr:`probs`
              will return this normalized value.
              The `logits` argument will be interpreted as unnormalized log probabilities
              and can therefore be any real number. It will likewise be normalized so that
              the resulting probabilities sum to 1 along the last dimension. :attr:`logits`
              will return this normalized value.

    See also: :func:`torch.distributions.Categorical` for specifications of
    :attr:`probs` and :attr:`logits`.

    Example::

        >>> m = OneHotCategorical(torch.tensor([ 0.25, 0.25, 0.25, 0.25 ]))
        >>> m.sample()  # equal probability of 0, 1, 2, 3
        tensor([ 0.,  0.,  0.,  1.])

    Args:
        probs (Tensor): event probabilities
        logits (Tensor): event log probabilities (unnormalized)
    """
```

Figure 4.2: A class comment in Python

Java and Python. On the one hand, Java is a general-purpose and statically-typed object-oriented programming language with wide adoption in the industry. Python, on the other hand, is dynamically-typed and supports object-oriented, functional, and procedural programming. We can observe differences in the notations used by Java and Python developers for commenting source code elements. For instance in Java, a class comment as shown in Figure 4.1 is usually written above the class declaration using annotations (*e.g.*, `@param`, `@version`, *etc.*), whereas a class comment in Python is typically written below the class declaration as "docstrings" which is shown in Figure 4.2.[1] Developers use dedicated annotations to denote specific types of information, for instance, Java developers use `@author` and `@see` *Javadoc* annotations to mention the author details and referenced classes. Python developers use similar docstring annotations, such as `See also:`, `Example:` and `Args:`, and they use tools, such as *Pydoc* and *Sphinx* to process them. However, not all languages support annotations and structured guidelines to write comments.

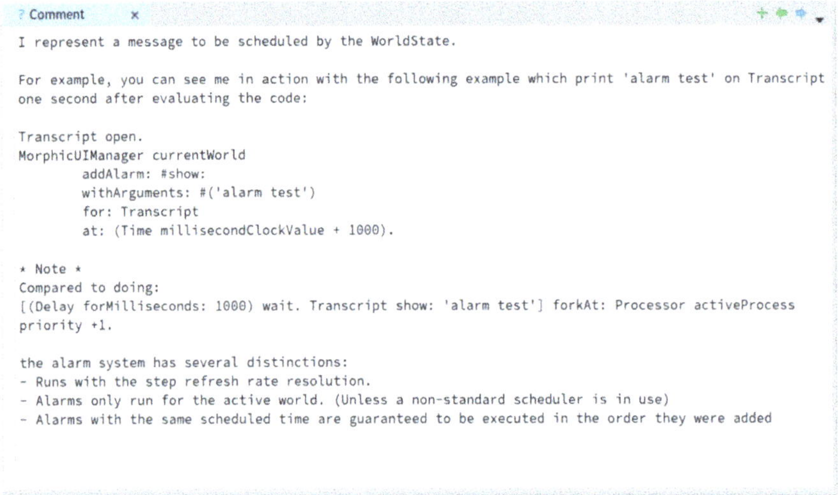

```
? Comment
I represent a message to be scheduled by the WorldState.

For example, you can see me in action with the following example which print 'alarm test' on Transcript
one second after evaluating the code:

Transcript open.
MorphicUIManager currentWorld
        addAlarm: #show:
        withArguments: #('alarm test')
        for: Transcript
        at: (Time millisecondClockValue + 1000).

* Note *
Compared to doing:
[(Delay forMilliseconds: 1000) wait. Transcript show: 'alarm test'] forkAt: Processor activeProcess
priority +1.

the alarm system has several distinctions:
- Runs with the step refresh rate resolution.
- Alarms only run for the active world. (Unless a non-standard scheduler is in use)
- Alarms with the same scheduled time are guaranteed to be executed in the order they were added
```

Figure 4.3: A class comment in Smalltalk

Smalltalk. Smalltalk is a pure object-oriented, dynamically-typed, and reflective programming language. It is still widely used in software systems, and has gained the second place for *most loved programming language* in the Stack Overflow survey of 2017.[2] Pharo is an open-source and live development environment incorporating a Smalltalk dialect. The Pharo ecosystem includes a significant number of projects used in research, and industry [117]. We computed the ratio of comment sentences to code lines in the most recent Pharo release (*i.e.*, Pharo 7) and found that 15% of the total lines are comments.

A typical class comment in Pharo (the Smalltalk environment) is a source of high-level design information about the class as well as low-level implementation details. For example, the class comment of the class `Morphic-Alarm` in Figure 4.3 documents (i) the intent of the class in the first line, followed by (ii) a code example to instantiate the class, (iii) a note explain-

---

[1] https://sphinxcontrib-napoleon.readthedocs.io/en/latest/example_numpy.html
[2] https://insights.stackoverflow.com/survey/2017/ last accessed on Aug 4, 2021

ing the corresponding comparison, and (iv) the features of the alarm system in the last paragraph. The class comment uses complete sentences, often written in the first-person form, and does not use any kind of annotations, such as @param or @see to mark the information type, as opposed to class comments in other languages [109, 111, 182]. We summarize the key characteristics that make Smalltalk ideal for our investigation of class commenting practices in object-oriented programming languages:

- Class comments are a primary source of documentation in Smalltalk.

- As a descendant of Smalltalk-80, Pharo has a long history of class comments being separated from the source code [62], and is thus appropriate to analyze various aspects (evolution aspect, information embedded in them, writing style) of class comments.

- Smalltalk has supported liveness for more than three decades, therefore, it can reveal interesting insights into code documentation in live programming environments.

- Class comments in Pharo neither use any annotations nor the writing style used in Javadocs or Pydocs, thus presenting a rather different aspect on commenting practices, and challenges for existing information identification approaches [115, 182].

- Pharo traditionally offers a default class comment template, which follows a CRC (Class-Responsibility-Collaboration) model, but no other standard guidelines are offered for the structure and style of the comments. The template follows a different and informal writing style compared to Java, Python, and C/C++, and it has evolved over the years.

Consequently, Pharo is appropriate as a case study to investigate what additional information developers embed in comments and to what extent developers follow the template in writing comments.

4.2 Study Design

By analyzing multiple languages that vary in their class comments, we can provide a more general overview of class commenting practices. To understand the multi-language nature of comments, we investigate RQ_1: *What kinds of information do developers write in comments across languages?* by formulating the following two subsidiary research questions (SRQs):

4.2.1 Research Questions

- SRQ_1: *To what extent do information types vary across programming languages?*

Rationale: As code comments are written using different notations and guidelines in various programming languages [52], commenting practices of developers may vary. Although previous works provide a taxonomy of code comments of a specific programming language, there is still a need to map these taxonomies to better understand developer commenting practices.

- SRQ_2: *What types of information are present in class comments across languages?*
  Rationale: Various types of code comments, such as inline, method, or class comments, exist in object-oriented languages, but not all types intend to contain the same type of information. Depending on the specific type of comment and the particular programming language, developers may embed different kinds of information in them. Since our SLR results highlight that class comments are rarely analyzed, we study class comments of three programming languages. Extracting class comment information types or simply *CCTM* (*Class Comment Type Model*) can further help in providing custom details to both novice and expert developers at different stages of development.

4.2.2 Data Collection

We selected popular, open-source, and heterogeneous projects for all the languages, *i.e.*, Java, Python, and Smalltalk. Such projects vary in terms of size, contributors, domains, ecosystems, and coding style or comment guidelines. As not all classes of a project contain class comments, we identified the classes with class comments. Afterward, we extracted a statistically significant sample of class comments to conduct a manual analysis.

To determine the minimum size of the statistically significant sample for each language dataset, we set the confidence level to 95%, and the margin of error to 5% [167]. Next, we selected the number of comments from each project based on the proportion of the project's class comments of all comments (from all projects). For instance, class comments from the Eclipse project in Java contribute to 29% of the total comments, *i.e.*, comments from all Java projects. Therefore, we selected the same proportion of sample comments, *i.e.*, 29% of the Java sample size from of Eclipse project (*110 class comments*) as shown in Table 4.1. To select representative sample comments from each project, we applied the *stratified random sampling strategy* and selected a proportional number of comments from each stratum. The strata were defined based on the length of comments (in terms of lines). In particular for each project, we first computed the quintiles based on the distribution of the comments' length and treated them as strata. For example, to choose 110 sample comments for Eclipse as shown in Table 4.1, we explored the distribution of the number of lines in comments and obtained quintiles as follows 1, 3, 4, 5, 7, and 1473. Hence, the five strata of comment lines are 1-3, 4-4, 5-5, 6-7, and 8-1473. Then from each stratum, we selected the proportional number of comments.

Java. We selected six open-source projects analyzed in previous work [115] to ease the comparison of our work with the previous achievements. Modern complex projects are commonly developed using multiple programming languages. For example, *Apache Spark* contains 72% Scala classes, 9% Java classes, and 19% classes from other languages [10]. In the context of our study, we only considered classes from the language under investigation. For each class, we parsed the Java code and extracted the code comments preceding the class definition using an Abstract Syntax Tree (AST)-based parser. During the extraction, we found instances of block comments, which start with /* symbol in addition to Javadoc class comments, which start with /** symbol before the class definition. In such cases, the parser detected the immediately preceding comment, *i.e.*, a block or Javadoc comment as a class comment, and treated the other comment above it as a dangling comment. To not miss any kinds of class comment, we adapted our parser to merge both comments, *i.e.*, the detected class comment and the dangling comment as the whole class comment.

Table 4.1: Comments found in Java projects

Project	% Java classes	# Java classes	# Class comments	% Dataset	# Sampled comments
Eclipse	98%	9 128	6 253	29%	110
Spark	9.3%	1 090	740	3.4%	13
Guava	100%	3 119	2 858	13%	50
Guice	99%	552	466	2.1%	10
Hadoop	92%	11 855	8 846	41%	155
Vaadin	55%	5 867	2 335	11%	41

We present an overview of the selected Java projects in Table 4.1 of which the corresponding raw files can be found in the replication package [129]. We established 379 class comments as the statistically significant sample size based on the total number of classes with comments. The number of lines in Java class comments varies from 1 to 4605 as shown in Figure 4.4. From each project's distribution, we established strata based on the measured quintiles, and then we selected the number of representative comments from each stratum. We followed the same approach for Python and Smalltalk to sample and select representative comments.

Python. Similar to Java, we selected seven open-source Python projects analyzed in previous work [182]. To extract class comments from Python

4. Comment Information Types (CITs)

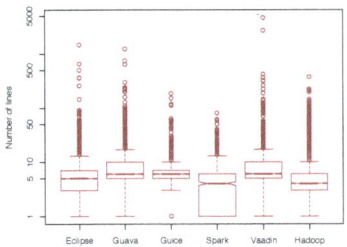
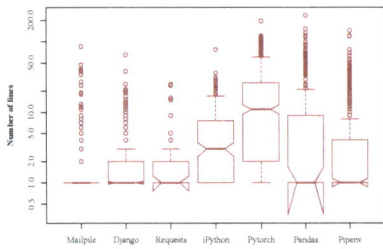

Figure 4.4: Distribution of Java projects **Figure 4.5:** Distribution of Python projects

classes, we implemented an AST-based parser and extracted the comments preceding the class definitions. The metadata related to the selected projects

Table 4.2: Comments found in Python projects

Project	# Python classes	# Class comments	% Dataset	# Sampled comments
Requests	79	43	1.1%	4
Pandas	1 753	377	9.9%	35
Mailpile	521	283	7.5%	26
IPython	509	240	6.3%	22
Djnago	8 750	1 164	30%	107
Pipenev	1 866	1 163	30%	107
Pytorch	2 699	520	13%	48

for Python is reported in Table 4.2, while the class comments are found in our replication package [129]. We measured 349 sample comments to be the statistically significant sample size.

Smalltalk-CCTM. In contrast to Java and Python, Smalltalk does not have an existing taxonomy of class comments or code comments. To prepare a Smalltalk taxonomy for class comments, we analyzed the core libraries of the latest stable version of Pharo, namely Pharo 7. The Pharo core environment presents a default template to write class comments and encourages developers to write them.[3] The initial categories of the taxonomy are constructed based on the content available in the template. Since each class has one class comment, every class of Pharo 7 that contains class comment contributed to the analysis dataset. This resulted in a dataset of 6 324 classes, which includes classes related to files, collections, sockets, streams,

---

[3] https://pharo.org/features

exceptions, graphical interfaces, unit tests, *etc.* Following the methodology described for Java and Python, we selected a statistically significant sample of 363 comments from 6 324 classes. The number of lines in the comments

Table 4.3: Comments found in Pharo 7 core

Stratum	# Class comments	% Dataset	# Sampled comments
1-1	3 040	48%	175
2-2	945	15%	54
3-6	1 224	19%	69
7-272	1 115	18%	65
Total	6 324	100%	363

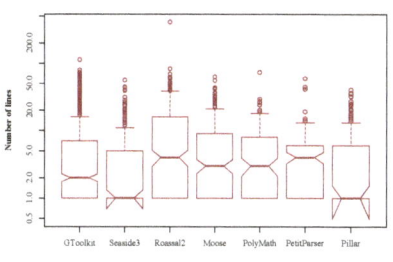
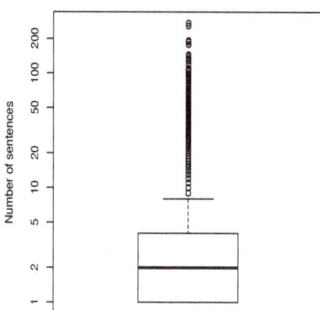

Figure 4.6: Distribution of Smalltalk projects   **Figure 4.7:** Distribution of Pharo7 comments

varied from 1 to 272 as shown in Figure 4.7, and provided the five quintiles 1, 1, 2, 3, 6, and 272. Based on the quintile values, we obtained comment strata shown in Table 4.3, and calculated the comment proportion of each stratum. Once we formulated the taxonomy for Smalltalk class comments, we verified it on external Smalltalk projects similar to Java and Python. We explain the selection criteria for these projects in the following paragraphs.

Smalltalk: To generalize the Smalltalk CCTM, verify the practices of Smalltalk core developers, and compare its commenting practices to Java and Python, we analyzed seven external open-source projects. We retrieved the external projects from GitHub[4] based on several criteria: (i) the project is not part of Pharo 7 core, (ii) it is an active project (it has an activity since 2019), (iii) the project history spans at least two years with at least 600 commits, (iv) it is not a repository for books, an article, or documentation, (v) it has more than five contributors, and (vi) the project does not contain more than 20% code from other programming languages to avoid polyglot

---

[4] https://github.com/topics/pharo?o=desc&s=stars

projects, *e.g.*, we did not consider *Opensmalltalk-vm* which contains 89% code from C, and *SmalltalkCI* which contains 35% shell scripts,[5] and (vi) the project contains more than 20 000 lines of Smalltalk code to remove small projects, such as *MaterialDesignLite*,[6] *Kendrick*,[7] and *PharoLauncher*.[8]

We sorted the projects based on commits and size (size is computed based on lines of code), and selected the top seven projects. These projects consequently vary in size, domain, and contributors. We selected 351 comments from the selected projects, following the methodology of selecting representative comments in Java and Python.

Table 4.4: Comments found in Smalltalk projects

Projects	Total classes	# Class comments	% Dataset	# Sampled comments
GToolkit	4 191	1 315	43%	148
Seaside	841	411	14%	46
Roassal	830	493	16%	56
Moose	1 283	316	10%	36
PolyMath	300	155	5%	17
PetitParser	191	99	3%	11
Pillar	420	237	8%	27

Table 4.4 shows the details of each Smalltalk project. We extracted a stable version of each project that is compatible with Pharo 7 except for GToolkit, which required Pharo 8 due to the lack of backward compatibility. We archived the selected projects and made them available in the replication package [129].

4.2.3 Analysis Method

Preparing Smalltalk-CCTM. Compared to Java and Python, a code comment taxonomy did not exist in Smalltalk. To prepare the class comment taxonomy for Smalltalk, three evaluators, *i.e.*, two Ph.D. candidates and one faculty member, each with at least four years of programming experience, manually analyzed the selected 363 comments. The 363 comments were equally divided among the three evaluators so that each subset (of size 121) had an equal number of randomly selected comments from each of the groups identified (see column *# Sampled comments* of Table 4.3). This ensured that each evaluator's dataset included comments of all lengths and

---

[5]https://github.com/OpenSmalltalk/opensmalltalk-vm
[6]https://github.com/DuneSt/MaterialDesignLite
[7]https://github.com/UNU-Macau/kendrick
[8]https://github.com/pharo-project/pharo-launcher

projects. At first, they constructed new categories and placed the comment sentences into them according to the intent of the sentence. Then, they used a two-step validation approach (described later in the section) to validate the content classification of the comment and the category name assigned to the content type. This way, all the categories were discussed by all the evaluators for a better naming convention, and whenever required, unnecessary categories were removed, and duplicates were merged using a majority voting mechanism.

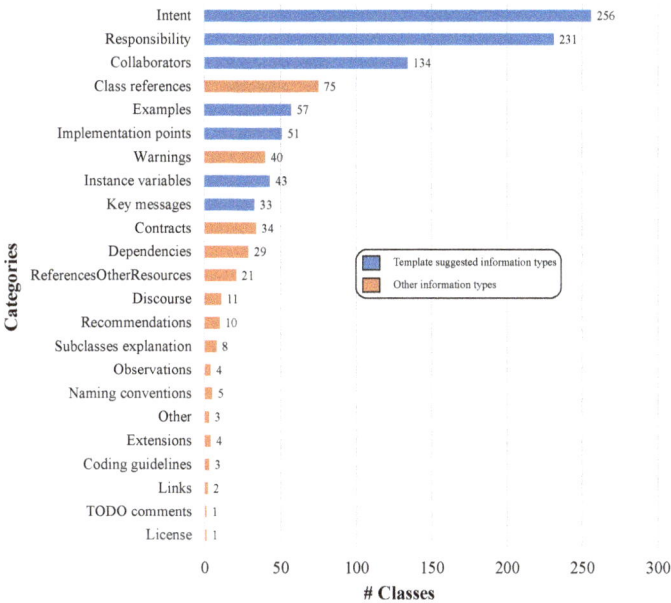

Figure 4.8: Information types found in Smalltalk comments

Resulting Smalltalk-CCTM. As a result of the Smalltalk-CCTM process, we identified 23 types of information (categories) in Smalltalk class comments as shown in Figure 4.8. Seven of the categories were inspired from the class comment template. We observed that developers had mentioned these categories more often than other categories. For instance, the *intent* and the *responsibility* categories (suggested by the template) were found in 65% of the sampled class comments, while the *warnings* category was found in 12% of them. This indicates the relevance of the template in terms of its suggested information types. However, to which extent developers follow the template in following the style of these information types is yet unknown.

Table 4.5 presents a detailed overview of this taxonomy. The column *Description* describes the category, *Implicitness level* defines the degree to

4. Comment Information Types (CITs)

Table 4.5: The 23 identified information types

Category	Description	Implicitness level	Keywords
Intent	Describes the purpose of a class	Often implicit	I represent, I am, I'm, This class is, A *Class* is
Responsibility	Lists responsibilities of a class	Often implicit	provide, implement, I do, I know, responsible
Collaborator	Lists interactions of a class with other classes	Implicit	use, interact, provide, collaborate
Key messages	Lists key methods and public APIs of a class	Sometimes implicit	Key Messages, Public API
Example	Provides code examples to instantiate a class and to use the APIs of the class	Often explicit	Usage, Example, For example, code examples
Implementation points	Provides internal details of objects, particular implementation logic, conditions about the object state, and settings	Often implicit	Internal representations, Implementation points:
Instance variables	Lists state variables of an object	Often explicit	instance variables:
Class references	Overlaps with Collaborator category but includes extra cases when developers refer to other classes in the class comment to explain the context of a class	Implicit	
Warnings	Warns readers about using various implementation details of the class	Often implicit	Note, do not, remarks, should
Contracts	Informs readers about potential conditions before or after using a class/method/component of a class	Often implicit	Precondition:, do..when..
Dependencies	Describes the dependency of a class on other classes/methods/components	Implicit	used by
Reference to other resources	Refers readers to additional internal or external resources	Often explicit	See, Look
Discourse	Informs the readers about a few class details in an informal manner	Implicit	developers use conversational language
Recommendation	Recommends improvements for the class implementation	Implicit	recommended, see, should be
Subclasses explanation	Describes details about its subclasses, the intent of creating the subclasses, and when to use which subclass	Implicit	My subclasses
Observations	Records developer observations while working with a class	Often implicit	
License	Stores the license information of the code	Often implicit	
Extension	Describes how to extend a class	Often implicit	extend, extension
Naming conventions	Records the different naming convention such as acronyms used in the code	Implicit	
Coding guideline	Describes coding rules for developers who write a class	Often implicit	
Link	Refers to a web link for detailed information	Sometimes implicit	
TODO comments	Records actions to be done or remarks for developers	Explicit	todo
Other	Includes code comments of other languages	Explicit	Javadoc

which information is hidden in the text, and *Keywords* lists the keywords and patterns observed during the manual analysis of each category. The *implicitness level* is taken from a five-level Likert scale with the labels: *implicit, often implicit, sometimes implicit, often explicit,* and *explicit.* A category is marked *implicit* when it is either in the same line or paragraph with other categories or without a header in the comment, making it challenging to identify. For example, the category *TODO* is always mentioned in a separate paragraph with a header "Todo", which makes it *explicit.* Moreover, a majority of the time the category *intent* is combined with *responsibility* in one line, thus make them *often implicit.* Based on the formulated criteria, one author evaluated the *implicitness level* of each category, and the other authors reviewed them and possibly proposed changes. All authors resolved their disagreements by the majority voting mechanism and refined the measurement criteria by mutual discussions. All categories, including examples and assigned comments are presented in the replication package [130]. In the *other* category, we observed a few comments having the source code of other languages and following the commenting style of other languages, such as C and Java.

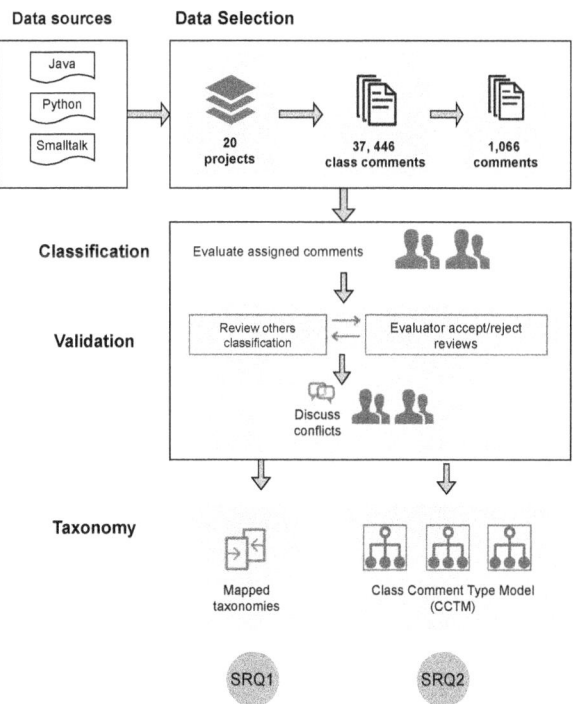

Figure 4.9: Research methodology to answer SRQ$_1$ and SRQ$_2$

Figure 4.9 depicts the research approach followed to answer SRQ$_1$ and

SRQ_2. The outcome of this research consists of a mapping taxonomy (SRQ_1) and a comprehensive taxonomy of class comment types called *CCTM* (SRQ_2), which are mined from the actual commenting practices of developers.

Mapping taxonomies. Before preparing the *CCTM*, we map earlier comment taxonomies, such as the code comment taxonomy for Java [115] and Python [182], and the class comment taxonomy for Smalltalk (Smalltalk-CCTM), since they are formulated using different approaches and focus on the different scope of comments and categories. For instance, the Python code comment taxonomy [182] is inspired by the Java code comment taxonomy [115], whereas the Smalltalk class comment taxonomy is formulated using an open-card sorting technique. Given the importance of mapping categories from heterogeneous environments [33], we establish a semantic interoperability of the categories from each taxonomy [50].

One evaluator mapped the categories from Smalltalk to Java and Python categories. Two other evaluators validated the mapping by reviewing each mapping and by proposing changes. The original evaluator accepted or rejected the changes. All the disagreement cases were reviewed by the fourth evaluator and discussed among all to reach a consensus. The categories that did not match the categories of other taxonomy were added as new categories in that taxonomy. For example, the *precondition* category from Smalltalk did not match any in Java or Python, and thus we added it as a new category in Java and Python. Thus, we proposed the *CCTM taxonomy*, which highlights the existing and new categories for class comments.

CCTM taxonomy. To understand the class commenting practices of developers, we mined class comments of 20 GitHub projects and extracted 1 066 class comments from a total of 37 446 class comments. We qualitatively classified them in the *classification* step and validated them in the *validation* step by reviewing and refining the categorization.

Classification: Four evaluators (two Ph.D. candidates and two faculty members), each with at least four years of programming experience, participated in the study. We partitioned the comments equally among all evaluators based on the distribution of the language's dataset to ensure the inclusion of comments from all projects and diversified lengths. Each evaluator classified the assigned class comments according to the CCTM taxonomy of Java, Python, and Smalltalk [115, 182, 136]. For example, the Python class comment in Figure 4.2 is classified into the categories *summary, warnings, parameters, etc.* shown in Figure 4.10.

Validation: The evaluators, after completing their individual evaluations, continued with the validation step. The evaluators adopted a three-iteration method to validate the correctness of the performed class comments classification shown in Figure 4.9. In the first iteration called *"Review others' classification"*, every evaluator was tasked to review 50% of the comments,

```
class OneHotCategorical(Distribution):
    r"""
    Creates a one-hot categorical distribution parameterized by :attr:`probs` or
    :attr:`logits`.

    Samples are one-hot coded vectors of size ``probs.size(-1)``.

    .. note:: The `probs` argument must be non-negative, finite and have a non-zero sum,
              and it will be normalized to sum to 1 along the last dimension. :attr:`probs`
              will return this normalized value.
              The `logits` argument will be interpreted as unnormalized log probabilities
              and can therefore be any real number. It will likewise be normalized so that
              the resulting probabilities sum to 1 along the last dimension. :attr:`logits`
              will return this normalized value.

    See also: :func:`torch.distributions.Categorical` for specifications of
    :attr:`probs` and :attr:`logits`.

    Example::

        >>> m = OneHotCategorical(torch.tensor([ 0.25, 0.25, 0.25, 0.25 ]))
        >>> m.sample()  # equal probability of 0, 1, 2, 3
        tensor([ 0., 0., 0., 1.])

    Args:
        probs (Tensor): event probabilities
        logits (Tensor): event log probabilities (unnormalized)
    """
```

- Summary
- Expand
- Development notes, Warnings
- Links
- Usage
- Parameters

Figure 4.10: The Python class comment classified in various categories

which were randomly assigned and classified by other evaluators. This step allowed us to confirm that each evaluator's classification is checked by at least one of the other evaluators. In reviewing the classifications, the reviewers indicated their judgment by labeling each comment with the *agree* or *disagree* label. In the second iteration, called *"Evaluator accept or reject reviews"*, the original evaluator examined the disagreements and proposed changes. They indicated their opinion for the changes by accepting the change or rejecting it, stating the reason. If the reviewer's changes were accepted, the classification was directly fixed. Otherwise, the disagreements were carried to the next iteration. The third iteration assigned all identified disagreements for review to a new evaluator, who had not yet looked at the classification. A decision was made based on the majority voting mechanism, and the classification was fixed according to the agreed changes. The levels of *agreement and disagreement* among the evaluators for each project and language can be found in the replication package [129].

After arriving at a decision on all comment classifications, we merged the overlapping categories or renamed the classes by applying the majority voting mechanism, thus converging on a final version of the taxonomy, *i.e.*, the CCTM. This way, all the categories were discussed by all the evaluators to select the best naming convention, and whenever required, unnecessary categories were removed, and duplicates were merged.

4.3 Results

4. Comment Information Types (CITs)

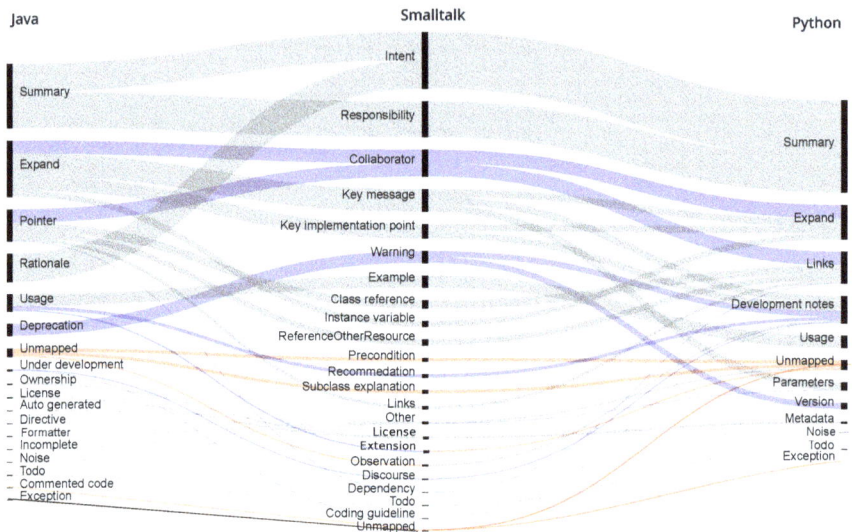

Figure 4.11: Mapping of Smalltalk categories to Java and Python

4.3.1 Mapping Taxonomies

As a first step to formulating the CCTM taxonomy, we systematically map the available taxonomies from previous works and identify the unmapped categories as shown in Figure 4.11. The mapping taxonomy shows several cases in which Java and Python taxonomies do not entirely fit the Smalltalk taxonomy, as shown by pink and violet edges in Figure 4.11. This figure shows the information types particular to a language (highlighted with red edges and unmapped nodes), such as *subclass explanations*, *observation*, *precondition*, and *extension* are found in the Smalltalk taxonomy, but not in the Python or Java taxonomy. However, our results in Figure 4.12 show that these information types are present in the class comments of Java and Python projects. We introduce such categories to the existing taxonomies of Java and Python, and highlight them in green in Figure 4.12. Moreover, the categories such as *commented code*, *exception*, and *version* are found in Java and Python class comments, but not in Smalltalk. One reason can be that the commented code is generally found in inline comments instead of documentation comments. However, information about *exception* and *version* is only found in Java and Python class comments, but not in those of Smalltalk.

The mapping taxonomy also highlights the cases where categories from different taxonomies match partially. We define such categories as subset categories and highlight them with violet edges. For example, the *deprecation* category in Java and the *version* category in Python are found under the *warning* category in Smalltalk, but their description given in the respective earlier work covers only a subset of that information type according to our investigation. Pascarella *et al.* defined the *deprecation* category as *"it contains explicit warnings used to inform the users about deprecated interface artifacts. The tag comment such as @version, @deprecated, or @since is used"* whereas Zhang *et al.* defined the category *version* as *"identifies the applicable version of some libraries"*, but did not mention the deprecation information in this category or any other category in their taxonomy [115, 182]. Thus, we define the *version* category as a subset or a partial match of the *deprecation* category. On the other hand, the *warning* category in Smalltalk (*"warns readers about various implementation details of a class"*) covers a broader aspect of warnings than the *deprecation* category, which does not mention the *version* information type [136]. We mark these categories as subset categories, and highlight them with violet edges. Similarly, the *collaborator* category in Smalltalk partially matches *expand* and *links* in Python. The categories such as *expand*, *links*, and *development notes* in Python combine several types of information under them compared to Smalltalk. For example, *expand* includes collaborators of a class, key methods, instance variables, and implementation-specific details. Such categories formulate challenges in identifying a particular type of information in a comment.

Finding. The Python taxonomy focuses more on high-level categories, which combines various types of information into each category, whereas the Smalltalk taxonomy is more specific to the information types.

4.3.2 CCTM Taxonomy

Using the categories from the mapping taxonomy, we analyze class comments of various languages and formulate the taxonomy for each language to answer SRQ_2. Figure 4.12 shows the frequency of information types per language per project. The categories shown in green are the newly-added categories in each taxonomy. The categories in each heatmap are sorted according to the frequency of their occurrence in total. For example in Java, *summary* appeared in 336 of 378 comments (88%) in six Java projects. Pascarella [115] proposed a hierarchical taxonomy by grouping the lower-level categories within the higher-level categories, *e.g.*, the categories *summary*, *rationale*, and *expand* within the *purpose* category. We show only lower-level categories that correspond with identified information types from other languages.

Figure 4.12 shows that a few types of information are found in class comments of all languages, such as the summary of the class (shown in the *summary*, and *intent* categories), the responsibility of the class (*responsibility*, *summary*), links to other classes or sources (*pointer*, *collaborator*, *links*), developer notes (*todo*, *development notes*), and warnings about the class (*warning*). Summary being the most prevalent category in all languages affirms the importance of summarizing the classes automatically [69, 106, 24, 103, 47]. As a majority of summarization techniques focus on

4. COMMENT INFORMATION TYPES (CITS)

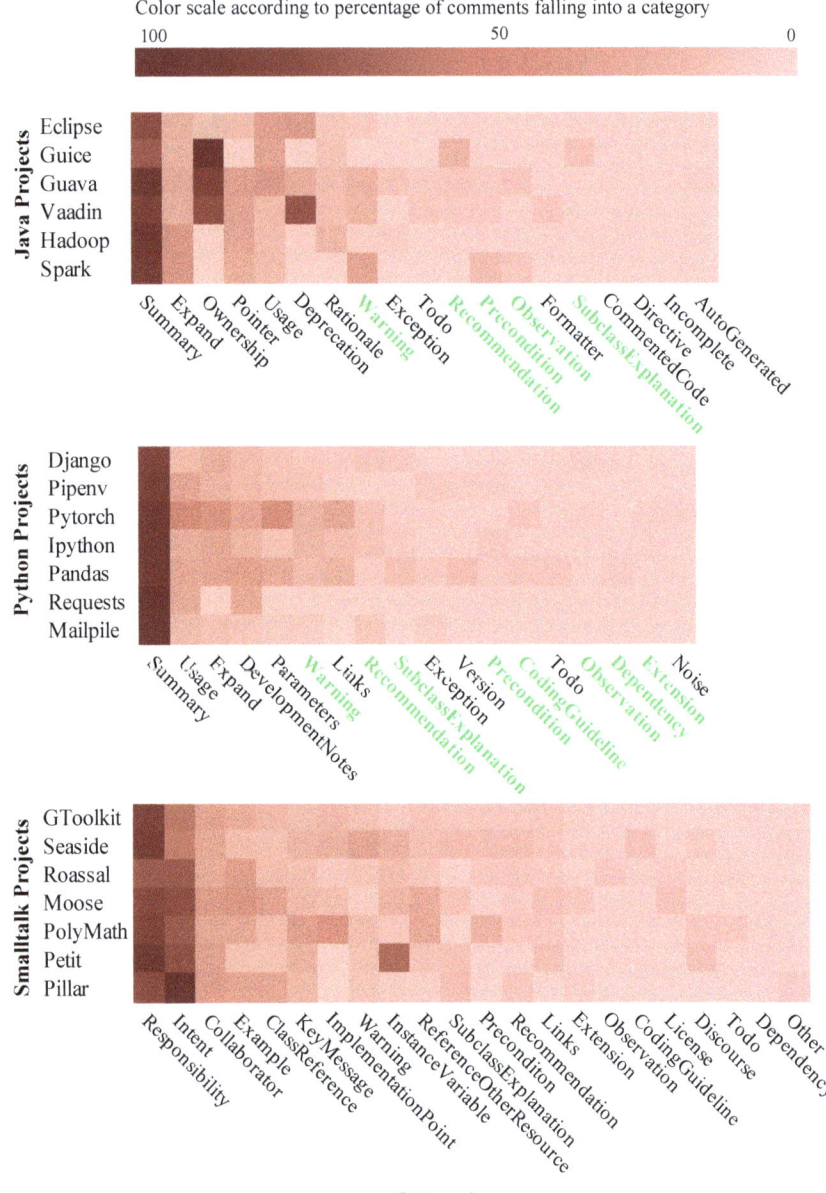

Figure 4.12: The categories found in class comments (*CCTM*) of various projects of each programming language shown on the y-axis. The x-axis shows the categories inspired from existing work in black and the new categories in green

generating the intent and responsibilities of the class for program comprehension tasks [103], other information types, such as *warning*, *recommendation*, and *usage*, are generally ignored even though developers often write them and coding style guidelines suggest them in documentation comments.

Our results indicate that developers mention them frequently, but whether they find these information types important to support specific development tasks, or they write them just to adhere to the coding guidelines, requires a more thorough analysis. Nevertheless, such information types present an interesting aspect to investigate in future work. For example, the usage of a class (*usage*), its key responsibilities (*responsibility*), warnings about it (*warning*), and its collaborators (*collaborator*) are found in significant numbers of comments in all languages. The coding guidelines often suggest these information types to support developers in various development and maintenance tasks. These information types can be included in the customized code summaries based on the development tasks of a developer. For instance, a developer seeking dependant classes can quickly find such classes from the class comment without reading the entire comment. Similarly, a developer expected to refactor a legacy class can quickly go through the warnings, if present, to understand the specific conditions better and thus can save time.

> **Finding.** Developers embed various types of information in class comments, varying from a high-level overview of the class to low-level implementation details of a class across the investigated languages.

According to Nurvitadhi *et al.* [109], a class comment in Java should describe the purpose of a class, its responsibilities, and its interactions with other classes. Our results indicate that Java class comments often contain the purpose and responsibilities of the class (*summary* and *expand*), but its interactions with other classes (*pointer*) less often. On the contrary in Smalltalk, the information about interactions with other classes, *i.e.*, *collaborator*, is the third most frequent information type after *intent* and *responsibility* compared to Java and Python. One of the reasons can be that Smalltalk class comments are guided by a CRC (Class, Responsibility, Collaborator) design template, and developers write the template-inspired information types more often than others.

Class comments in Java also contain many other types of information. The most frequent type of information present in class comments is *summary*, which shows that developers summarize most classes. Pascarella *et al.* found *usage* to be the second most prevalent category in code comments. In contrast, we find *expand* to be the second most prevalent category in class comments, and *usage* to be the fifth most prevalent type of information [115]. However, the most prevalent categories vary across projects of a language, and also across programming languages. For example, *usage* is mentioned more often than *expand* in Google projects (Guice and Guava), whereas in Apache projects (Spark, Hadoop) it is not. In contrast to Java, Python class comments contain *expand* and *usage* equally frequently, thus showing that Python targets both end-user developers and internal developers.

We notice that Python and Smalltalk class comments contain more low-level implementation details about a class compared to Java. For instance, Python class comments contain details about the class attributes and the instance variables of a class with a header "*Attributes*" and "*Parameters*", its public methods with a header "*Methods*", and its constructor arguments in the *parameters* and *expand* categories. Additionally, Python class comments often contain explicit warnings about a class, *i.e.*, with a header "*warning:*" or "*note:*" in the new line, making the information easily noticeable, whereas such behavior is rarely observed in Java. Whether such variations in the categories across projects and languages are due to different project comment style guidelines or developers' personal preferences is unknown. We observe that developers use common natural language patterns to write similar types of information. For example in Listing 1, a Smalltalk developer described the collaborator class of the `PMBernoulliGeneratorTest` class. Similarly, a Java developer described the collaborator of the `SequenceFileRecordReader` as shown in Listing 2. This reveals a common pattern *"[This class] for [other class]"* to describe the collaborating classes. This information type is captured in the categories *collaborator* in Smalltalk and *pointer* in Java.

```
1  A BernoulliGeneratorTest is a test class for testing the
2  behavior of BernoulliGenerator
```

Listing 1: Collaborator mentioned in the `PMBernoulliGeneratorTest` class in Smalltalk

```
1  An {@link RecordReader} for {@link SequenceFile}s.
```

Listing 2: Collaborator mentioned in the `SequenceFileRecordReader` class in Java

Identifying such patterns can help in easily extracting the type of information from a comment, and they can support a developer by highlighting the required information necessary for a particular task, *e.g.*, to modify dependent classes in a maintenance task.

In contrast to earlier studies, we observed that developers mention details of their subclasses in a parent class comment in all languages. We grouped this information under the *subclass explanation* category. In the Javadoc guidelines, this information is generally indicated by a special *@inherit* tag in method comments, but we did not find such a guideline for Java class comments. Similarly, we found no such guideline to describe subclasses for Smalltalk class comments or method comments. In contrast, the standard Python style guideline [121] suggests to add this information to the class comment, but other Python style guidelines, such as those from Google[9]

---

[9]https://sphinxcontrib-napoleon.readthedocs.io/en/latest/example_google.html

and Numpy[10] do not mention this information type. However, we found instances of class comments containing subclass information in the *IPython* and *Pytorch* projects that follow the Numpy and Google-style guidelines respectively. Investigating which information types each project style guidelines suggest for the comments, and to what extent developers follow these style guidelines in writing class comments requires further analysis.

> **Finding.** Not all information types found in class comments are suggested by the corresponding project style guidelines.

4.4 Implications and Discussion

Disagreements in classification. In the process of validating the taxonomies, reviewers (evaluators reviewing the classification) marked their disagreement for the classification, stating their reason and proposing the changes. A majority of disagreements in the first Smalltalk iteration were due to the long sentences containing different types of information (*intent* and *responsibility* information types were commonly interweaved), and the assignment of information to the categories *implementation point* and *collaborator*. In Java and Python, we observed that disagreements were due to the broad and loosely defined categories, such as *expand* in Java and *development notes* in Python. Several information types, such as *warning, recommendation, observation,* and *development notes* are not structured by special tags and thus pose a challenge for automatic identification and extraction. On the contrary, a few categories such as *example* and *instance variable* in Smalltalk, and *deprecation, links,* and *parameters* in Java and Python were explicitly marked by the headers or the tags in comments, such as `usage`, `instance variable`, `@since`, `@see`, `@params` respectively. We observed that developers use common keywords across languages to indicate a particular information type. For example, notes were mentioned in the comments by using the keyword "note" as a header as shown in Listing 3, Listing 4, and Listing 5.

```
1 Note that even though these
2 * methods use {@link URL} parameters, they are usually not appropriate for
3 * HTTP or other non-classpath resources.
```

Listing 3: Explicit note mentioned in the `Resources` class in Java

```
1 .. note::
2
3 Depending on the size of your kernel, several (of the last)
4 columns of the input might be lost, because it is a valid
5 `cross-correlation`_, and not a full `cross-correlation`_.
6 It is up to the user to add proper padding.
```

Listing 4: Explicit note mentioned in the `Conv3d` class in Python

---

[10]https://numpydoc.readthedocs.io/en/latest/format.html

```
1 Note: position may change even if an element has no parent
```
Listing 5: Explicit note mentioned in the BlElementPositionChangedEvent class in Smalltalk

Lack of comment conventions. The project-specific style guidelines suggest several information types, but not their exact syntax, whereas they do not mention many information types, which we found in our results. Due to the lack of conventions for these information types, developers use their own conventions when writing comments. For instance, developers write subclass details (*subclass explanation*) in class comments, but no tag or header information is suggested by the style guidelines to write this detail [121, 76]. In Smalltalk, we found developers using a different syntax for writing examples (*example*), warnings (*warning*), and extensions (*extension*). This analysis indicates the need to revise the comment conventions suggested by the coding style guidelines.

Identifying specific information types. Maalej et al. [91] demonstrated that developers consult comments in order to answer their questions regarding program comprehension. However, different types of information are interweaved in class comments, and not all developers need to know all types of information. Cioch et al. presented the documentation information needs of developers depending on the stages of expertise [34]. They showed that experts need design details and low-level details, whereas novice developers require a high-level overview with examples. The task of accessing the type of information embedded in comments depends on the kind of information (warning, rationale), the level of detail (design level or implementation level) developers seek, the type of development activities they are performing, and the type of audience (user or developers) accessing them. Tools to automatically identify these information types can reduce developers' and other stakeholders' efforts to read code comments when gathering particular types of information. In addition, on top of these automated tools, visualization strategies could be implemented to highlight and organize the content embedded in the comments to ease further the process of obtaining the required information. Our results highlight that a substantial number of comments contain a *warning* information, *i.e.*, a note about the code, or behavior of the class, an important point to keep in mind while extending the class. Identifying such warnings from the comments can help to turn them into executable test cases, so that developers can automatically check that the mentioned warnings are respected. Similarly, automatically identifying code examples from the comments and executing them can ensure that they are up to the date.

Pascarella et al. built a machine learning-based approach to automatically identify information types for Java [115]. Similarly, Wang et al. developed such an approach for Python [182]. However, which specific information types from comments can support developers in which specific tasks and how these information types should be presented to developers require further investigation. Additionally, given the increasing trend of open-source systems written in multiple programming languages, these approaches can be of limited use for developers contributing to these projects [165]. Our work has the aim to foster language-independent tools for comment analyses based on comprehensive taxonomies.

4.5 Threats to Validity

Threats to construct validity. This mainly concerns the measurements used in the evaluation. We did not consider the full ecosystem of projects in each language but selected a sample of projects for each language. To alleviate this concern to some extent, we selected heterogeneous projects used in the earlier comment analysis work of Java and Python [115, 182]. The projects in each language focus on different domains, such as visualization, data analysis, or development frameworks. They originate from different ecosystems, such as from Google and Apache in Java, or from the Django Foundation, and community projects in Python. Thus, the projects follow different commenting guidelines or coding style guidelines. Additionally, the projects are developed by many contributors, which further lowers the risk towards a specific developer commenting style.

Another critical issue could be the sampling of only a subset of the extracted class comments. However, (i) the sample size limits the estimated imprecision to an error of 5% for a confidence level of 95%, and (ii) to limit the subjectiveness and the bias in the evaluation, three evaluators manually analyzed the resulting sample. To reduce the possibility that the chosen comments are not representative of the whole population, we used a stratified sampling approach, thus considering the quintiles of the comment distribution from various projects.

A second threat involves the taxonomy definition since some categories could overlap or be missing in the *CCTM*. To alleviate these issues, we used the categories defined by the earlier works in comment analysis [115, 182] and performed a broader validation which involved three evaluators on three programming languages.

Threats to internal validity. This concerns confounding factors that could influence our results. The main threat to internal validity in our study is related to the manual analysis carried out to prepare the *CCTM* and the mapping taxonomy. Since human subjects performed it, it could be biased. Indeed, there is a level of subjectivity in deciding whether a comment type belongs to a specific category of the taxonomy or not, and whether a category of one language taxonomy maps to a category in another language taxonomy or not. To counteract this issue, the evaluators of this work were two Ph.D. candidates and two faculty members, each having at least four years of programming experience. We performed a two-level validation step. This validation step involved a further discussion among the evaluators whenever they had divergent opinions until they reached a final decision. All the decisions made during the evaluation process and validation steps are reported in the replication package to provide evidence of the non-biased evaluation, and we discussed a few instances in section 4.4

Threats to external validity. This concerns the generalization of the results. The main aim of this chapter is to investigate the class commenting practices for the selected programming languages. The results may vary in other programming languages or projects. To limit this threat, we considered both static and dynamic object-oriented programming languages with different commenting styles and guidelines. To reduce the threat related to the project selection, we chose diverse projects that have been used in previous studies about comment analysis and assessment. The projects vary in terms of size, domain, contributors, and ecosystems. Thus, our empirical investigation is currently limited to these ecosystems and might not be generalizable to other programming languages. For instance, our results highlight how comments in Java contain information like exceptions, IDE directives, bug references, formatters, and author ownership, however, they do not apply to the Smalltalk environment.

Finally, during the definition of our taxonomy, *i.e.*, *CCTM* we mainly rely on a quantitative analysis of class comments, without involving the actual developers of each programming language. Specifically, for future work, we plan to involve developers with surveys and interviews. This step is particularly important to improve our work results and design and evaluate further automated approaches that can help developers achieve a high quality of comments.

4.6 Summary and Conclusion

Class comments provide a high-level understanding of the program and help one to understand a complex program. Different programming languages have their own commenting guidelines and notations. Thus, identifying a particular type of information from them is essential to generalize the class commenting practices but, a non-trivial task.

We investigated class commenting practices of 20 projects from three programming languages: Java, Python, and Smalltalk. The multi-language taxonomy (CCTM) highlights the information types found in class comments and provides the patterns developers use to write them. We utilize these patterns in the next chapter and develop a language-independent approach to automatically identify frequent information types from class comments of these languages. Once the information types are identified, they

4.6. Summary and Conclusion

can be verified for their quality and can be recommended to developers to support them in suitable software development and maintenance tasks.

Our results highlighted many instances of specific information types found in class comments, but their respective coding style guidelines do not mention them. For instance, the Smalltalk template suggests seven types of information to write in class comments, but developers embedded 16 other types of information. This indicates the need to study the extent to which developer commenting practices adhere to these guidelines. We argue that such an analysis can help in evaluating the quality of comments, which has also been suggested by previous works [111, 70, 159]. Therefore, in chapter 6, we extract the coding style guidelines of these heterogeneous projects and compare the extracted guidelines with the identified comment information types in this chapter.

5

Automated Identification of CITs

The previous chapter showed that class comments contain various types of information in various programming languages. These information types can help developers to gain knowledge about program behavior, reasons behind certain implementations inside the program, or recommendations about modifying the program, regardless of the programming language they are using. The automated identification of such information types can help developers in completing their code comprehension and maintenance tasks faster. Additionally, it can support them in assessing the quality of their class comments. The programming languages present different language-specific code commenting notations and guidelines, which complicates the task of identifying the relevant information from class comments for developers.

To handle this challenge, this chapter proposes an approach that leverages two techniques — namely Natural Language Processing (NLP) and Text Analysis (TA) — to automatically identify *class comment types* (CCTM), *i.e.*, the specific types of semantic information found in class comments.

The chapter is based on the journal article:
"P. Rani, S. Panichella, M. Leuenberger, A. Sorbo, and O. Nierstrasz. How to identify class comment types? A multi-language approach for class comment classification, JSS'21" [132]

5. Automated Identification of CITs

SOFTWARE maintenance and evolution tasks require developers to perform program comprehension activities [53, 69]. Though comments support developers in various software engineering tasks, and well-documented code simplifies software maintenance activities, many programmers often delay code commenting tasks or overlook comment quality [36, 103, 112, 113]. Developers overlook the comment quality aspect because code comments are written in a mixture of natural languages and code. Consequently, developers in various object-oriented programming languages adopt different code commenting notations, guidelines, and tools [52], and they embed different kinds of information in the comments. Indeed, our results from the previous chapter confirm it.

On the one hand, having comments in natural language sentences enables developers to express the overview and the rationale behind the code more freely. On the other hand, natural language makes it hard for other developers to identify the specific information from the comment required for their tasks. It also makes assessing the overall comment quality a nontrivial task as comments are not usually checked by the built-in tools or external plug-ins tools for their content. For example, if a style guide requires a class comment to have information about its public methods, or instance variables for the completeness of class comments, it is important to individually identify the public methods and instance variables from the comment and verify their quality.

The identification of various information types has many additional benefits in improving comment quality. We identified 21 QAs that are used to assess comment quality, *e.g.*, *accessibility*, *correctness*, *conciseness etc.* Several of the QAs can be measured more easily with respect to each information type. For instance, *accessibility* and *content relevance* QAs measure the ease to find a specific type of information in comments. Separating the information types can help developers to easily find such information in comments, thus improving the *accessibility* and *content relevance* of comments. This chapter aims to establish an approach to identify these information types automatically according to the CCTM in a language-independent manner. We achieve this objective by answering the research question SRQ_1: *Can machine learning be used to automatically identify class comment types according to CCTM?*

We propose an approach that leverages NLP and TA techniques to infer relevant features characterizing the class comment types, *i.e.*, CCTM and then classify the comment types accordingly. These features are then used to train various machine learning models on our manually labeled dataset of class comments. Our results confirm that these techniques can be used to classify class comments with high accuracy for all the investigated languages. We believe that our solution can serve as a crucial component for tools to assess the quality and evolution of code comments in several programming languages because it can automatically detect the presence or absence of various CITs required for program comprehension tasks.

5.1 Motivation

Previous work has focused on identifying information types from code comments scattered throughout the source code, from high-level class overviews to low-level method details [159, 115, 182, 60]. These works have focused individually on code comments in Java, Python, C++, and COBOL. In the case of class comments, researchers focused on mainly three types of information, *i.e.*, class intent, responsibilities, and examples in class comments [47, 181]. However, there exist many other types of information in class comments, and the majority of the comment analysis studies focus on mainly code comments of Java. Different from our study, none of these works attempted to automatically identify information types in class comments across multiple languages. We are interested in exploring strategies that can achieve this goal in multiple languages, such as Python, Java, and Smalltalk.

5.2 Study Design

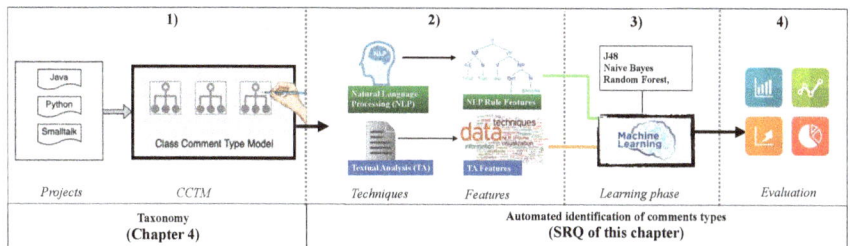

Figure 5.1: Research methodology to answer SRQ$_1$

As shown in Figure 5.1, the goal of this study is to build a recommender system that can automatically identify the different types of information in class comments based on the obtained understanding of class comment types. Such a system can provide custom details to both novice and expert developers, and assist them at various stages of development without much manual effort.

5.2.1 Data Collection

Our previously established dataset includes 37 446 class comments from 20 projects and 1 066 class comments manually classified according to the CCTM [129]. In this chapter, we utilize this labeled dataset to apply our approach.

5.2.2 Analysis Method

Based on the definition of CCTM, we propose an approach, called TESSERACT (auTomated multi-languagE claSSifiER of clAss CommenTs), which leverages machine learning (ML) techniques and automatically classifies class comments according to CCTM. The approach consists of four main phases:

1. *Preprocessing*: All the manually-labeled class comments were used as a ground truth to classify the unseen class comments. It is important to note that we split the comments into sentences, because the classification was sentence-based. We changed the sentences to lower case and removed all special characters. Moreover, we applied additional preprocessing steps to the sentences [14] *e.g.*, stop-word removal for TA features, but not for NLP features to preserve the word order and to capture the important n-gram patterns that we observed in class comments.

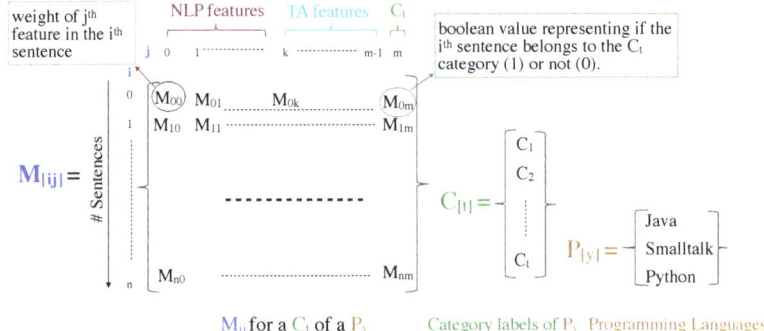

Figure 5.2: Matrix representation of a classifier

2. *NLP feature extraction*: In this phase, we focused on extracting the NLP features, which we added to to the initial term-by-document matrix M shown in Figure 5.2, where each row represents a *comment sentence i.e.*, a sentence belongs to our language dataset composing CCTM and each column represents the extracted feature. To extract the NLP features, we used a tool named NEON that has been proposed in previous work [43]. The tool can automatically detect NLP patterns, *i.e.*, recurrently used predicate-argument structures for specific intents [42], which are available in natural language descriptions composing various types of software artifacts, *e.g.*, mobile user reviews, emails *etc.* [43]. We used the tool to infer all NLP patterns characterizing comment sentences modeled in the matrix M. We then added the identified NLP patterns as feature columns to M, where each column models the presence or absence (using binomial features) of an NLP pattern in the comment sentences. More formally, the boolean

presence or absence of a j−th NLP feature in a generic i−th sentence in M is modeled by 0 (absence) and 1 (presence), respectively. The output of this phase is the matrix M, where each i−th row represents a comment sentence and each j−th column represents an NLP feature.

3. **TA features**: In this phase, we added TA features to the matrix M. To extract the TA features, we preprocessed the comment sentences by applying stop-word removal[1] and stemming [90].[2] The output of this phase corresponds to the matrix M, where each row represents a *comment sentence*, *i.e.*, a sentence that belongs to our language dataset composing CCTM, and each column represents a term contained in it. More formally, each entry $\mathbf{M}_{[i,j]}$ of the matrix represents the weight (or importance) of the j−th term contained in the i−th *comment sentence*.

   For the TA features, terms in M were weighted using the *tf-idf* score [14], which can identify the most important terms in the sentences. In particular, we used *tf-idf* as it downscale the weights of frequent terms that appear in many sentences. Such a weighting scheme had been successfully adopted in recent work [102] for performing code comment classification. The output of this phase consisted of the weighted matrix M, where each row represents a comment sentence, and a column represents the weighted term contained in it.

   It is important to note that a generic i−th comment sentence could be classified into multiple categories according to CCTM. To model this state, we prepared the matrix M for each category ($\mathbf{C}_{[t]}$) of each language ($\mathbf{P}_{[y]}$). The generic (last) column $\mathbf{M}[m]$ of the matrix $\mathbf{M}$, where $m-1$ is the total number of features extracted from all sentences, represents the category $\mathbf{C}_{[t]}$ of a language $\mathbf{P}_{[y]}$ as shown in Figure 5.2. More formally, each entry $\mathbf{M}_{[im]}$ of the matrix represents the boolean value if the i−th sentence belongs to the matrix $C_{[t]}$ (1) or not (0).

4. **Classification**: We automatically classified class comments by adopting various ML models and a 10-fold cross-validation strategy. These models were fed with the aforementioned matrix M. Specifically, to increase the generalizability of our findings, we experimented with the *Weka* tool [175], and used several ML techniques, namely, the standard probabilistic *Naive Bayes classifier*, the *J48 tree* model, and the *Random Forest model*. It is important to note that the choice of these techniques was not random, but based on their successful usage in recent work on code comment analysis [159, 115, 182, 148] and classification of unstructured texts for software maintenance purposes [114, 41].

---

[1] http://www.cs.cmu.edu/~mccallum/bow/rainbow/
[2] https://weka.sourceforge.io/doc.stable/weka/core/stemmers/IteratedLovinsStemmer.html

5. AUTOMATED IDENTIFICATION OF CITS

Table 5.1: Top frequent comment categories with at least 40 comments

Language	Categories	# Comments
Java	Summary	336
	Expand	108
	Ownership	97
	Pointer	88
	Usage	87
	Deprecation	84
	Rationale	50
Python	Summary	318
	Usage	92
	Expand	87
	Development notes	67
	Parameters	57
Smalltalk	Responsibility	240
	Intent	190
	Collaborator	91
	Examples	81
	Class reference	57
	Key message	48
	Key implementation point	46

Evaluation metrics & statistical tests. To evaluate the performance of the tested ML techniques, we adopted well-known information retrieval metrics, namely *Precision, Recall,* and the *F-measure* [14]. During our empirical investigation, we focused on the best configuration of features and ML models as well as alleviating concerns related to overfitting and the selection bias. Specifically, (i) we investigated the classification results of the aforementioned ML models with different combinations of features (NLP, TA, and TA+NLP features), and by adopting a 10-fold validation strategy on the term-by-document matrix M; (ii) to avoid potential bias or overfitting problems, we trained the model for the categories having at least 40 manually validated instances in our dataset. The average number of comments that belong to a category varied from 43 comments to 46 comments across all languages. Therefore, we selected the categories with a minimum of 40 comment instances. The top categories selected from each language with the number of comments are shown in Table 5.1. In order to determine whether the differences between the different input features and classifiers were statistically significant or not, we performed a *Friedman test*, followed by a post-hoc *Nemenyi test* as recommended by Demšar [40].

5.3 Results

Haiduc *et al.* [69] performed a study on automatically generating summaries for classes and methods and found that the experimented summarization techniques work better on methods than classes. More specifically, they discovered that while developers generally agree on the important attributes that should be considered in method summaries, there were conflicts concerning the types of information, in particular whether class attributes and method names should appear in class summaries. We found that while Smalltalk and Python developers frequently mention class attributes or method names in class comments, it rarely happens in Java. Automatically identifying various kinds of information from comments can generate customized summaries based on what information individual developers consider relevant for their task at hand, *e.g.*, maintenance task. To this aim, we empirically experimented with an ML-based multi-language approach to automatically recognize the types of information available in class comments.

Table 5.2 provides an overview of the average precision, recall, and F-measure results considering the top frequent categories for all languages shown in Table 5.1. The results are obtained using multiple ML models and various combination of features: (i) TA features only, (ii) NLP features only, (iii) both NLP and TA features. All results can be found in the replication package [129]. The results in Table 5.2 show that the NLP+TA configuration achieves the best results with the Random Forest algorithm with a relatively high precision (ranging from 78% to 92% for the selected languages), a recall (ranging from 86% to 92%), and an F-measure (ranging from 77% to 92%). Figure 5.3 shows the performance of the different algorithms with NLP+TA features for the most frequent categories in each language.

> **Finding.** Our results suggest that the Random Forest algorithm fed by the combination of NLP+TA features achieves the best classification performance for the different programming languages.

According to Table 5.2, NLP features alone achieve the lowest classification performance for both Java and Python, while we observe that this type of feature works well when dealing with Smalltalk class comments. Class comments can often contain mixtures of structured information, *e.g.*, code elements such as class and attribute names and unstructured information, *i.e.*, natural language. We used the NEON tool to leverage models trained on general-purpose natural language sentences to construct the parse tree of the sentences. The tool relies on the generated parse trees to identify common NLP patterns. We found that the presence of code elements degrades NEON's capability to generate accurate parse trees, and consequently complicates its pattern recognition task.

Table 5.2: Results for Java, Python, and Smalltalk obtained through different ML models and features

Language	Model	TA			NLP			NLP + TA		
		Precision	Recall	F-measure	Precision	Recall	F-measure	Precision	Recall	F-measure
Java	J48	**0.91**	**0.92**	**0.91**	**0.84**	0.81	0.81	0.89	0.90	0.88
	NB	0.86	0.83	0.83	**0.84**	0.81	0.81	0.86	0.84	0.84
	RF	**0.91**	**0.92**	**0.91**	**0.84**	**0.87**	**0.82**	**0.92**	**0.92**	**0.92**
Python	J48	0.73	0.83	0.73	0.68	0.80	0.66	0.81	0.83	0.79
	NB	0.78	0.69	0.72	0.75	0.77	0.75	0.79	0.72	0.74
	RF	**0.84**	**0.85**	**0.83**	**0.78**	**0.81**	**0.78**	**0.85**	**0.86**	**0.84**
Smalltalk	J48	0.60	0.87	0.58	0.61	**0.88**	0.59	0.72	**0.88**	0.70
	NB	**0.84**	0.80	**0.82**	**0.85**	0.83	**0.83**	**0.86**	0.82	**0.84**
	RF	0.75	**0.90**	0.73	0.82	**0.88**	0.82	0.78	**0.90**	0.77

5.3. Results

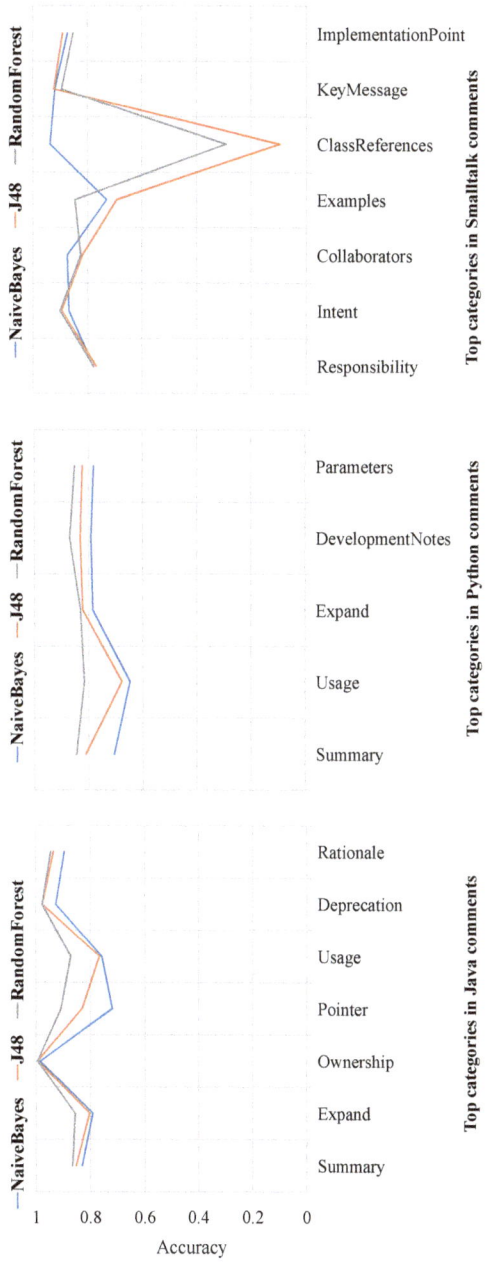

Figure 5.3: Performance of the different classifiers based on the F-measure for the NLP + TA feature set

```
1 Terms subclasses Bag with support for handling stop words etc.
2
3 example: string
4 | terms |
5 terms := Terms new.
6 terms addString: string using: CamelCaseScanner new.
7 terms withCountDo: [ :term :count |term -> count ].
```

Listing 6: Smalltalk Code in MalTerms comment resembles natural language

Smalltalk code often resembles natural language phrases in English, *e.g.*, the method `addString: using:` shown in Listing 6 takes two parameters `string` and `CamelCaseScanner new` written in a natural language sentence-style. Similarly, class comments in Smalltalk are written in a more informal writing style often using the first-person form, and use complete sentences as shown in Figure 4.3. In contrast, Java and Python suggest writing class comments in a more formal way using phrases and the third-person form. As demonstrated in previous works [114, 42], the usage of predicate-argument patterns is particularly well-suited when dealing with classification problems in highly unstructured and informal contexts.

> **Finding.** When dealing with the sentences that contain mixtures of code elements and natural language texts, NLP tools based on parse trees fail to correctly identify well-suited NLP features. The usage of these features is otherwise recommended when class comments are mostly unstructured.

Table 5.3: Results for Java using the Random Forest classification model

Category	NLP + TA		
	Precision	Recall	F-measure
Summary	0.87	0.88	0.87
Expand	0.86	0.87	0.86
Ownership	0.99	0.99	0.99
Pointer	0.91	0.91	0.91
Usage	0.88	0.88	0.87
Deprecation	0.98	0.98	0.98
Rationale	0.95	0.95	0.95

For the sake of brevity, we base the following analysis on the NLP+TA configuration in combination with the Random Forest classifier. Table 5.3, Table 5.4, and Table 5.5 report the precision, recall, and the F-measure respectively for the top frequent categories (shown in Table 5.1) obtained through the Random Forest model with the NLP+TA features.

According to Table 5.3, the categories *deprecation, ownership*, and *rationale* achieve high F-measure scores ($\geq 95\%$), while *expand, summary* and *usage* achieve the lowest F-measure values, but still higher than 85%. This means that for the most Java categories, the Random Forest model achieves very accurate classification results. However, we observed a certain variability in the results, depending on the categories presented in Table 5.1. While in our manually validated sampled comments the *summary* and *usage* categories occurred more frequently than others, they achieved a lower classification performance than *deprecation* and *ownership* (see Table 5.3). This outcome can be due to the presence of specific annotations or words that often occur in sentences belonging to the *deprecation* (*e.g.*, @since) and *ownership* (*e.g.*, @author) categories. Although we removed all the special characters (including annotation symbols) from the sentences, the techniques based on the NLP+TA features could well capture the specific terms that frequently occurred and were useful for identifying these categories. For instance, in the *Vaadin* project, the *ownership* category always contained "Vaadin" in the @author field. Similarly, in the other Java projects, author name patterns were included in the NLP+TA feature set.

In contrast with the *deprecation* and *ownership* categories, we did not observe recurrent annotations or words in the sentences of the *rationale* category. However, sentences in this category are more accurately classified compared to the sentences in the *summary*, and *expand* categories. This could depend on the quantity and quality of the NLP features captured in these categories, jointly with a lower variability in the structure of comments falling in the *rationale* category. In particular, we observed that for the *rationale* category, twelve unique NLP features have higher *information gain* values than 0.01, whereas two unique NLP features for the *summary* category, and only one NLP feature for the *expand* category have *information gain* scores higher than 0.01. In terms of quality, the top-ranked NLP feature of the *summary* category, *i.e.*, "Represents [something]" occurs in only 3% of the overall comments that fall in this category, whereas the top-ranked feature of the *rationale* category, *i.e.*, "Has [something]" occurs in 8% of the total comments belonging to this category. Nevertheless, the NLP patterns of various categories are not mutually exclusive since one sentence can be classified into multiple categories. For instance, the NLP patterns that occur in the sentences that belongs to the *expand* category are also frequent in the instances of the *pointer* and *usage* categories, making it harder to correctly predict the type of the sentences falling in these categories. Specifically, the NLP pattern with the highest *information gain* score, *i.e.*, "See [something]" for the *expand* category (with an information gain of 0.00676) is also relevant for identifying sentences of the *pointer* category, exhibiting an information gain value higher than the one observed for the *expand* category (*i.e.*, 0.04104). A careful selection of suitable features exclusive to a specific category could further improve our approach.

In the case of Python, the F-measure results are still positive ($> 80\%$) for all the considered categories as shown in Table 5.4. Similar to Java, more frequent categories do not achieve the best performance. For example, the category *parameter* is the least frequent among the categories considered,

Table 5.4: Results for Python using the Random Forest classification model

Category	NLP + TA		
	Precision	Recall	F-measure
Summary	0.86	0.86	0.85
Usage	0.83	0.83	0.82
Expand	0.83	0.86	0.83
Development notes	0.87	0.89	0.87
Parameters	0.86	0.86	0.85

but still achieves a higher performance than most of the other categories. In contrast to Java, Python developers frequently use specific words, *e.g.*, `params`, `args`, or `note`, rather than annotations to denote a specific information type. We observe that these words frequently appear in sentences of the *parameter* and *development note* categories and these terms are captured in the related feature sets. In the Python classification, the *usage* category reports the lowest F-measure due to its maximum ratio of incorrectly classified instances, *i.e.*, 17% among all categories. This outcome can be partially explained by the small number of captured NLP heuristics, *i.e.*, one heuristic *"[something] defaults"* is selected according to the information gain measure with a threshold of 0.005. We also observe that instances of the *usage* category often contain code snippets mixed with informal text, which increases the difficulty of identifying features that would be good predictors of this class. Similarly, the instances in the *expand* category also contain mixtures of natural language and code snippets. Separating code snippets from natural language elements and treating each portion of the mixed text with a proper approach can help (i) to build more representative feature sets for these types of class comment sentences, and (ii) to improve overall classification performance.

Table 5.5: Results for Smalltalk using the Random Forest classification model

Category	NLP + TA		
	Precision	Recall	F-measure
Responsibility	0.79	0.82	0.78
Intent	0.92	0.92	0.90
Collaborator	0.83	0.94	0.83
Example	0.85	0.84	0.85
Class references	0.29	0.98	0.29
Key messages	0.92	0.92	0.89
Key implementation points	0.87	0.89	0.85

Concerning Smalltalk, the Random Forest model provides slightly less stable results compared to Python and Java as shown in Table 5.2. Moreover, Table 5.5 shows that the *intent* category achieves the highest F-measure. However, for most categories, the F-measure values are high (> 78%), except for the *class references* category. The *class references* category captures the other classes referred to in a class comment. For this category, the Random Forest model achieves the worst results, *i.e.*, F-measure of 29%. However, the Naive Bayes model achieves an F-measure score of 93% for it. Similarly, for the *collaborator* category, the Naive Bayes model achieves better results compared to the Random Forest model. Both categories can contain similar information, *i.e.*, the name of other classes the class interacts with. We noticed in Smalltalk comments that the camel case class names are generally split into separate words, which makes it more difficult to identify them as classes from the text. Nevertheless, as demonstrated in previous work [115], the Naive Bayes algorithm can achieve a high performance in classifying information chunks in code comments containing code elements, *e.g.*, *pointer*, while its performance degrades when dealing with less structured texts, *e.g.*, *rationale*. We observed similar behavior for the *links* category in the Python taxonomy. Figure 4.11 shows that all these categories, such as *links*, *pointer*, *collaborator*, and *class references* contain similar types of information. In contrast, developers follow specific patterns in structuring sentences that belong to other categories, such as *intent* and *example* as shown in the previous chapter. In future work, we plan to combine various ML algorithms to improve our results [5].

To qualitatively corroborate the quantitative results and understand the importance of each considered NLP heuristic, we computed the popular statistical measure *information gain* for the NLP features in each category, and ranked these features based on their scores. We used the default implementation of the information gain algorithm and the ranker available in Weka with a threshold value of 0.005 [122]. Interestingly, for each category the heuristics that have the highest information gain values also exhibit easily explainable relations with the intent of the category itself. For instance, for the *responsibility* category in Smalltalk, which lists the responsibilities of the class, we observed that *"Allows [something]"* and *"Specifies [something]"* are among the best-ranked heuristics. Similarly, the heuristics *"[something] is used"* and *"[something] is applied"* are among the heuristics that have the best information gain values for the *collaborator* category which lists the interactions of the class with other classes. Furthermore, the heuristics *"[something] is class for [something]"* and *"Represents [something]"* have higher information gain values when used to identify comments of the *intent* category, which describes the purpose of the class. These heuristics confirm the patterns identified by us in our manual analysis of Smalltalk class comments [136]. We observed similar results for the other languages. More specifically, for the *summary* category in Java the heuristics *"Represents [something]"* and *"[something] tests"* are among the NLP features with the highest information gain. Instead, in the case of the *expand* and *pointer* categories, we observed a common relevant heuristic: *"See [something]"*. The analysis of the top heuristics for the considered categories highlights that developers follow similar patterns (*e.g.*, *"[verb] [something]"*) to summarize the purpose and responsibilities of the class across the different programming languages. However, no common patterns are found when discussing specific implementation details, *i.e.*, *expand* and *usage* in Java and Python, and *example* in Smalltalk.

> **Finding.** In all the considered programming languages, developers follow similar patterns to summarize the purpose and the responsibilities of a class. No common patterns are observed when implementation details are discussed.

Statistical tests. To further confirm the reliability of our results, we complemented our results with relevant statistical tests. In particular, the *Friedman test* reveals that the differences in performance among the classifiers is statistically significant in terms of the F-measure. Thus, we can conclude that when comparing the performance of classifiers and using different input configurations, the choice of the classifier significantly affects the results. Specifically, to gain further insights about the groups that statistically differ, we performed the *Nemenyi test*. The test results suggested that the Naive Bayes and the J48 models do not statistically differ in terms of the F-measure, while the Random Forest model is the best performing model with statistical evidence ($p-value < 0.05$).

To analyze how the usage of different features (NLP, TA, or NLP+TA) affects the classification results, we executed a *Friedman test* on the F-measure scores obtained by the Random Forest algorithm for each possible input combination. The test concluded that the difference in the results with different inputs is statistically significant ($p-value < 0.05$). To gain further insight into the groups that statistically differ, we performed a *Nemenyi test*. The test revealed a significant difference between the NLP and NLP+TA combinations ($p-value < 0.05$). This result confirms the importance of both NLP and TA features when classifying class comment types in different languages. The input data and the scripts used for the tests are provided in the replication package [129].

5.4 Implications and Discussion

Specific information types. Rajlich presented a tool that gathers important information, such as a class's responsibilities, its dependencies, member functions, and authors' comments to facilitate the developer's need to access the particular information types [125]. We advanced the work by automatically identifying and extracting several other frequent information types from the class comments. Researchers have suggested various ways to

5.4. Implications and Discussion

satisfy the information needs of developers, such as On-Demand Developer Documentation (OD3) [139]. Such a system (OD3) would automatically generate a high-quality response for a developer query based on a mixture of information extracted from various artifacts, such as source code, documentation, and Q&A posts. This requires an automatic identification of relevant information types from other artifacts as well. Our work provides leads in this direction by presenting an approach to identify the comments according to the comprehensive class comment taxonomy extracted from various programming languages.

Quality attributes for various information types. Identifying various information types in comments can help to improve comment content quality with respect to several QAs identified in chapter 3. Table 5.6 presents such QAs in the column *QA* and how can they facilitate assessment of comments in the column *Description*. For instance, the *correctness* quality attribute can be measured with respect to certain information, and thus incorrect information types can be indicated to the developers to update or delete them.

Improvements in our approach. Our approach can be further improved by focusing on several aspects. First, various other types of comments, such as method comments and inline comments, and other artifacts, such as wikis, bug reports, Q&A posts, commit messages, and mailing lists, can be added as data sources. The NEON tool, used to extract natural language patterns, is already tested successfully on the mailing lists artifact for user reviews[42]. To avoid the longer training time and memory consumption of ML strategies, Kallis *et al.* used *fastText*, a tool using linear models that achieved comparable results in classification to various deep-learning-based approaches, to classify the issues reports on GitHub. Since *fastText* is tailored and trained on natural language datasets, it can be more effective in classifying comments. Second, more algorithms based on unsupervised ML and deep learning can be used to identify various types of information in comments. Third, our automatically extracted features can be further refined by employing more advanced word embedding, text processing, and feature selection techniques. This can help identify not only a specific type of information, but also refine the related information types. For example, *intent* and *responsibilities* information types in Smalltalk often occur together and are found mixed within one sentence. Such refinement approaches can help to separate the part of the sentence indicating the *intent* and *responsibilities* information. Fourth, the patterns related to specific domains, such as visualization, file systems can be extended to other domains, languages, and artifacts.

Table 5.6: Assessment of the information types based on QAs (identified in chapter 3)

QA	Description
Accessibility	Easiness to find specific information from comments, *e.g.*, if a comment contains warnings they can be easily accessed
Readability	Whether the specific information is easily readable, *e.g.*, the example to instantiate a class is readable with other available information
Trustworthiness	Whether an information type is reliable
Author-related	If an author information is present in a comment
Correctness	Whether an information type is correct
Completeness	If specific information, important to support developers in various tasks, is available
Similarity	Given information type is already mentioned in a comment
Consistency	Given information type follows a consistent style as suggested by its style guideline, or consistent to other sources, such as code or external documents
Up-to-dateness	The information type is kept up-to-date with software evolution, *e.g.*, if a class is deprecated then the deprecation information should be updated in class comment
Accuracy	Given information is enough precise or not, *e.g.*, usage information about the class includes a code example or not.
Organization	The Information types are organized or structured as suggested by the project guidelines, *e.g.*, summary information should be in the first line of a comment followed by parameters *etc.*
Format	Given information follows the correct writing style, includes visuals or code examples, *e.g.*, summary is written using phrases rather than complete sentences
Conciseness	Given information type is succinct and necessary in a comment
Content relevance	The information is relevant to developers to support them in a particular purpose, such as documentation, communication
Maintainability	The extent to which an information can be maintained easily, *e.g.*, certain information types require more update than others, such as the deprecation information might require less update than the frequently updated responsibilities of the class
Understandability	To what extent specific information contributes to understandability, *e.g.*, summary help developers understand a class more than author information
Internationalization	The information can be correctly translated to other natural languages

5.5 Threats to Validity

Threats to construct validity. This mainly concerns the measurements used in the evaluation. We did not consider the full ecosystem of projects in each language, but selected a sample of projects for each language. To alleviate this concern to some extent, we selected heterogeneous projects used in the earlier comment analysis work of Java and Python [115, 182]. The projects in each language focus on different domains, and originate from different ecosystems. Thus, the projects follow different comment guidelines (or coding style guidelines).

Threats to external validity. This concerns the generalization of our results. The main aim of our proposed approach is to automate the identification of comment information types of the selected programming languages. The approach may achieve different results in other programming languages or projects. To limit this threat, we considered both static and dynamic object-oriented programming languages with different commenting styles and guidelines. While we believe that the comments from these diverse projects and languages will represent comments in other projects and languages, we do not expect to reach any general conclusion. We plan to train the classifiers with more labeled comments of other software systems to generalize our results.

Threats to internal validity. This concerns the problem of overfitting the ML algorithms. For instance, certain models such as the Random Forest model can be prone to overfitting, thus providing too optimistic results. To alleviate this threat, we trained different models, and tested them using tenfold cross-validation. Our analysis only includes three traditional supervised ML algorithms, *i.e.*, Naive Bayes, J48, and Random Forest. Nevertheless, there can be other algorithms based on unsupervised ML and deep learning, and other configurations worthy of investigation.

Threats to conclusion validity. This concerns the relationship between treatment and outcome. Appropriate statistical procedures have been adopted to draw our conclusions. We investigated whether the differences in the performance achieved by the different ML models with different combinations of features were statistically significant. To perform this task, we used the Friedman test, followed by a post-hoc Nemenyi test, as recommended by Demšar [40].

5.6 Summary and Conclusion

In this chapter, we built various classifiers using supervised ML algorithms to automate the identification of specific information types from comments defined in CCTM. We used the manually labeled class comments of Java, Python, and Smalltalk as a dataset for training and testing various classifiers. We proposed an approach based on natural language processing (NLP) and text analysis (TA) techniques. The approach classifies the most frequent information types of all the investigated languages using ML models with a high accuracy.

We found that the Random Forest model fed by the combination of NLP+TA features achieves the best classification performance over the different programming languages. The approach identified the cases where NLP tools (based on parse tree) fail to identify well-suited NLP features for the sentences that contain a mixture of code elements and natural language texts. However, these features are recommended when class comments are mostly unstructured. Based on this approach, we plan to implement a tool, e.g., a browser plugin to filter various relevant information types for developers. We also plan to verify our approach based on deep learning algorithms, specifically CNN-based approaches.

Although, we characterized developer commenting practices (chapter 4 and 5) in terms of what developers embed in class comments, how they write such information, but do they follow coding style guidelines in writing comments is unknown. In chapter 6, we extract the coding style guidelines of the projects, and evaluate the adherence of code comments to the guidelines.

6

Comment Adherence to Conventions

Previous chapters showed that developers embed various types of information in class comments, and they follow different syntax and style to write the same kind of information. Several coding style guidelines have been created with an aim to encourage developers in writing informative, readable, and consistent comments. However, it is not yet clear from the research which specific aspects of comments these guidelines cover, *e.g.*, syntax, content, or structure, and to which extent developers follow these guidelines when they write code comments.

We analyze various style guidelines used in several programming languages, and uncover that most of them address more the content aspect of the comments than the syntax or format aspect. However, when considering the different types of information developers embed in comments of Java, Python, and Smalltalk, existing comment conventions are not yet specified clearly enough, nor do they adequately cover important concerns.

The chapter is mainly based on the paper:
- "P. Rani, S. Abukar, N. Stulova, A. Bergel, and O. Nierstrasz. *Do comments follow commenting conventions? A case study in Java and Python, SCAM'21*" [132], and partly based on the journal article:
- "P. Rani, S. Panichella, M. Leuenberger, M. Ghafari, and O. Nierstrasz. *What do class comments tell us? An investigation of comment evolution and practices in Pharo Smalltalk, EMSE'21*" [136].

6. Comment Adherence to Conventions

APART from the syntax given by a programming language to write code, there are various other aspects of code that can be written in several ways, such as, naming variables, formatting the code statements, or writing comments. Other than code, code comments are usually written in a semi-structured manner using natural language sentences, and they are not verified overall by the compiler. Therefore, developers have quite much freedom to write comments in numerous ways [95, 6]. To encourage developers to write consistent, readable, and informative code comments, programming language communities and several large organizations, such as Google and Apache provide coding style guidelines that suggest comment-related conventions [76, 121, 65]. These conventions cover various aspects of comments, *e.g.*, syntax, style, and content. For example, *"Use 3rd person (descriptive), not 2nd person (prescriptive)"* is an example of a stylistic comment convention for Java documentation comments [76]. However, which other comment aspects different style guidelines and languages cover is unknown. Understanding various commenting conventions the guidelines suggest can help the community to know what our current style guidelines lack, and where developers need the most tool support.

Software that adheres to coding standards or style guidelines improves maintainability and readability of code [46], and fosters a common understanding among developers [85]. Developers perceive the adherence to code convention as important [150], but they find it difficult to comply with [48]. There is no universal set of rules that apply to comments of all programming languages. Instead, different languages follow various standard style guidelines. For example, Java and Python have widely accepted standard coding guidelines [76, 121, 65]. In contrast, Pharo (a Smalltalk-based environment) traditionally offers a concise template that consists of commenting guidelines to write class comments for the newly-created classes. However, it remains largely unknown whether developers who write code comments in these languages adhere to their style guidelines or not. Studying the adherence aspect is crucial to encourage them to follow commenting conventions, and in designing tools to assess the overall comment quality. In this chapter, we study RQ_3: *To what extent do developers follow the style guidelines in their comments?*

We analyzed 1 089 sampled class comments of 20 projects written in Java, Python, and Smalltalk. We identified the coding style guidelines of each project, extracted commenting conventions from them, and manually compared the conventions to the sampled comments.

Our results for Java and Python show that the majority of style guidelines propose more content-related conventions, *i.e.*, what information to write in comments than other types of conventions, *e.g.*, how to format comments. However, compared to various information types developers actually embed in comments, it is clear that existing comment conventions are neither adequate, nor precise enough. Similarly in Smalltalk, the template provides an example of how a class comment should look like, but it is not precise about which syntax to follow to write what information, and the required formatting conventions. Overall, our results highlight the mismatch between the conventions suggested by the style guidelines and conventions developers follow in their projects and vice versa.

6.1 Motivation

Coding style guidelines across languages provide conventions with an aim to help developers in writing high-quality comments.

Java. On the one hand, there exist various style guidelines in Java that suggest commenting conventions. Not all style guidelines provide the same level of detail for writing comments. For instance, Oracle provides documentation guidelines, which suggest summarizing a class in the first sentence of a class comment and then listing various other tags or information types [76]. On the other hand, Google provides very limited documentation guidelines [65]. In addition to the standard guidelines offered by the languages, various major open-source projects modify conventions of the standard guidelines, *e.g.*, Apache Spark extends the Oracle documentation guideline [10].

Python. Similar to Java, Python offers the standard *PEP8* or *PEP257* guidelines to write code comments [121], which suggest using the *docstring* format to write class comments. In contrast to Java, the PEP8 and PEP257 guidelines recommend writing public methods and instance variables in a class comment using different syntax and style conventions. Furthermore, the *Numpy* guideline proposes to add warnings, notes, and references to external sources to class comments.

Smalltalk. Pharo, the Smalltalk-based environment, offers a semi-structured default template to guide developers in writing a class comment as shown in the Pharo 7 template in Figure 6.1. The template encourages developers to write different types of information, such as *intent*, *responsibilities*, *collaborators*, and *key messages* to document important properties and implementation details of a class. Not all versions of the template suggest embedding all these information types. Pharo and its template have evolved over the years in different versions, but it is still unclear how developers adopt the template when writing comments.

An overall understanding of comment conventions and their use across projects can help researchers and practitioners to build a recommender system for comments. We envision such a recommender system to automatically identify comment-related conventions from a guideline, and to measure the mismatch between commenting practices of developers and the used conventions. Such a system should be adaptable to project-specific guidelines,

6. Comment Adherence to Conventions

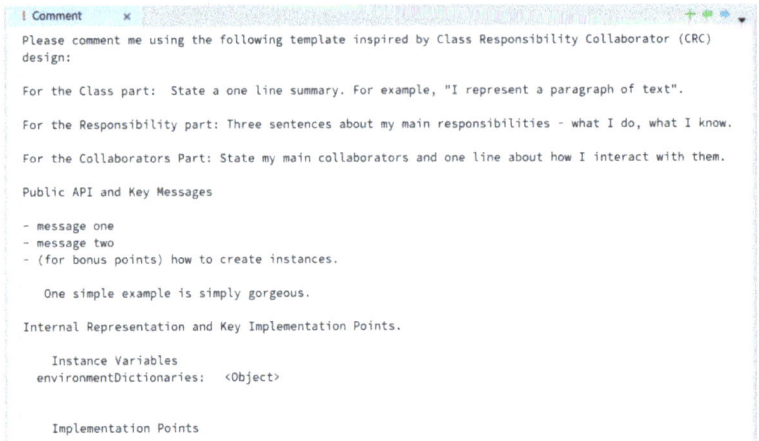

Figure 6.1: Class comment template in Pharo 7

and thus can reduce the developers' effort in maintaining high-quality comments. Additionally, the knowledge of developer practices in following the comment conventions can provide insight into how developers write various information types, and whether they follow conventions or not. In this chapter, we collect various kinds of empirical evidence to enable designing such a system. It can help us to improve the guidelines to define comment assessment measures, and to design methodologies to encourage developers to write high-quality comments.

6.2 Study Design

This chapter aims to further understand developer commenting practices by answering two subsidiary research questions (SRQs) that eventually answer RQ_3.

6.2.1 Research Questions

- SRQ_1: *Which type of class comment conventions are suggested by various style guidelines?*
  Rationale: Coding style guidelines suggest comment conventions that relate to the syntax of class comments, *i.e.*, syntax conventions, how to format comments, *i.e.*, format conventions, and what content to write in comments, *i.e.*, content conventions. However, these conventions are scattered across pages, sections, and paragraphs in the guidelines. It is unknown which comment aspects are covered and to what extent in these style guidelines.

6.2. Study Design

- SRQ$_2$: *To what extent do developers follow commenting conventions in writing class comments?*
  Rationale: Commenting conventions are provided to help developers in writing informative, consistent, and maintainable comments. However, whether developers follow these guidelines or not is unknown. For instance, we do not know yet whether they write their comments as stated by the guideline or write additional information in comments.

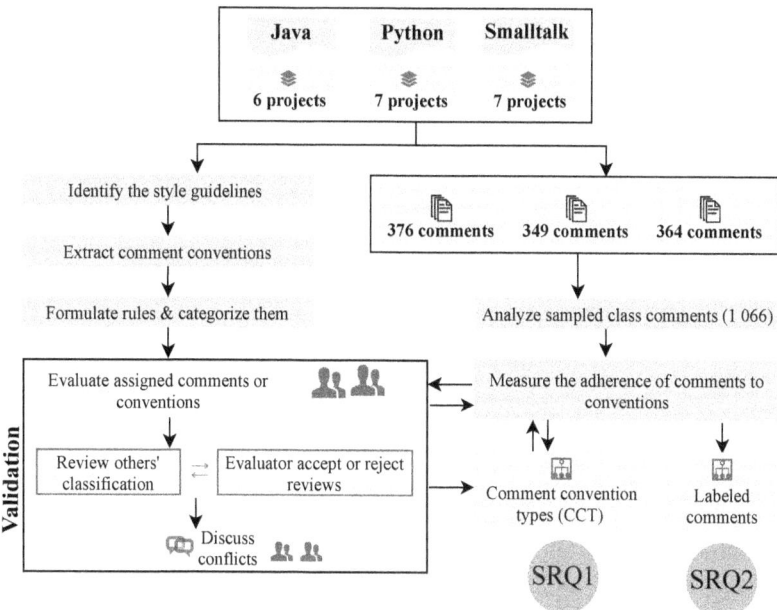

Figure 6.2: Research methodology to answer SRQ$_1$ and SRQ$_2$

Figure 6.2 presents the methodology followed to answer these SRQs. We consider the sampled labeled class comments of Java, Python, and Smalltalk from chapter 4 to understand what syntax, structure, and content developers follow when they write the comments.

6.2.2 Data Collection

Java and Python. We considered all Java and Python projects that we have reported in subsection 4.2.2. That is, we considered six projects for Java: *Eclipse, Hadoop, Vaadin, Spark, Guava,* and *Guice*; and seven projects for Python: *Django, Requests, Pipenv, Mailpile, Pandas, iPython,* and *Pytorch*. These projects belong to different ecosystems, *i.e.*, Apache, Google, and Eclipse, and they follow a variety of coding style guidelines including project-specific guidelines. The projects indicate the coding style guidelines they refer to in their corresponding web pages, GitHub repositories, or mailing lists.

Smalltalk. We considered the *Pharo 7 core* project, *i.e.*, the 363 sampled class comments that we have analyzed in chapter 4 to construct the Smalltalk CCTM. However, we excluded the external Smalltalk projects shown in Table 4.4 for two reasons: (i) some external projects lacked a web page that indicates the coding style guidelines they use, and (ii) the ones that had a project web page did not mention which documentation guidelines they followed to write class comments.

The Pharo core environment presents a default comment template for new classes and encourages developers to write class comments.[1] We expect that Pharo core developers are more aware and exposed to the template than other Smalltalk developers who are working on external projects. Pharo has evolved over the years, and many classes in Pharo 7 originate from previous Pharo versions. Similarly, the comment template in Pharo 7 has evolved since the first version of Pharo, *i.e.*, Pharo 1. In the Pharo environment, the default template appears only when a developer adds for the first time a class comment to a class. To ensure that a developer had a chance to look at the template of that version, the classes chosen for the analysis should be the newly added classes of that version. Therefore, for each comment in the sample set, we identified the original Pharo version when the comment was first added to a class. We then extracted that class comment and compared it to the corresponding comment template, *e.g.*, we compared a class comment added in Pharo 2 to the corresponding template in Pharo 2. Thus, we analyzed classes from Pharo version 1 to 7 and their corresponding template.

6.2.3 Analysis Method

SRQ$_1$: Comment conventions. The goal of SRQ$_1$ (*Which type of class comment conventions are suggested by various style guidelines?*) is to investigate the type of the comment conventions that various style guidelines offer. The term *comment convention* refers to suggestions or rules about various comment aspects, such as syntax, format, content, or writing style. In Table 6.1, we show the identified coding style guidelines the projects mentioned on their web page. We show the standard guidelines in column *Standard guideline*. Each project might refer to project-specific guidelines in addition to the standard guidelines to customize its coding style. We show if a project supports project-specific commenting guidelines (✓) or not (×) in the column *Project guideline*. The project-specific guidelines extend, clarify,

---

[1] https://github.com/pharo-project/pharo

Table 6.1: Overview of the selected projects and their style guidelines.

Language	Project	Standard guideline	Project guideline
Java	Eclipse	Oracle	✓
	Hadoop	Oracle	✓
	Vaadin	Oracle	✓
	Spark	Oracle	✓
	Guava	Google	✗
	Guice	Google	✗
Python	Django	PEP8/257	✓
	Requests	PEP8/257	✓
	Pipenv	PEP8/257	✗
	Mailpile	PEP8/257	✗
	Pandas	Numpy	✓
	iPython	PEP8/257, Numpy	✓
	Pytorch	Google	✓
Smalltalk	Pharo 1	Template v1	✗
	Pharo 2	Template v2	✗
	Pharo 3	Template v2	✗
	Pharo 4	Template v3	✗
	Pharo 5	Template v4	✗
	Pharo 6	Template v4	✗
	Pharo 7	Template v4	✗

or conflict with the standard guidelines such as Pandas.[2] For Smalltalk, we considered the default class comment template provided by Pharo.

Identifying the style guideline version. Coding style guidelines evolve over time, and new conventions are changed, added, or deleted. Therefore, we first identified the referenced coding style guidelines, and then we determined the version available at the time of the snapshot of our projects. Since the snapshots of Java and Python projects date from the end of 2019, we had to trace the version of the style guideline that was available at that time and compare it to the current online version of the style guideline. As the content of the Java and Python style guidelines are often stored as a text file in a GitHub repository, we traced back older versions of the style guidelines. We then compared the online version from which we extracted the rules to the version that dates from the end of 2019. We found that most style guidelines did not change at all or did not change any comment-related conventions. *Pandas* has changed the wording of conventions, however, the meaning is still the same. We could not find any versioning of project-specific conventions defined for *Eclipse*. Therefore, we used the conventions available on its website at the time of writing. To guarantee the reproducibility of the work, we provide a copy of each style guideline version that is considered

---

[2]https://pandas.pydata.org/pandas-docs/stable/development/contributing_docstring.html

in the thesis in the replication package [127]. In the case of Smalltalk, we found that the template had been updated in specific Pharo versions, *i.e.*, Pharo 1, Pharo 2, Pharo 4, and Pharo 5. Thus, we analyzed the template of all these versions, as shown in Table 6.1.

Identify comment conventions. Once we found the referenced style guidelines of each project, we started to identify the comment related conventions in these guidelines, and turned them into rules. We organized these rules into a taxonomy of the five main categories: *content, structure, format, syntax*, and *writing style* as described in Table 6.2. If a rule does not fit any of these categories, we assigned it to the *other* category. The rationale behind the taxonomy is that the approaches to evaluate comment quality can focus on a specific aspect of comments that they want to improve. To answer SRQ_1, we analyzed the frequency of these rule categories in the style guidelines.

Table 6.2: Types of comment conventions or rules

Category	Description
Content	Contains the rules that describe the type of information comments should contain
Writing style	Contains natural-language specific rules, such as grammar, punctuations, and capitalization
Format	Contains the rules related to indentation, blank lines, or spacing in comments
Structure	Contains the rules about text organization, and location of the information, *e.g.*, how tags/sections/information should be ordered in comments
Syntax	Contains the syntax rules to write specific types of comments, *e.g.*, which symbol to use to denote a class comment
Other	Contains the rules that do not fit into one of the other categories

Java and Python. Various code conventions exist in a typical coding style guideline, such as to name variables, methods, or classes, the syntax to write and format them, or add comments to them. Moreover, comment conventions can be scattered across multiple paragraphs or pages. We scanned every sentence of a style guideline and selected those that mentioned any comment convention as shown in Figure 6.3. To preserve the context of the conventions, we extracted the section titles and examples in the guidelines.

6.2. Study Design

```
Multi-line Docstrings                    Content                          Format
①
Multi-line docstrings consists of a summary line just like a one-line docstrings, followed ②
                ③
by a blank line, followed by a more elaborate description. The summary line may be used by
                               ④
automatic indexing tools; it is important that fits on one line and is separated from the
                               ⑤
rest of the docstring by a blank line. The summary line may be on the same line as the
                          ⑥
opening quotes or on the next line. The entire doctoring is intended the same as the
quotes at its first time.
```

Figure 6.3: Comment conventions in Python PEP 257 Docstring conventions [a]

[a] https://www.python.org/dev/peps/pep-0257/

In the next step, we turned these conventions into individual rules that can be validated for a comment type. For instance, the shown convention ① was turned into the rule: *"Multi-line docstrings should consist of a summary line."* A convention can target various types of comments, such as class, package, or inline comments, or it can target a part of a comment, *e.g.*, a summary, or parameters. In case a sentence targeted multiple comment types, we formulated the rule for each type. In total, we collected 600 comment-related rules. Since we focused on class comments, we could filter rules related to class comments, which skip 210 rules.

Three evaluators participated in the study and independently analyzed each style guideline. They scanned each guideline and extracted the corresponding comment conventions in more details. The first evaluator identified and converted the conventions to rules and categorized them according to the taxonomy. The remaining evaluators validated the classification using an iterative process where each of them reviewed their assigned classification. In case any evaluator disagreed with the first evaluator, the third evaluator who had not yet seen the classification validated it. The final decision was taken based on the majority voting mechanism.

Smalltalk. In contrast to Java and Python, many *syntax* and *format* rules did not apply to the template as it is limited to class comments, and class comments in Pharo (shown in Figure 4.3) are written into a separate pane rather than mixed with the code. For instance, the Java and Python guidelines describe the syntax to write a class comment in terms of symbols (/** .. */, or ''' a comment '''), or to indent with respect to the code, whereas such rules are not found in Smalltalk. Additionally, we did not extract the *format* conventions from the template due to these conventions not being apparent in the initial stages like Java or Python. The *format* conventions were clearly mentioned in Java and Python style guidelines, *e.g.*, *"Four spaces should be used as the unit of indentation"* or *"limit the line length to 80 characters"* and thus only became apparent later on.

For each version of the template, we manually extracted the information types hinted by the template, and then extracted the syntax, structure, and

6. COMMENT ADHERENCE TO CONVENTIONS

writing style guidelines hinted for each information type. Three evaluators participated in the analysis of a template, discussed each extracted guideline, and formulated several rules for each information type. Next, we used a two-step validation approach, thus validating the content classification of the template and the name assigned to the classified content. Specifically, the content classification was validated by an iterative evaluation process, where each evaluator reviewed the other's content classification. This way, all the information types were discussed by all the evaluators to achieve a better naming convention and classification.

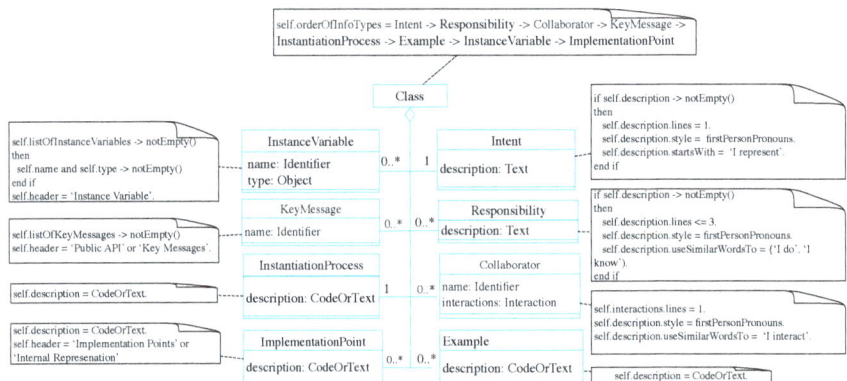

Figure 6.4: Comment convention rules formulated from the Pharo 7 template

For example, we identified the `For the Class part` section in the Pharo 7 template shown in Figure 6.1 as the *intent* information type. For this information type, we extracted the guidelines from the keywords `State one line, I represent` and converted them into rules, such as *"description should be one line, the subject should be first person"*, and that it should follow the pattern *<subject>*, *<verb>* from the keywords `I represent`. Figure 6.4 shows the final rules for each information type in the Pharo 7 template. In total, we could identify 128 rules from all versions of the template. A complete list of all rules, their examples for each Pharo version, and the process of finalizing the rules can be found in the replication package [136]. There were a few intermediate Pharo versions where the template had not changed; in such cases, we used the same guidelines from the earlier template.

SRQ$_2$: Adherence of comments to conventions. The goal of SRQ$_2$ (*To what extent do developers follow commenting conventions in writing class comments?*) is to verify whether developers follow the comment conventions that we identified in the previous SRQ in their projects.

6.2. Study Design

Collecting sample class comments. Classifying all comments into various information types and comparing them to corresponding conventions is a time-consuming and tedious task. To restrict the scope, we focused on the adherence of class comments to class comment conventions.

Java and Python. Currently, there are no tools available that can automatically check comments against all types of rules. Therefore, we manually validated a sample of class comments against all related rules. We used the statistically significant sample of 700 class comments from the projects shown in Table 6.1. We used 390 class comment-related rules extracted from standard and project-specific guidelines. For the scope of this work, we focused on the rule types that require manual validation due to limited tool support *i.e.*, all types of rules except *format*. Thus, we could validate 270 rules against the sampled class comments.

Smalltalk. We used the dataset of 363 classes from Pharo 7, of which many classes originated in previous Pharo versions. Moreover, the template appears only once when a class comment is added for the first time, therefore, each class comment of a version should be compared to the template of that corresponding version.

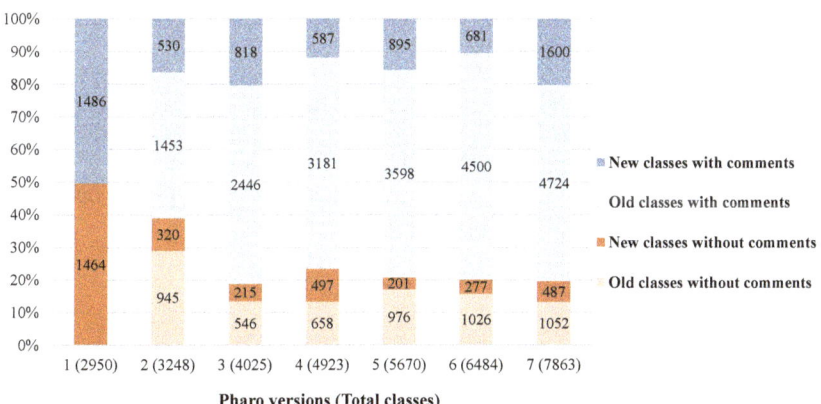

Figure 6.5: The trend of classes with and without comments in Pharo versions.

Identifying the origin of the classes led to an unequal number of classes from various Pharo versions, thus giving an unbalanced number of representative classes of each Pharo version. To balance the sampled classes from each version, we set a lower threshold of 52 classes for each Pharo version, increasing from a total of 363 classes to 364 classes. For each Pharo version in which the number of classes was lower than 52, we sampled newly added classes with comments shown in the top dark blue segment of Figure 6.5. We followed the same approach to choose representative class comments in the Smalltalk-CCTM study, *i.e.*, according to the distribution of comments based on the number of sentences present in a comment. Similarly, we removed the classes from Pharo versions where there were more than 52 classes, *i.e.*, Pharo 1, Pharo 6, and Pharo 7, based on the distribution of comments of each version.

In summary, we grouped 364 comments according to their original Pharo versions so that we could differentiate the comments of one version from another version, and compare them to the corresponding template of that version. Then, we identified the comment information types for the newly added class comments, following the same methodology that we used for the Smalltalk-CCTM study.

Adherence measurement. In this step, we compared the 1 064 sampled class comments from Java, Python, and Smalltalk to the 270 class comment-related rules from Java and Python, and 128 rules for Smalltalk. In case a comment followed a particular rule, we labeled the rule as *followed*, otherwise as *not followed*. There were often cases where a rule was not applicable to a comment due to missing information in the comment. For instance, the rules related to syntax, content, or style of a version information in a class comment could not be verified if the information was not mentioned in the comment. In such cases, we labeled rules as *not applicable* to the comment. We excluded a few rules that could not be verified with the current dataset due to the abstract nature of a rule, the unavailability of the symbols that denote the class comment, or code associated with the class, *e.g.*, to verify the Oracle rule *"for the @deprecated tag, suggest what item to use instead"*, the class comment is not enough and requires code of the class to verify the mentioned replacement item.

Finally, we measured how many comments followed a particular rule and how many did not. One author labeled the comments, and another author reviewed the labeled comments. In cases where they disagreed, the third author was consulted, and conflicts were resolved using the majority voting mechanism (Cohen's kappa = 0.80).

Impact of templates on comments. To find the impact of the template on comments, we assessed the adherence of comments to the template via two main aspects: *content* and *content style*.

Content adherence: In SRQ_1, we identified the information types the templates contain, and formulated them as *content* type rules. Then, we compared them to each version's comment information types. For example, we compared the information types of a class comment in Pharo 2 to the information types suggested by the template in Pharo 2. Thus, we can compare what developers typically write in their comments to the information recommended by the template.

Content style adherence: The templates suggest specific styles for various information types, *e.g.*, which header to use for what information type, or in which order these information types should be written. In SRQ_1, we clustered these rules into various categories, such as *syntax*, *style*, or *structure*. Some rules identified from the template can be verified automatically for comments, and do not require manual intervention. However, this could lead to less reliable results due to the freedom of writing free text in comments, non-availability of formatting standards, and limited patterns available in the template. Additionally, there were chances to miss the cases where selected patterns are not present. Instead, developers used synonyms to describe the same detail in a comment or did not describe the detail under a specific section header inside the comment, *e.g.*, *Instance variables*, and just wrote the instance variables without any header. We, therefore, manually analyzed 364 comments, *i.e.*, 52 comments from each version. We used the same setup from our previous manual analysis performed in chapter 4 to identify the information types, *i.e.*, we followed the same iterative approach for evaluating and validating the rules. In addition, we used the pair sorting approach to decide whether a sentence in the comment *follows* the rules, and whether the template influences it. Similar to Java and Python, there were often cases in Smalltalk class comments where a rule did not apply to a comment due to missing information, thus marking such rules as *not applicable* to the comment.

6.3 Results

6.3.1 Comment Conventions Suggested by the Guidelines

Figure 6.6 shows a total of 600 conventions from Java and Python for each standard guideline from Oracle and Google, and project-specific guidelines that include conventions from the standard guidelines on the y-axis. The numbers in parentheses, *e.g.*, 149 for Oracle, indicate the number of comment-related rules found in the respective style guideline. The x-axis indicates the ratio of conventions belonging to a particular category from our taxonomy. We observed that the numbers of comment-related rules vary across projects and guidelines, because not all guidelines provide the same details for comment conventions. For instance, the Oracle Java code convention has an entire coding style guideline dedicated to code comments. In contrast, the Google Java style guideline has dedicated only a small section to code comments. Thus, the Oracle guideline contains 149 rules, whereas the Google Java guideline contains only 19 rules.

Moreover, Figure 6.6 shows the distribution of rule types for Python style guidelines. The Numpy style guideline and the projects following it (*Pandas* and *iPython*) contain the most rules about what type of information to write in comments and how to write it, compared to other standard guidelines, such as those of Google, PEP, and Oracle. For example, the Numpy guideline suggests to write both a short and an extended summary of the class, usage examples, notes, and warnings in a class comment. It

6. Comment Adherence to Conventions

	Format	Content	Syntax	Structure	Writing style	Other
Oracle (149)	14%	38%	21%		14%	11% 1%
Google (19)	26%	21%	11%	26%		16%
Spark* (190)	13%	42%	22%		12%	11% 1%
Eclipse* (153)	14%	39%	22%		14%	11% 1%
Hadoop* (152)	14%	39%	21%		14%	11% 1%
Vaadin* (150)	15%	38%	21%		14%	11% 1%
Guava (19)	26%	21%	11%	26%		16%
Guice (19)	26%	21%	11%	26%		16%

Percentage of comment conventions in Java

	Format	Content	Syntax	Structure	Writing style	Other
Numpy (111)	10%	48%		29%	11%	1%
Google (59)	15%	42%	12%	14%		17%
PEP8/257 (55)	27%	38%		9%	15%	11%
Pandas* (213)	9%	42%		30%	7%	10% 3%
iPython* (170)	18%	44%		22%	12%	5%
Pytorch* (102)	21%	40%	11%	18%		11%
Django* (66)	30%	36%		9%	12%	12%
Requests* (66)	30%	33%	11%	12%		14%
Pipenv (55)	27%	38%		9%	15%	11%
Mailpile (55)	27%	38%		9%	15%	11%

Percentage of comment conventions in Python

Figure 6.6: Convention types in Java and Python guidelines

also provides syntax and style conventions to follow when writing these types of information. Class comments of *iPython* and *Pandas* contain all of these information types and follow the syntax conventions to write them. Interestingly, developers write such types of information in all other projects [182, 135] regardless of whether the project guideline suggests or not, but they write them in inconsistent ways. Previous comment analysis studies of Java and Python showed that developers embed other types of information in comments, such as *usage, expand, rationale,* or *pointer*. Still, we did not find conventions to write such types of information in their corresponding style guidelines (Google, PEP, Oracle) [115, 182]. However, whether such detailed conventions in the Numpy guideline are one of the reasons for the low number of questions on *Stack Overflow* about the Numpy documentation (only 50 questions with the *numpydoc* tag) compared to the 2 784 Java questions with the *javadoc* tag, requires further investigation.[3]

> **Finding.** The Numpy style guideline provides more rigorous content conventions for comments compared to other style guidelines, such as Oracle, PEP257, or Google.

Our results further show that the majority of style guidelines present more rules about the content to write in comments, *i.e., content* conven-

---
[3]https://stackoverflow.com/questions/tagged/numpydoc accessed on Oct, 2021

tions, except for the Google style guideline in Java, which contains more rules on how to format and structure comments, *i.e.*, *format*, and *structure* conventions. Since the Oracle guideline is used as a baseline in several Java projects, project-specific guidelines suggest only few additional comment conventions. These additional conventions often either clarify or conflict with the baseline conventions. For example, comment conventions, such as *"line length limit"* and *"indentation with two spaces, four spaces, or tab"* are often among such conflicting rules across projects. Identifying such rules and ensuring they are properly configured in tools can help developers in following them automatically.

> **Finding.** The majority of the style guidelines in Java and Python predominately propose content and format-related comment conventions. However, content conventions are not easy to locate in style guidelines.

We observed that although style guidelines are meant to encourage and help developers to write good comments, comment conventions are scattered across multiple sources, documents, and paragraphs. Thus, it is not always easy to locate conventions particular to one entity like class, function, or inline, which causes developers to seek conventions in online sources [133].

Figure 6.7 shows the total number of class comment conventions that we extracted from standard and project-specific guidelines on the y-axis. In the case of Smalltalk, it denotes the total class comment conventions extracted from the template of each Pharo version. The x-axis indicates the ratio of conventions that belongs to a particular category from our taxonomy.

Our results show that the majority of the Java style guidelines present more content-related rules, whereas Python style guidelines except Numpy focus rather on the format aspect of comments. In contrast, the Pharo template focuses on the syntax of various information types. This fosters the understanding of Pharo templates, and the differences among them. Table 6.3 shows that the template in the initial three versions of Pharo suggested only a few information types for class comments. Later on, the template suggested seven types of information. Similarly, early versions suggested to write comments in the third-person form, whereas later ones suggested the first-person form.

6.3.2 Adherence of Comments to Conventions

Figure 6.8 shows the distribution of comments within each project that follow the rules, does not follow them, or to which the rules are not applicable. For example, in Eclipse, on average 27% of the comments follow the rules, whereas 3% of the comments violate the rules, and 70% of the comments do not hold enough relevant information to check them against a rule. The high ratio of non-applicable rules to selected comments indicates that the style guidelines suggest various comment conventions, but developers rarely

6. Comment Adherence to Conventions

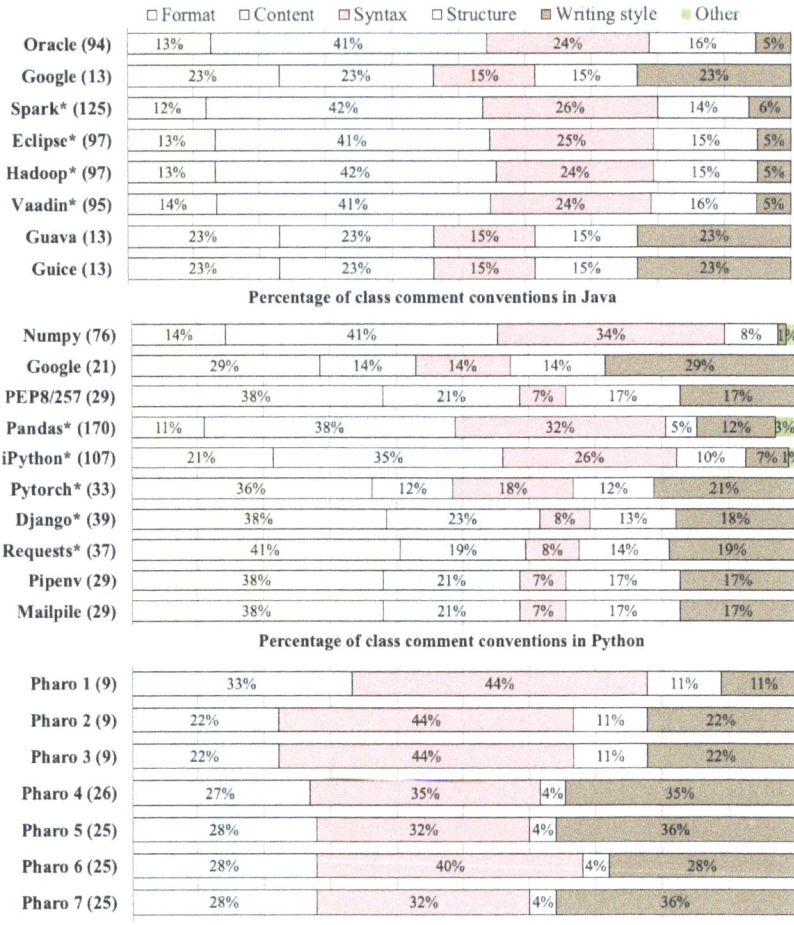

Figure 6.7: Types of class comment conventions in Java, Python, and Smalltalk guidelines

adopt them. For instance, the Oracle rules, such as *"use FIXME to flag something that is bogus or broken"*, or *"use @serial tag in class comment"* are not applicable to comments due to the general unavailability of the `FIXME` or `@serial` information in comments and thus showing the developers' lack of interest in adopting such rules. Similarly, some rules in Python such as *"Docstrings for a class should list public methods and instance variables"* are also rarely adopted. Similarly in Smalltalk, the high ratio of non-applicable rules is due to the unavailability of the suggested information types in the template, such as *instance variable*, *key messages*, or *implementation point*.

Finding. Style guidelines suggest various comment conventions, but not all of them are adopted by developers in their comments.

6.3. Results

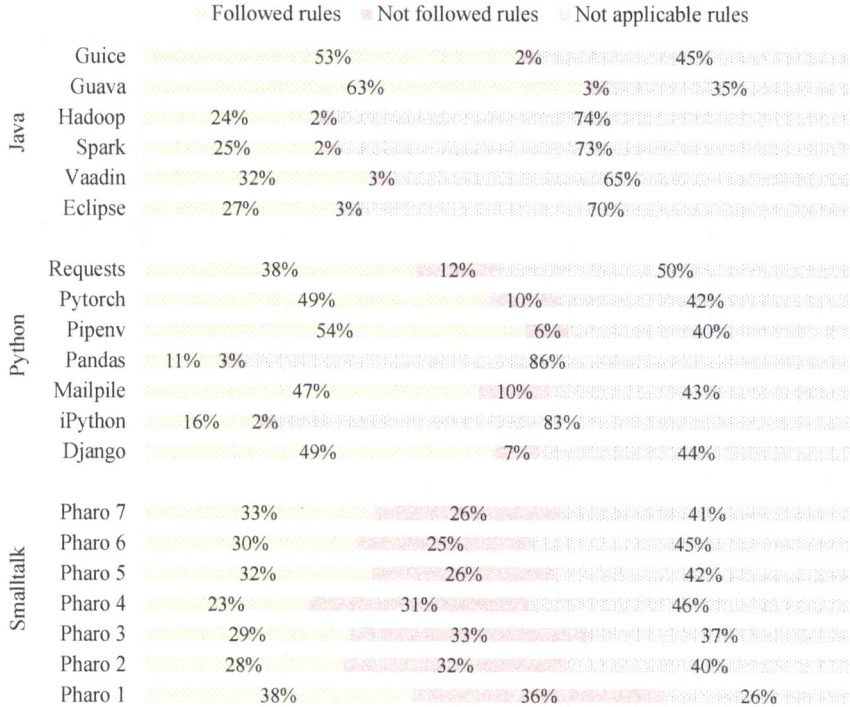

Figure 6.8: Percentage of comments that follow the rules, do not follow them, or to which rules are not applicable.

Finding. Compared to Python, Java class comments violate rules less often (see Figure 6.8).

Figure 6.9 shows the rules that are applicable to comments. The rules *writing style* and *content* are more often followed than *syntax* and *structure* rules in Java and Python. In contrast, Smalltalk developers follow *structure* and *writing style* rules more often than others. However, comparing the frequency of the information types suggested by the template to other information types found in comments, we observed that they mention the template suggested information types more often than other types of information. For instance, *intent* and *responsibility* are present in 65% of the sampled class comments, while *warnings* (not suggested by the template) are present in 12% of the sampled class comments, which indicates the relevance of the template in terms of its information types. Figure 6.9 also shows the rules that comments do not follow. For instance, the *structure* rules are often violated in Java and Python. In contrast, Smalltalk developers violate *content* and *syntax* rules more often than others.

107

6. Comment Adherence to Conventions

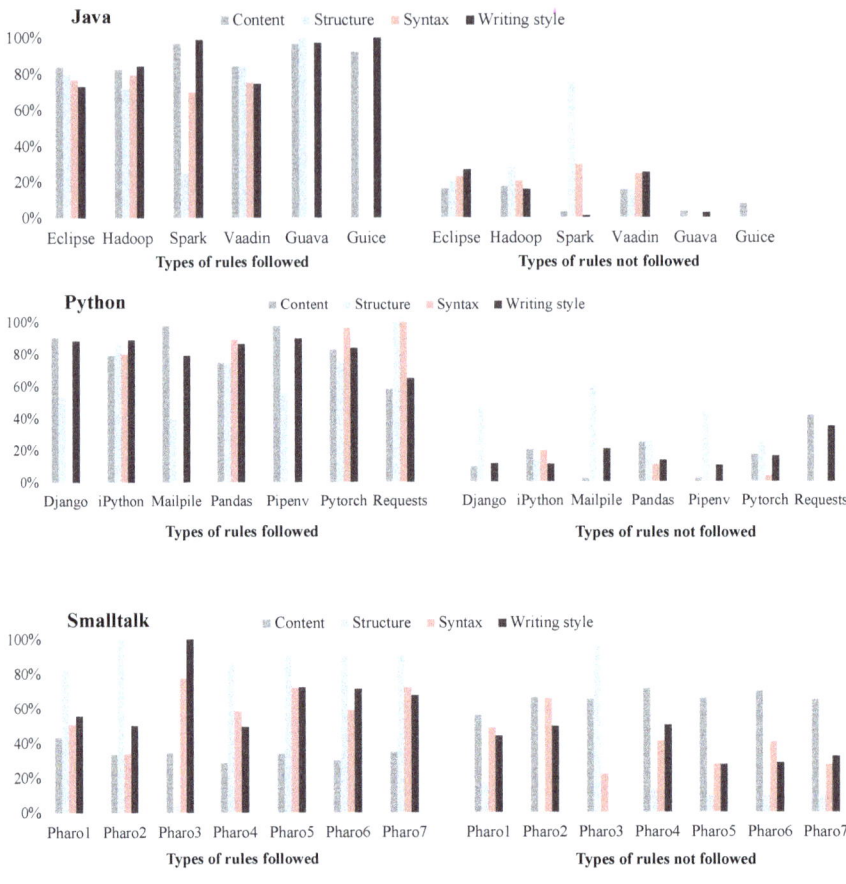

Figure 6.9: Types of rules followed or not in Java, Python, and Smalltalk projects

> **Finding.** Most Class comments in Java and Python often follow writing style and content conventions, but about every third comment violates structure conventions (kindly refer to Figure 6.9). In contrast, Smalltalk developers follow structure conventions in about three of four comments and less frequently writing style conventions. However, every third comment violates content conventions.

Furthermore, we realized that some rules are often followed, whereas others are frequently violated. For instance, in *Pandas*, the rule *"a few sentences giving an extended summary of the class or method after the short (one-line) summary"* is often followed, but the rule *"there should be a blank line between the short summary and extended summary"* is often violated. Similarly, in Pharo 2 and 3, the rules *"describe the intent behind the class"* and *"Instance variables should be written after the intent information"* are almost always followed, whereas *"describe the instance variables of the class"* is rarely followed. We found only one structure convention that is about the order of information types in the template, which developers often follow (78%). This can be the reason for achieving a high rate of comments that follow the structure convention. By surveying developers, such conventions can be further investigated to know the specific factors behind their adherence or violation, such as the usage of linters for comments, the team strictness, or developer awareness.

Although the project-specific guidelines in Java and Python provide few additional conventions, these conventions are followed more often in projects compared to the conventions provided by their standard guidelines. Precisely, 85% of Python class comments and 89% of Java class comments follow the project-specific conventions, whereas 81% of their comments follow standard guideline conventions. One such example is the rule *"Do not use @author tags"*, which is specific to Hadoop and in contrast with the Oracle style guideline, however, it is always followed in Hadoop comments. It would be an interesting future work to explore the reasoning behind such conventions.

Finding. Project-specific class comment conventions are followed more often than conventions suggested by the standard guidelines.

Impact of templates on comments. We measured the adherence of Smalltalk comments to the template by assessing *content adherence*, and *content style adherence* to see the impact of templates on comments.

Content adherence: The analysis of the information embedded in the comments shows that developers document different kinds of information in the class comments to make their classes more understandable and maintainable. However, whether the practice of embedding different information in class comments has recently emerged or it has been there since initial Pharo versions, is unexplored and unknown.

In Figure 6.10, the x-axis lists the information types and the y-axis shows the Pharo versions with the number of classes considered for each Pharo version. A darker shade of orange indicates a large number of comments that have a particular type of information, and a lighter shade indicates a smaller number of comments that fall into an information type. From our analysis, we found that most of the information types are present in the comments since Pharo 1 except *Todo comments*, *coding guidelines*, and *observations*. A few information types like *intent*, *responsibility*, *collaborators*, and *examples* are highly frequent in all versions of Pharo. Table 6.3 shows that the templates suggest only a few information types to write in a class comment. Still, there exist other information types mentioned by developers than those recommended by the templates. For example, the Pharo 1 template mentions only three types of information shown in Table 6.3, but Smalltalk developers have mentioned 20 other types of information shown

6. Comment Adherence to Conventions

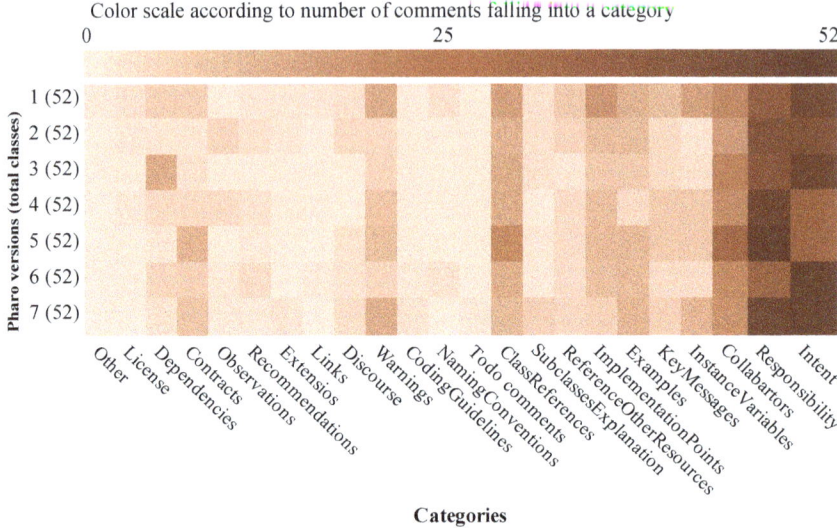

Figure 6.10: The trend of information types in Pharo versions

in Figure 6.10. In Pharo 7, 23 types of information are found in comments, but its template mentions only seven types.

> **Finding.** Most of the information types in comments are available since Pharo version 1. A few information types like, *Todo comments*, *coding guidelines*, and *observations* do not exist in the initial version.

> **Finding.** The template-suggested information types are mentioned more frequently in the comments than other types of information.

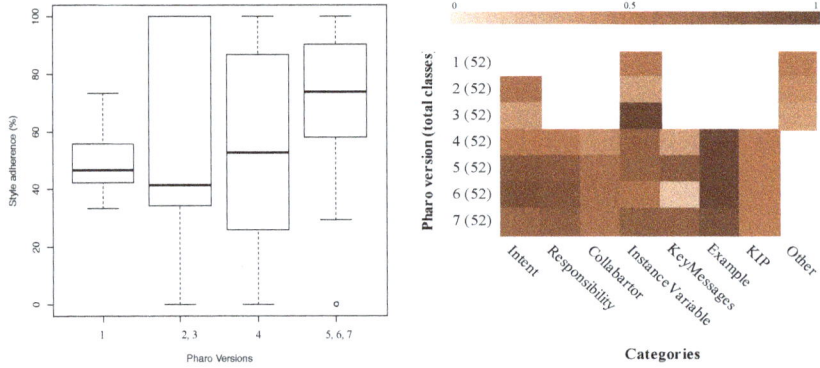

Figure 6.11: Distribution of style adherence differences between Pharo versions

Figure 6.12: The trend of following content style rules across Pharo versions

110

Content style adherence: In Figure 6.11, we see that Pharo 1 comments follow the content style rules 50% of the time, whereas since Pharo 4, the trend of comments adhering to the rules increased to 75%. To understand these differences between Pharo versions, we grouped comments of various Pharo versions according to the changes in the template *e.g.*, Pharo 2 and Pharo 3 templates are identical and therefore, we grouped Pharo 2 and Pharo 3 comments. We then measured the percentage of comments that adhere to content style rules. After the grouping, we used the *Wilcoxon* test as well as the *Vargha-Delaney* $\hat{A}_{12}$ measure to observe potential statistically significant differences in the results. The results of the *Wilcoxon* test highlight a marginally significant difference, *i.e.*, a p-value of 0.0673 has been observed between Pharo 1 and the Pharo 4, 5, 6 groups. For these groups, the *Vargha-Delaney* measure also revealed a large difference.

Finding. Since Pharo 4, Developers adhere rather to content style guidelines, especially in describing the *intent, responsibilities*, and *instance variables* of a class.

In Figure 6.12, we further explored the differences between Pharo versions by measuring the adherence of comments to specific information types of each template version. We found that *example* and *KIP* (*Key Implementation Points*) are always inconsistent due to the unavailability of strict guidelines to write or format them. Developers, therefore, follow various conventions when they mention examples, such as using the dedicated headers *usage, examples*, and *code examples*. Similarly, for *KIP*, one of the rules just suggests to write the header *Internal representation and Implementation points* when mentioning the implementation details, but this is rarely followed by developers.

```
I am a base class for commands which perform operations with
  collection of methods.

Internal Representation and Key Implementation Points.

Instance Variables
methods:        <Collection of<CompiledMethod>>

```

Listing 7: *Key Implementation Points* header present in the SycMethodCommand class

Our analysis found several comments where only the header was present without any further details mentioned below it. We believe that this is due to a lack of attention from developers in deleting unused section headers. One of the cases we encountered is in the class `SycMethodCommand` shown in Listing 7, where the developers have not provided any details under the *Internal representation and Implementation points* section, but the header is still present. In the case of the *instance variable* information, its header is mostly mentioned with the instance variables. One of the reasons for such a behavior can be the Pharo feature which automatically adds an instance variable section to the class comment template if a class is created with instance variables. This indicates a careful consideration for the approaches that aim to generate comments automatically.

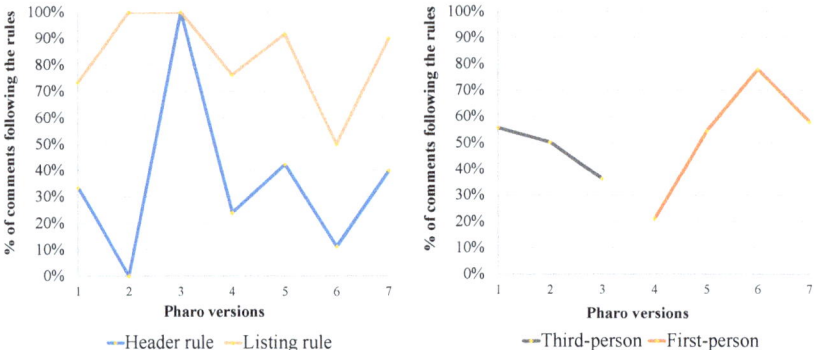

Figure 6.13: Comments following formatting guidelines

Figure 6.14: Comments following subject-form guidelines

We observed a high degree of inconsistency in using headers to delimit different information types in class comments. Figure 6.13 (Header rule) shows that the use of headers fluctuates significantly across all Pharo versions. We noted a similar fluctuation in the adherence to the listing rules, which document instance variables and Key APIs as lists. This indicates the need to have a better and consistent standard for formatting and providing headers for different information types. For a few rules, we noticed the consistent declining rate in following them. For instance, in Pharo 1 the rules ask developers to write specific information types in the third person. Instead, developers often write this information in the first person. Since Pharo version 5, such rules are respected more than 50% of the time, showing increased use of the first-person. We confirmed our observation by mining the rules related to the first and third person from all information types in all versions as shown in Figure 6.14. We found that the use of the third person started to decline in the initial versions even though the template proposed to use it. Since Pharo 4, the use of the first person and active-voice rules have been increasing, however, they are still not entirely followed. These results indicate the need to have standard and detailed rules to consistently write various information in the comment template.

Finding. Developers use various verb forms to describe the top three information types *intent*, *responsibilities*, and *collaborators* of a class, but mainly adhere to the template's use of the first-person pronouns.

6.3. Results

> **Finding.** In most Pharo versions, fewer than 40% of the comments make use of the headers suggested by the comment template. Where headers are used, developers often use different and inconsistent headers for the same information types.

Table 6.3: The information types from the CCTM suggested or not by the guidelines

Java	Eclipse	Hadoop	Vaadin	Spark	Guava	Guice	
Summary	✓	✓	✓	✓	✓	✓	
Expand	✓	✓	✓	✓	✓	✓	
Ownership	✓	x	✓	✓	-	-	
Pointer	✓	✓	✓	✓	-	-	
Usage	✓	✓	✓	✓	-	-	
Deprecation	x	✓	✓	✓	✓	✓	
Rationale	✓	✓	✓	✓	-	-	
Warning	✓	✓	✓	✓	-	-	
Exception	x	x	x	x	✓	✓	
Todo	-	-	-	✓	-	-	
Recommendation	-	-	-	-	-	-	
Precondition	✓	✓	✓	✓	-	-	
Observation	-	-	-	-	-	-	
Formatter	x	x	x	x	-	-	
Subclass explanation	-	-	-	-	-	-	
Commented code	-	-	-	-	-	-	
Directive	-	-	-	-	-	-	
Incomplete	x	x	x	x	-	-	
Auto generated	-	-	-	-	-	-	
Python	**Django**	**Pipenv**	**Pytorch**	**iPython**	**Pandas**	**Requests**	**Mailpile**
Summary	✓	✓	✓	✓	✓	✓	✓
Usage	✓	✓	✓	✓	✓	✓	✓
Expand	✓	✓	✓	✓	✓	✓	✓
Development notes	✓	-	✓	✓	✓	-	-
Parameters	x	x	✓	✓	✓	x	x
Warning	-	-	✓	✓	✓	-	-
Links	-	-	-	✓	✓	-	-
Recommendation	-	-	-	✓	✓	-	-
Subclass explanation	✓	✓	-	✓	-	✓	✓
Exception	-	-	✓	✓	✓	-	-
Version	-	-	-	✓	✓	-	-
Precondition	-	-	-	-	-	-	-
Coding guideline	-	-	-	✓	✓	-	-
Todo	-	-	-	-	-	-	-
Observation	-	-	-	-	✓	-	-
Dependency	-	-	-	-	-	-	-
Extension	-	-	-	-	-	-	-
Noise	-	-	-	-	-	-	-
Smalltalk	**Pharo1**	**Pharo2**	**Pharo3**	**Pharo4**	**Pharo5**	**Pharo6**	**Pharo7**
Intent	✓	✓	✓	✓	✓	✓	✓
Responsibility	-	-	-	✓	✓	✓	✓
Collaborators	✓	-	-	✓	✓	✓	✓
Instance variables	✓	✓	✓	✓	✓	✓	✓
Key messages	-	-	-	✓	✓	✓	✓
Examples	-	-	-	✓	✓	✓	✓
Implementation points	-	-	-	✓	✓	✓	✓
Refer other resources	-	-	-	-	-	-	-
Subclass explanation	-	-	-	-	-	-	-
Class references	-	-	-	-	-	-	-
Todo	-	-	-	-	-	-	-
Naming conventions	-	-	-	-	-	-	-
Coding guideline	-	-	-	-	-	-	-
Warnings	-	-	-	-	-	-	-
Discourse	-	-	-	-	-	-	-
Links	-	-	-	-	-	-	-
Extensions	-	-	-	-	-	-	-
Recommendations	-	-	-	-	-	-	-
Observations	-	-	-	-	-	-	-
Contracts	-	-	-	-	-	-	-
Dependencies	-	-	-	-	-	-	-
License	-	-	-	-	-	-	-
Other	-	-	-	-	-	-	-

113

Overall, our results highlight the mismatch between developer commenting practices and commenting guidelines. Figure 6.8 indicates the number of conventions the style guidelines suggest, but developers do not adopt them. Table 6.3 shows various information types found (in the column *Information types*) for each language and highlight which of them are suggested (✓) or not (x) by their style guidelines. The symbol '-' denotes that the style guideline does not mention the information type.

6.4 Implications and Discussion

Java and Python. There are some conventions that the guidelines suggest to write in comments, but developers do not seem to adopt them. For example, the Oracle style guideline suggests to write `@version` information in class comments, but we found no instance of this tag in our sampled class comments. In contrast, there were some information types that the guidelines suggested to avoid, but developers nevertheless wrote. For example, the Oracle style guideline suggests *"Documentation comments are meant to describe the specification of the code, from an implementation-free perspective"*, but we found developers writing implementation details in class comments under the *expand* category. In contrast, the guideline suggests to write such details in block comments. We found similar instances for Python where the guidelines suggest to write ownership information, but comments did not contain that. We highlighted some of these mismatches in Table 6.3. However, whether writing the implementation information in class comments is due to the ease of embedding the information, or the laziness of developers, would require surveying the developers.

Smalltalk. When we analyzed the content style aspect, we found that developers follow a mix of the first person and third person to express the same information about the class. Although more than 75% of the comments in recent versions follow the style conventions of the template, there is a substantial proportion of comments that are written differently, creating an inconsistent style across projects. This suggests a need for better structure conventions, as the template does not follow any strict structural guidelines to organize the content, thus forcing developers to look through the entire comment to find a piece of information. Encouraging developers to follow structural guidelines in the text, and writing comments with standard headers will allow other developers to easily extract information from them. We suggest that the Pharo comment template should impose a formatting and markup style to structure the details in comments.

Impact of coding conventions. Coding style guidelines impact program comprehension and maintenance activities. However, not all conventions from the guidelines have the same impact on these activities. Binkley *et al.*

evaluated the impact of identifier conventions on code comprehension, but the conventions were limited to identifiers [23]. Smit et al. [151] ranked 71 code conventions that are most important to maintainable code. However, they accounted only for missing or incomplete Javadoc comments on public types and methods, and did not account for other comment-related conventions, especially about their content. Similarly, most previous work has focused on building tools for formatting and naming conventions for code entities, while being very limited on comment conventions [6, 11]. Therefore, assessing the impact and importance of comment conventions depending on a specific domain and project, and on various development tasks appears to be another potential direction. We labeled a dataset of 1 050 class comments of three languages and 687 comment conventions. This dataset can help researchers rank the specific comment conventions to find out their importance and impact on program comprehension and maintenance activities, and thus help in developing comment quality tools based on supervised machine-learning approaches.

Adherence of comment conventions. Previous works, including Bafatakis et al. and Simmons et al., evaluated the compliance of Python code to Python style guidelines [15, 149]. However, they included only a few comment conventions and missed other types of conventions, such as *writing style*, or *content*. Our study found various comment conventions that developers often follow, such as grammar rules, and rules governing the syntax for writing different types of information, but these are not covered in previous studies. We measured the adherence of Smalltalk class comments to the default comment template and found that developers write the template suggested information types more often and follow the writing conventions to write them. Java and Python do not provide any default template to write comments, but our results show that developers follow content and writing style conventions suggested by the style guidelines, thus indicating the need for the future studies to include such conventions in their analysis.

To ensure developers follow such guidelines, various automated style checkers or linters, *e.g.*, Checkstyle,[4] Pylint,[5] and ESLint[6] turn such guidelines into rules and then evaluate the rules against comments automatically. However, these style checkers are not available for all programming languages, and for the supported ones, they provide limited rules for addressing code commenting guidelines. The majority are limited to detecting missing comments and to verifying formatting guidelines, but not checking the adherence to guidelines that concern the content and style of comments. Furthermore, the results indicated the need to conduct extensive studies on (i) which comment-related conventions linters provide, (ii) how well linters

---
[4]https://checkstyle.org/checks.html
[5]https://www.pylint.org/
[6]https://eslint.org/

cover comment conventions from various style guidelines, and (iii) building tools and techniques to reduce the mismatch between developer commenting practices and style guidelines. Our dataset provides relevant data to observe which commenting guidelines developers frequently follow in their comments and which they do not. We plan to survey some popular tools to see the extent they support various comment conventions that we identified. Thus, it can help enhance the rule set of these tools and conduct studies in other languages.

Comment quality attributes. We identified several quality attributes (QAs), such as *completeness*, or *consistency* to assess comment quality. However, the results show that several studies either fail to specify the definition of QAs, or refer to different terminologies for the same attribute. The guidelines suggest various comment conventions that describe QAs, such as how to write concise, precise, or consistent comments. Collecting such conventions can define the QAs for comment content in a uniform and standard way. For instance, the *completeness* quality attribute measures how complete a comment is [183], and the style guidelines suggest which types of information should be written for which type of comment, *e.g.*, a class comment should contain a summary of the class, *i.e.*, summary information type, or a method comment should have its parameter details. Thus, according to the guideline, the *completeness* quality attribute can be defined as 'the information types suggested by the guideline for a particular comment type (class, or method comment) are available or not in the comment'. If all of the information types are available in a comment, then the comment can be considered complete. Table 6.4 presents our identified QAs in the column *QA* and their definition based on the style guidelines in the column *Description*. For instance, *completeness* can be measured with respect to the availability of certain information types, and thus missing information types can be indicated to developers to add them.

Table 6.4: Various QAs emerged from the style guidelines

QA	Description
Accessibility	To what extent the information available in comments is easy to find or access
Readability	To what extent the comment is readable, and use of certain words
Author-related	Author information is written as required by the guidelines
Completeness	Types of information suggested by a guideline are mentioned in the comment
Similarity	The information is already available in comments
Consistency	The comment follows the consistent style that is described in the style guideline
Accuracy	The information is enough precise, *e.g.*, usage information about the class includes a code example as required by the guideline
Organization	Information types are organized or structured as suggested by the guidelines, *e.g.*, summary information should be on the top of a comment
Format	The information type follows the correct writing style, includes visuals or code examples, *e.g.*, a summary is written using phrases rather than complete sentences
Conciseness	The information is succinct and necessary in comments according to the guideline, *e.g.*, a summary should be one line
Internationalization	Comment can be correctly translated to other natural languages

6.5 Threats to Validity

Threats to construct validity. This mainly concerns the measurements used in the evaluation. First, we are aware that we sampled only a subset of the extracted class comments. However, (i) the sample size limits the estimation imprecision to 5% of error for a confidence level of 95%, and (ii) to limit the subjectiveness and the bias in the evaluation, three evaluators (three authors of this work) manually analyzed the resulting sample.

Another threat to construct validity concerns the definition of the rule taxonomy, information types, and writing rules from the template, which are performed on data analyzed by three subjects. Indeed, there is a level of subjectivity in deciding whether a convention belongs to a specific taxonomy category or not and whether a comment follows the rule. To counteract this issue, we performed a two-level validation step. This validation step involved further discussion among the evaluators, whenever they had divergent opinions, until they reached a final decision.

Threats to internal validity. This concerns confounding factors that could influence our results. To analyze whether developers follow a rule in their comments or not, we performed a manual analysis. The main threat to internal validity in our study is that the assessment is performed on data provided by human subjects; hence it could be biased. To counteract this issue, the evaluators of this work were two Ph.D. candidates and one faculty member, each having at least four years of programming experience. To make all decisions drawn during the evaluation process transparent, all results of the various validation steps are shared in the replication package (to provide evidence of the non-biased evaluation) and described in detail in the paper.

A second threat involves the rule taxonomy definition since some categories could overlap or be missing. To alleviate these issues, the authors performed a pilot study that involved a validation task on a Pharo comment template and then extended this work to Java and Python style guidelines. Then a wider validation was performed involving the three evaluators.

Threats to external validity. This concerns the generalization of the results. Our main aim is to investigate the commenting conventions and developer commenting practice characterizing the comments of three programming languages. Programmers developing different kinds of applications such as end-user applications, might follow different commenting guidelines and have entirely different commenting practices. To alleviate this concern to some extent, we analyzed a sample set of comments from a combination of projects from different ecosystems of Pharo, Java, and Python. Thus, our empirical investigation is currently limited to these ecosystems and not generalizable to other programming languages. On the other hand, our results highlight how various languages provide commenting guidelines, *e.g.*, Pharo provides a comment template, whereas Java and Python provide standard documentation guidelines. However, it is important to point out that variables such as developer experience could have influenced the results and findings of this work, *e.g.*, more experienced developers could be more prone to following or violating the rules or be more aware of the actual commenting guidelines.

Finally, during the definition of our rule taxonomy, we mainly relied on a quantitative analysis of coding style guidelines, without directly involving the actual developers. Thus, for future work, we plan to involve developers in the loop, via surveys and face-to-face or conference call interviews.

Conclusion threats. This concerns the conclusion derived from the results. We supported our findings by using appropriate statistical tests, such as the Wilk-Shapiro normality test to verify whether the non-parametric test could be applied to our Smalltalk data. Finally, we used the Vargha and Delaney $\hat{A}_{12}$ statistical test to measure the magnitude of the differences between the studied distributions.

6.6 Summary and Conclusion

Given the importance of code comments and consistency concerns in projects, we studied various style guidelines and diverse open-source projects in the context of comment conventions. We highlighted the mismatch between what conventions the style guidelines suggest for class comments, and how often developers adopt and follow them, and what conventions they follow, but are not suggested by the style guidelines. Similarly, in Java and Python we highlighted certain rules that developers often follow or violate. We found that developers follow the content and writing style rules, but violate structure and syntax rules in Java and Python.

However, automatically identifying this mismatch is not yet fully achieved. This indicates the need to automate the software documentation field further. Our results also indicate the need to conduct extensive studies on various linters and quality assessment tools to know the extent they cover comment conventions and improve them to support the missing conventions.

7

Commenting Practice Concerns

The previous chapter showed the varying standards for code comments, availability of numerous coding style guidelines for a project, and scattered commenting conventions within the guidelines. This makes it hard for developers to find relevant commenting conventions. Given the unstructured or semi-structured nature of comments and availability of numerous guidelines, developers become easily confused (especially novice developers) about which convention(s) to follow, or what tools to use while writing code documentation. Thus, they post related questions on external online sources to seek better commenting practices. In this chapter, we analyze code comment discussions on online sources Stack Overflow (SO) and Quora to shed some light on the questions developers ask about commenting practices.

Our results highlight that on SO nearly 40% of the questions discuss how to write or process comments in documentation tools and development environments. In contrast on Quora, developer questions focus rather on background information (35% of the questions) or asking opinions about whether to add comments to code or not (16% of the questions).

The chapter is based on the papers:
"P. Rani, M. Birrer, S. Panichella, M. Ghafari, and O. Nierstrasz. What do developers discuss about code comments?, SCAM'21" [133] and
"P. Rani, M. Birrer, S. Panichella, and O. Nierstrasz. Makar: A Framework for Multi-source Studies based on Unstructured Data, SANER'21" [26].

7. Commenting Practice Concerns

THERE exist various coding style guidelines or project documents to guide developers in writing code comments. However, the availability of multiple syntactic alternatives for comments, the freedom to adopt personalized style guidelines,[1] the challenges in finding relevant comment conventions, and the lack of tools for assessing comments, confuse developers about which commenting practice to adopt [6], or how to use a tool to write and verify comments.

To resolve potential confusion and learn best commenting practices, developers post questions on various Q&A forums. SO, one of the most popular Q&A forums, enables developers to ask questions to experts and other developers [157]. Barua *et al.* determined the relative popularity of a topic across all SO posts and discovered that the "coding style" topic is the most popular [17]. Similarly, Quora [123] is another platform widely adopted by developers to discuss software development aspects [84]. However, what specific problems developers report about code comments, such as challenges in locating conventions, writing comments in development environments, or lack of commenting conventions, is unknown. Consequently, we gather developer concerns by answering RQ_4: *What do developers ask about commenting practices on Q&A forums?*

Our results show that developers frequently ask the best syntactic conventions to write comments, ways to retrieve comments from the code, and background information about various comment conventions. Specifically, the questions about how to write or process comments, *i.e.*, *implementation strategy* in a development environment, *e.g.*, documentation tool, integrated development environment (IDE) are frequent on SO. In contrast, the questions concerning background information behind various conventions or opinions on the best commenting practices are frequent on Quora. Our analysis shows that developers are interested in embedding various kinds of information, such as code examples and media, *e.g.*, images in their code comments, but lack the strategies and standards to write them. Additionally, developers ask about the ways of automating the commenting workflow with documentation tools or IDEs to foster commenting practices and to assess them. This shows the increasing need to improve the state of commenting tools by emphasizing better documentation of the supported features, and by providing their seamless integration in the development environments.

7.1 Study Design

7.1.1 Research Questions

To get an insight into developer needs and challenges, we answer RQ_4 by formulating the following subsidiary research questions (SRQs):

---

[1]https://github.com/povilasb/style-guides/blob/master/cpp.rst

SRQ_1: *What **high-level topics** do developers discuss about code comments?* Our interest is to identify high-level concerns and themes developers discuss about code comments on Q&A platforms.

SRQ_2: *What **types of questions** do developers ask about code comments?* Developers may ask *how* to write comments, or *what* is the problem in their comments, or *why* a specific comment convention should be used *etc.* Our aim is to identify the *types of questions* developers frequently ask and which platform they prefer for which types of questions.

SRQ_3: *What **information needs** do developers seek about commenting practices?* Developers may face problems in writing or using comments in a specific development environment, *e.g.*, language, tool, or IDE. Such questions may include how to *set up a tool* to write comments in an IDE, what is the *syntax* to write a class comment, how to *format* inline comments *etc.*

SRQ_4: *What specific **commenting conventions** are recommended by developers?* Developers may face a dilemma in adopting various commenting conventions. Expert developers on Q&A forums may support such developers by recommending the best commenting practices, or describing the limitations of current tools and conventions. Our aim is to collect such recommendations.

7.1.2 Data Collection

SO. To identify the relevant discussions concerning *commenting practices*, we used an approach similar to Aghajani [4]: we selected the initial keywords (Ik), such as *comment, convention*, and *doc* to search them on the SO tag page.[2] The search converged to a set of 70 potentially relevant tags, referred to as *initial tags* (It).

Two authors independently examined all the tags, their descriptions, and the top ten questions in each tag, and selected the relevant tags. We observed that certain tags are ambiguous due to their usage in different contexts. For example, the *comment* tag with 5 710 questions on SO contains questions about development frameworks *e.g., Django*, which can attach comments to a website or other external sources, *i.e.*, 478 questions tagged with the *wordpress* tag, or about the websites where users add comments to a post, *i.e.*, 512 questions tagged with the *facebook* tag. We discarded posts where co-appearing tags were *wordpress* and *facebook*, or *django-comment*. The resulting set of tags (It) contains 55 tags out of the 70 initial tags, and can be found in the Replication Package (RP) [128].

We extracted all questions tagged with at least one tag from the It set, which resulted in 19 705 unique questions. For each question, we extracted

---

[2]https://stackoverflow.com/tags (accessed on Jun 2021)

various metadata fields, such as ID, title, body, tags, creation date, and view count from SO using the *Stack Exchange Data Explorer* interface [156]. The interface facilitates the users to query all Stack Exchange sites in an SQL-like query language.[3]

Quora. Extracting data from Quora is non-trivial due to the lack of publicly available datasets, its restrictive scraping policies [116], and the absence of a public API to access that data. Thus, to extract its data, we implemented a web scraper in Python using the *Selenium* framework, and *BeautifulSoup* to parse the HTML code [19, 145]. In Quora, the notion of topics is the same as for tags on SO, so a question in Quora can be tagged with multiple topics. Unlike the SO tag page, Quora provides neither an index page that lists all its topics, nor a list of similar topics on a topic page. We, therefore, used the relevant SO tags as initial Quora topics, searched for them on the Quora topic search interface, and obtained 29 topics, such as *Code Comments*, *Source Code*, and *Coding Style*. The list of all Quora topics and their mapping to SO tags can be found in the RP [128].[4] We scraped all questions with their metadata, such as the URL, title, body, and topics, which resulted in 3 671 questions.

7.1.3 Analysis Method

Since each SRQ focuses on a different aspect of the questions, we analyzed the questions at various levels, such as focusing only on the title of the question, the entire question body, or the answers to the question. The rationale behind each level is that future approaches for identifying and automating developers' intent, needs, and recommendations can focus on that specific aspect of comments they want to evaluate and improve. Our manually labeled questions for SRQs, *i.e.*,SRQ_2, SRQ_3, and SRQ_4 can serve as an initial dataset for building such approaches. Figure 7.1 illustrates the steps of identifying and extracting relevant posts from the selected sources, and analyzing them for each SRQ.

SRQ_1: High-Level Topics. To answer SRQ_1, (*What **high-level topics** do developers discuss about code comments?*), we used a semi-automated approach involving LDA [27], a well-known topic modeling technique used in SE, to explore topics from the SO and Quora posts [17, 173, 179, 119]. LDA infers latent discussion topics to describe text-based documents. Each document can contain several topics, and each topic can span several documents, thus enabling the LDA model to discover ideas and themes in a corpus. We applied LDA to the SO dataset, but excluded the Quora dataset as it contains nearly 80% irrelevant posts based on the manually analyzed sampled

---
[3]File 'Stack-exchange-query.md' in our RP
[4]File Tags-topics.md in the RP

7.1. Study Design

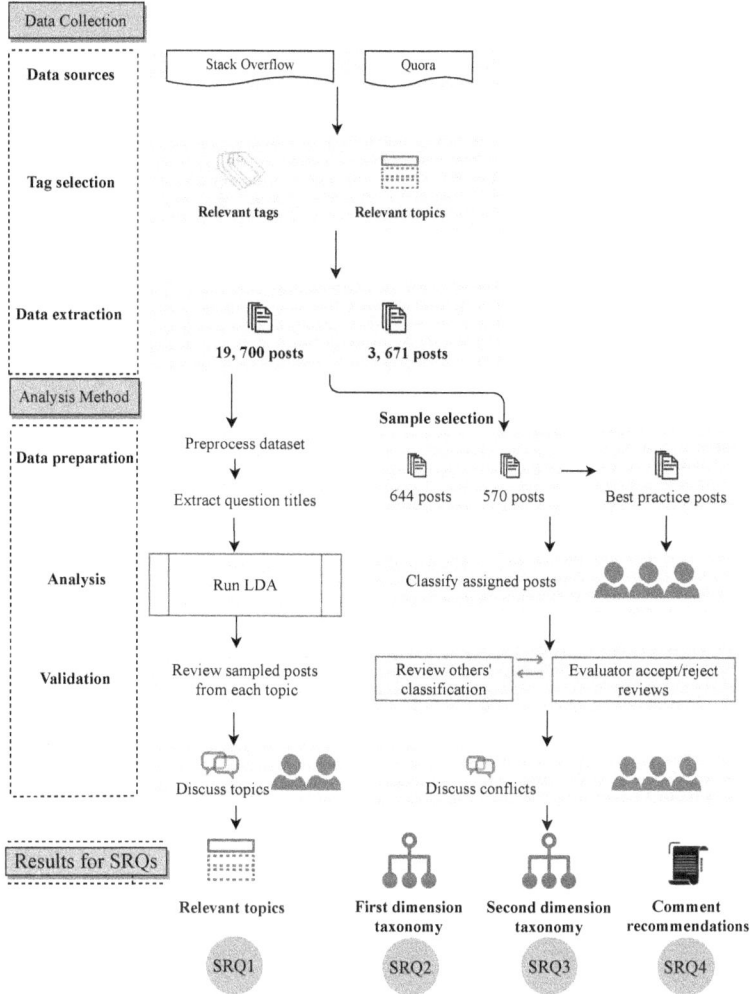

Figure 7.1: Research methodology to answer the SRQs

questions shown in Table 7.1. Additionally, as LDA uses the word and co-occurrence frequencies across documents to build a topic model of related words, having a high number of irrelevant posts can impact the model quality. Since our objective is to discover the high-level concerns of developers, we extracted only titles of the SO questions. The title summarizes the main concern, whereas the body of a question adds irrelevant information, such as details of the development environment, the strategies that the developer has tried, or already referred sources.

To achieve reliable high-level topics from LDA, we performed the following preprocessing steps on the question titles: removal of HTML tags, code elements, punctuation, and stop words using the Snowball stop word list[5], and applied Snowball stemming[31]. We used the data management tool, *Makar*, to prepare the data for LDA [26]. We provide the concrete preprocessing steps *Makar* performed on the data in the *Case study* subsection A.1.2. The preprocessed *title* field of the questions served as the input documents for LDA. We used the *Topic Modeling Tool* [49], *i.e.*, a GUI for MALLET [97] that uses a Gibbs sampling algorithm, and facilitates augmenting the results with metadata. The input data used for the MALLET tool and its output can be found in the RP [128].

LDA requires optimal values for the k, α, and β parameters to be chosen, which depends on the type of data under analysis, however, selecting optimal parameters remains an open challenge in SE tasks. Wallach *et al.* pointed out that choosing a smaller k value may not separate topics precisely, whereas a larger k does not significantly vary the quality of the generated topics [170]. Therefore, to extract distinct topics that are both broad and high-level, we experimented with several values of k ranging from 5 to 25, as suggested by Linares-Vásquez *et al.* [87]. We assessed the optimal value of k by analyzing the *topic distribution*, the *coherence* value (large negative values indicate that words do not co-occur together often)[6] [140], and the *perplexity* score (a low value indicates that a model correctly predicts unseen words) [73] for each value of k from the given range [29]. This process suggested $k = [10]$ as the most promising value for our data (with the lowest perplexity of –6.9 and a high coherence score of –662.1) as fewer redundant topics were selected with these values.

In the next iterations, we optimized the hyperparameters α and β by using the best average probability of assigning a dominant topic to a question, inspired by the existing studies [141]. We selected the initial values of hyperparameters $\alpha = \frac{50}{k}$, $\beta = 0.01$ using the de facto standard heuristics [22], but allowed these values to be optimized by having some topics to be more prominent than others. We ran the model optimizing the hyperparameters after every ten iterations in a total of 1000 iterations. Thus, we concluded that the best hyperparameter configuration for our study is $k = 10$, $\alpha = 5$, and $\beta = 0.01$. As LDA does not assign meaningful names to the generated topics, we manually inspected a sample of 15 top-ranked questions from each topic to assign the topic names.

Table 7.1: Posts or questions extracted from SO and Quora

Source	# Extracted	# Sampled	# Relevant
SO	19 700	644	415
Quora	3 671	565	118

---

[5]http://snowball.tartarus.org/algorithms/english/stop.txt
[6]http://mallet.cs.umass.edu/diagnostics.php

7.1. Study Design

SRQ$_2$, SRQ$_3$: Taxonomy Study. To answer SRQ$_2$ (*What types of questions do developers ask about code comments?*) and SRQ$_3$ (*What information needs do developers seek about commenting practices?*), we analyzed a statistically significant sample set of posts from the SO and Quora posts reaching a confidence level of 99% and an error margin of 5%. Thus, the resulting sample set contained 644 posts for SO and 565 posts for Quora as shown in Table 7.1. We selected the sampled posts using the *random sampling approach without replacement* approach. We then derived a taxonomy of *question types* and *information needs* for SRQ$_2$ and SRQ$_3$ respectively.

Table 7.2: Categories of *question types*

Category	Description	Keywords and examples
Implementation strategy	The questioners are not aware of ways to write or process comments, and ask questions about integrating different information in their comments, or using features of various tools	"How to", *e.g.*, *How to use @value tag in javadoc?*
Implementation problem	The questioners tried to write or process a comment, but they were unsuccessful	"What is the problem?", *e.g.*, *Doxygen \command does not work, but @command does?*
Error	The questioners post an error, exception, crash, or any warning produced by a documentation tool while writing or generating comments	Contain an error message from the exceptions or stack trace
Limitation and possibility	The questioners seek information about limitations of a comment related approach, tool, or IDE, and various possibilities to customize a comment	"Is it possible or allowed", *e.g.*, *Is there a key binding for block comments in Xcode4?*
Background information	The questioner seek background details on the behavior of comments in a programming language, a tool, or a framework.	"Why something", *e.g.*, *Why in interpreted languages the # usually introduces a comment?*
Best practice	The questioners are interested in knowing the best commenting practice, guidelines, or a general advice to tackle a comment-related problem or convention	"Is there a better way to", *e.g.*, *What is the proper way to reference a user interaction in Android comments?*
Opinion	The questioners are interested in knowing the judgment of other developers for a comment convention	"What do you think", *e.g.*, *Are comments in code a good or bad thing?*

Classification: We classified the sampled posts into a *two-dimensional* taxonomy, which mapped the concepts of the selected questions. The first dimension *question types* aims to answer SRQ$_2$, and the second dimension *information needs* answers SRQ$_3$. The first dimension, which is inspired from an earlier SO study [21], defines the categories that concern the kind of question, *e.g.*, if a developer is asking *how* to do something related to comments, *what* is the problem with their comments, or *why* comments are written in a particular way. We renamed their categories to fit our context, *e.g.*, we renamed their *what* type of questions to *implementation problem* [21]. We used the closed card-sorting technique to classify the sampled questions in the first dimension categories as shown in Table 7.2.

The second dimension *information needs* dimension outlines more fine-grained categories about the types of information developers seek [68], *e.g.*, development environment-related needs, such as comments in programming languages, tools, or IDEs, or about comments in general. The majority of these categories are based on the software documentation work by Aghajani et al. [4]. The questions were classified into those categories using the hybrid card-sorting technique [100]. In the development environment-related needs, we identified if a question is about *IDE and editors*, *e.g.*, Intellij, Eclipse, *programming languages*, *e.g.*, Java, Python, or *documentation tools*, *e.g.*, Javadoc, Doxygen. The further sublevels of the *information needs* taxonomy focus on specific information a questioner is seeking in these development environments, such as asking about the syntax to add a comment in code, or specific information in the Javadoc comment [68]. For instance, the question *"How to reference an indexer member of a class in C# comments"* [*SO:341118*][7] is asking *how to* refer to an element in C# comments, and thus gets classified into the *implementation strategy* category according to the first dimension. In more detail, the question is about the C# language and asking for the syntax required to refer to a member in a class comment, thus it gets classified into the three hierarchical levels *Programming languages—Syntax and format—Class comment* according to the second dimension taxonomy shown in Figure A.9.

Execution and Validation: Three evaluators, *i.e.*, a Ph.D. candidate, a master's student, and a faculty member, each having more than three years of programming experience, participated in the evaluation of the study. The sampled questions were divided into three equally-sized subsets of questions, and random questions were selected for each subset to ensure that each evaluator got a chance to look at all types of questions. We followed a three iteration-based approach to categorize the questions. In the first iteration, we classified the posts into the first and second-dimension categories. In the second iteration, each evaluator (as a reviewer) reviewed the classified questions of the other evaluators and marked their agreement or disagreement with the classification. In the third iteration, the evaluator agreed or disagreed with the decision and the changes proposed by the reviewers. In the case of disagreements, another reviewer who has not yet been involved in that particular classification reviewed it and decided. Finally, if all evaluators disagreed, we chose the category based on the majority voting mechanism. This way, it was possible to ensure that at least one other evaluator reviewed each classification. In case of a question belonging to more than one category, we reviewed the other details of the question, such as tags and comments of the questions, and chose the most appropriate one. We finalized the category assignment and their names based on the majority voting mechanism.

Based on the validation approach, all three evaluators checked the relevance of their assigned questions, and then they reviewed the questions that the other evaluators marked as irrelevant. The third evaluator reviewed and

---

[7]We use the notation *SO:<id>* to refer to Stack Overflow hyperlinks that are generated according to the structure: https://www.stackoverflow.com/questions/<id>

resolved the disagreement cases using a majority voting mechanism (Cohen's k = 0.80). As a result, 415 questions of SO and 118 questions of Quora were found relevant to our study. In the end, the irrelevant questions were once again manually inspected, but no new relevant topic could be identified.

SRQ$_4$: Recommended comment conventions. Various organizations and language communities present numerous comment conventions to support the consistency and readability of their comments. However, not all of these conventions are recommended by developers in actual practice, and some conventions are even discouraged, depending on a development environment. We observed some cases in which developers assumed that conventions were feasible, *e.g.*, overriding docstrings of a parent class in its subclasses. Still, other developers pointed them out as a limitation of current documentation tools or environment. We collected such comment conventions recommended by developers in their answers on SO and Quora. From the classified questions in SRQ$_2$, we chose the questions categorized in the *best practice* category. Based on the accepted answers of these questions, we identified the *recommendation* or *limitation* of various comment conventions. In case a question had no accepted answer, we referred to the top-voted answer.

7.2 Results

7.2.1 High-Level Topics

Table 7.3 shows the 10 topics generated by the LDA analysis, where the column *Relevance* denotes if a topic is relevant (R) or irrelevant (IR) in the context of code comments, and *Topic name* is the assigned topic label. The column *Topic words* shows the words generated by LDA, which are sorted in the order of their likelihood of relevance to the topic.

In the first topic *syntax and format*, developers mainly ask about the syntax of adding comments, removing comments, parsing comments, or regular expression to retrieve comments from code. Occasionally, the questions are about extracting particular information from comments to provide customized information to their clients, such as obtaining descriptions, or to-do comments. Depending on a programming language or a tool, strategies to add information in the comments vary, such as adding a description in XML comments [*SO:9594322*], in the R environment [*SO:45917501*], or in the Ruby environment [*SO:37612124*]. This confirms the relevance of recent research efforts on identifying the comment information types in various programming languages [115, 182, 135].

7. COMMENTING PRACTICE CONCERNS

Table 7.3: Ten topics generated by LDA considering the most important topic words

Relevance	Topic name	Topic words
R	Syntax and format	line code file c python doxygen block php html text remov string tag javascript style add regex command script singl
R	IDEs and editors	javadoc generat studio eclips visual file xml java project code class c android sourc maven tag doc intellij show netbean
R	R documentation	r rmarkdown markdown tabl output pdf html file knitr code render chunk text packag chang latex error knit plot add
R	Code conventions	function class method jsdoc type doxygen paramet c object variabl return python phpdoc javadoc name refer properti convent valu docstr
IR	Development frameworks for thread commenting	api doc rest rail generat spring rubi test net swagger web rspec where asp creat find develop googl rdoc what
IR	Open-source software	code sourc what open can app where whi get find anyon websit develop program if android mean softwar doe someon
R	Documentation generation	sphinx file doxygen generat python html link doc page includ modul make creat build custom autodoc rst restructuredtext imag output
IR	Thread comments in websites	facebook post wordpress page get php whi plugin user box like show youtub section display form system repli delet add
IR	Naming conventions and data types	convent name what java python develop c whi sql tabl valu case mysql string data x program code variabl column
R	Seeking documentation and learning language	what code software best program way write good language develop standard requir tool project c practic need learn are which

The *IDEs and editors* topic contains questions about adding or removing comments in the code in various IDEs, or setting up documentation tools to write comments. The *R Documentation* topic groups questions about documentation features provided in the R language such as creating various formats of documents including Markdown, Latex, PDF, or HTML. "R Markdown", a documentation format available in the *knitr* package, provides these features in R. The *Code convention* topic groups the questions concerning best practices, such as printing the docstrings of all functions of an imported module, or conventions to check types in Javascript. This topic also includes questions where developers ask for the reasons behind code conventions, such as having only one class that contains the main method in Java, or using particular symbols for comments. In the *documentation generation* topic, developers inquire about problems in automatically generating project HTML documentation from comments using various documentation tools, such as Sphinx, or Doxygen. Besides code comments, software projects support other forms of documentation, such as wikis, user manuals, API documentation, or design documentation. As a project documentation is divided into various components, developers post questions about locating them in the topic *seeking documentation*. Additionally, developers also showed interest in learning various programming languages and thus sought documentation to learn them.

Overall, developers complained about the inability to locate various syntax or format-related conventions, and guides describing the use of the documentation tools in their development environment, and their integration. Developers were also interested in automating their code documentation and thus asked for related features.

7.2.2 Question Types

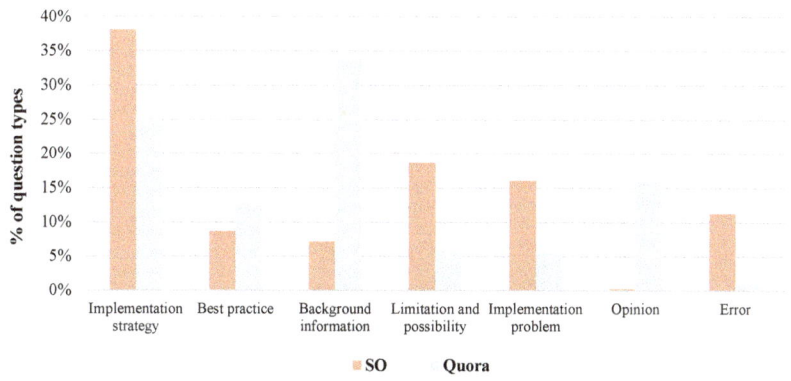

Figure 7.2: Types of questions identified on SO and Quora

To get insights into the types of questions developers ask about comments and where they ask these questions more often, we categorized the sampled questions from SO and Quora according to the (*question type*). Figure 7.2 shows such categories on the x-axis with respect to both sources, and the y-axis indicates the percentage of questions belonging to a category out of the total question of that source. The figure highlights that *implementation strategy* (how-to) is the most frequent category on SO, confirming prior study results [20, 7, 173, 17]. Different from previous studies, we found *best practice* and *background information* questions to arise more frequently than questions about *implementation problem*.

We also observed that different types of questions are prevalent on the investigated platforms, *i.e.*, developers ask *implementation strategy* questions and *implementation problem* questions more frequently on SO compared to Quora. Despite Quora being an opinion-based Q&A site, we observed commenting *best practice* and *background information* questions. This shows how developers rely on Quora to gather knowledge behind numerous conventions and the features provided by a development environment. Such questions are also found on SO, but to a lesser extent. For instance, we observed the question: "*What are these tags @ivar @param and @type in python docstring*" [*SO:379346*] on SO. Based on the thousands of views the post has received, we can say that the question has attracted the attention of many developers. Uddin *et al.* gathered developers' perceptions about APIs in SO by mining opinions automatically [168]. Our study provides the evidence to include Quora as another source to validate their approach and mine developer's opinions.

Finding. Different kinds of questions are prevalent on SO and Quora *e.g.*, *implementation strategy* and *implementation problem* questions are more common on SO, whereas *best practice* and *background information* questions besides opinion-based questions are more prevalent on Quora. This suggests that Quora can be a useful resource to understand how developers perceive certain development aspects, whereas SO can be useful to understand what technical challenges they face during development.

Finding. The *implementation strategy* category questions are the most frequently viewed questions on SO and *limitation and possibility* questions are the second most viewed questions based on their view count. Based on the answer count of questions, *best practice* questions trigger the most discussions along with *implementation strategy*.

7.2.3 Developer Information Needs

To gain a better insight into developer needs, we analyzed the questions from two different perspectives in Figure 7.3. The x-axis shows the kinds of problems developers face with code comments in their development environments, whereas the y-axis shows the types of questions developers ask,

7.2. Results

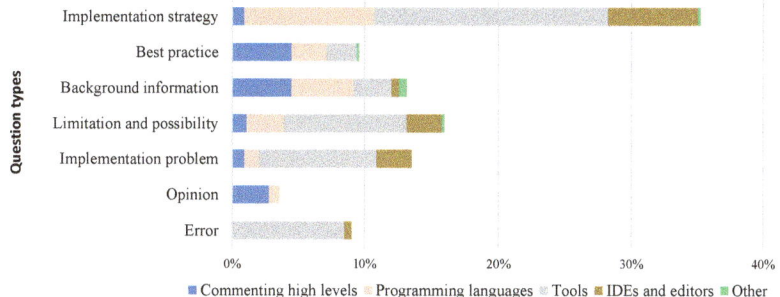

Figure 7.3: Distribution of *question types* and *information needs* categories

e.g., implementation strategy, problem. For example, the most frequent category *implementation strategy* contains questions about how to do something (comment-related) in a development environment, be it specific to a programming language, a documentation tool, or the IDE itself. Furthermore, many developers discuss possible features of the *tools* and *IDEs and editors* in the *limitation and possibility* category. This category highlights the developers' struggle in locating feature details in the documentation of such tools and indicates the vital need for improving this aspect. However, which specific features and syntaxes of comments developers seek in the development environment is essential information required to progress in this direction. Therefore, we first separated general questions about comment conventions to the *commenting high levels* category, and moved other development environment-related questions to the *programming languages*, *tools*, and *IDEs and editors* categories, which are first level categories shown in Figure A.9. We then added subcategories, such as *syntax and format*, *asking for feature*, *change comment template etc.* under each first level category to highlight the specific need related to it. This is explained in Table 7.4 and illustrated in Figure A.9 [133]. Table 7.4 shows the hierarchy of categories with the definition (D) and one example (E) of each category in the column *Definition and Example*. The example uses only the titles of the questions taken from SO or Quora due to space reasons. In the following paragraphs we explain the most prevalent second level categories.

Table 7.4: Types of Information developers seek on SO and Quora

First level	Second level	Definition and Example
Languages	Adopt other language style	D: Questions about adopting the commenting style of another programming language. E: *Is it a bad practice to use C-style comments in C++ code?*
	Asking for feature	D: Questions regarding whether a feature is supported or not and if not, then how a problem can be solved in the language. E: *How do I put code examples in .NET XML comments?*
	Asking tool existence	D: User asks whether there is a tool for a particular programming language to document code. E: *Are there documentation tools for SOAP web services?*
	Change comment template	D: Questions about modifying the template of a specific programming language or environment. E: *How to propose some revision to RFC(s) for JSON to account for comments?*
	Process comments	D: Questions about processing comments of a particular programming language. Processing includes stripping, removing, extracting, or cleaning comments. E: *Remove comment blocks bounded by "#——...—#" in textfile - python*
	Syntax and format	D: Questions about the syntax of comments in a specific programming language. E: *How to add comment in a batch/cmd?*
	Understand documentation	D: Questioner faces difficulties with the understanding of code documentation of functions, classes, or projects. E: *How to interpret cryptic Java class documentation?*
	Using features	D: User is aware about the feature, but they do not know how to use it. E: *What are these tags @var @param and @type in python docstring?*
Tools	Asking for features	D: Question regarding whether a feature is supported, or how a problem can be solved with the tool. E: *How to properly write cross-references to external documentation with intersphinx?*
	Change comment template	D: Questions about modifying the comment template provided by the tool. E: *Cannot remove "Release" appearing in sphinx-doc generated pdf*
	Error	D: Questioner needs help with some error or warning received through the tool while writing documentation. E: *Stylecop doesn't understand <inheritdoc>*
	Process comments	D: Questions about processing comments in a tool. Processing includes stripping, removing, extracting, or cleaning comments. E: *Regex for splitting PHPDoc properties*
	Report bug	D: Questioner reports a (potential) bug. E: *Doxygen C# XML comments and generics do not generate links in HTML output?*
	Setup	D: Questioner asks about configuring a tool.

Continued on the next page

7.2. Results

Table 7.4 – *Continued from the previous page*

First level	Second level	Definition and Example
	Syntax and format	E: *How to link third party libraries in Ant's Javadoc task?* D: Questioner asks ways to document specific code elements, such as classes, methods, or parts of code in a documentation tool. E: *How do I refer to classes and methods in other files my project with Sphinx?*
	Using feature	D: Questions regarding how to use a certain feature of the tool. E: *How to use @value tag in Javadoc?*
	Asking for feature	D: Questions regarding whether a feature is supported, or how a problem can be solved in the environment. E: *Eclipse: How can I find all (public) classes/methods without Javadoc comments?*
IDEs and editors	Change comment template	D: Questions about modifying the template of the IDE or editor. E: *Add different default and custom tags to Visual Studio XML Documentation*
	Process comments	D: Questions about processing comments in an IDE or editor. Processing includes stripping, removing, extracting, or cleaning comments. E: *How do I get rid of XXX Auto-generated method stub?*
	Shortcut	D: Question regarding how to achieve certain functionality with a shortcut (keyboard). E: *Finding Shortcuts in Aptana Studio 3.0 to Comment Code*
	Syntax and format	D: Questions about the syntax of comments in the IDE or editor. E: *How to comment SQL statements in Notepad++?*
	Tool setup	D: Questions on setting up a documentation tool in the IDE or editor. E: *How to generate Javadoc using ubuntu + eclipse to my project*
	Using features	D: User is aware about the feature but does not know how to use it. E: *How can I get Xcode to show my documentation comments during option-hover?*
	Add comments	D: General questions about adding comments without mentioning a specific programming language, tool, or IDE. E: *How can you comment code efficiently?*
Commenting high levels	Versioning comments	D: Questioner asks about best practices for comments in code versioning tools like Git or SVN. E: *Comments that only you can see*
	Comments example	D: Questioner asks for specific (funny, helpful, silly) examples of code comments they have seen. E: *What's the least useful comment you've ever seen?*
	Grammar rules	D: Questions about following grammar rules in writing comments. E: *Should .net comments start with a capital letter and end with a period?*
	Maintain comments	D: General questions about maintaining comments over time. E: *Maintenance commenting*
	Other	D: General conceptual questions about code comments. E: *What's a good comment/code ratio?*

Continued on the next page

Table 7.4 – *Continued from the previous page*

First level	Second level	Definition and Example
	Syntax and format	D: General questions about the syntax and format of comments irrespective of a development environment. E: *Documentation style: how do you differentiate variable names from the rest of the text within a comment?*
Other		D: The questions that do not belong to any of the above categories. E: *How do I write code requiring no comments?*

7.2. Results

Finding. One-third of the commenting questions are about their specific development environment. The top two most frequent questions concern the categories *syntax and format* and *asking for feature* indicating developers' interest in improving their comment quality. The rest focus on setting up or using documentation tools in IDEs to generate comments automatically.

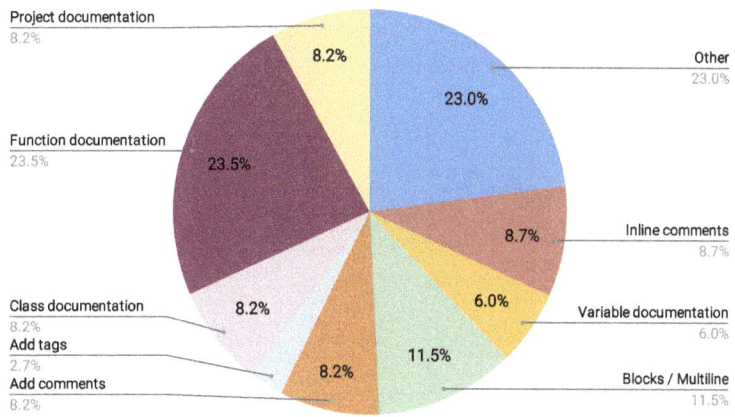

Figure 7.4: Distribution of comments' syntax and format discussions

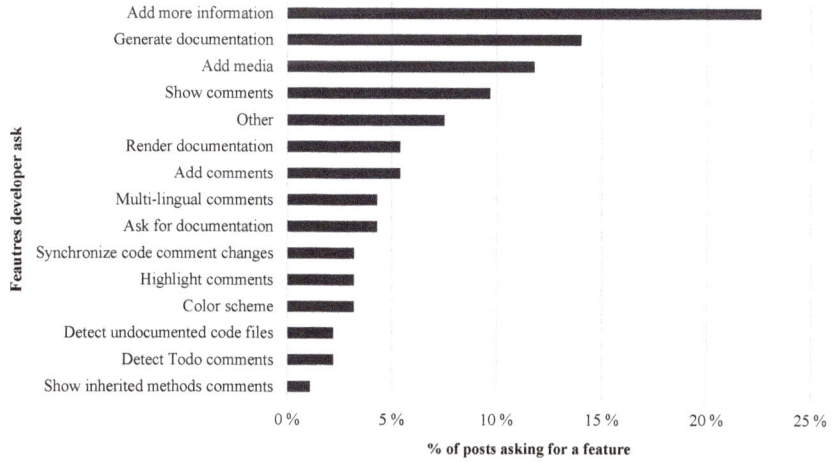

Figure 7.5: Distribution of the features developers are interested in

In the *syntax and format* category shown in Figure 7.4, developers discuss syntax to add various kinds of comments to the code, such as function comments, class comments, block comments, and different tags. Specifically, the syntax of writing function comments is asked more frequently, *i.e.*, nearly 24% of questions, showing the importance of improving API documentation. In this analysis, we found 23% of the questions marked as *other* are either about the syntax of writing comments in a programming language or a tool without stating the kind of comment (class/function/block), or concerning the intent of syntax conventions. Such background questions are more often posted on Quora compared to SO.

> **Finding.** Developers often ask about the syntax to write method comments compared to other kinds of comments like class, or package, showing the trend of an increasing effort towards API documentation. Another frequently asked question on SO concerns the conventions to add different kinds of information to code comments, such as code examples, media, or custom tags, indicating developers' interest in embedding various information in comments.

Asking for feature is another frequent information that developers seek on SO to locate various features provided by the documentation tools. We rarely found such questions on Quora. We report such inquiries, as shown in Figure 7.5, and in the category *asking for feature* under all development environment categories in Figure A.9. Figure 7.5 shows that developers frequently need to add different kinds of information to the code comments, such as code examples: "*How to add code description that are not comments?*" [*SO:45510056*], performance-related: "*Javadoc tag for performance considerations*" [*SO:39278635*], and media-related [*SO:43556442*]. Additionally, developers ask about features to add comments automatically, detect various information from the comments, or synchronize the comments with code changes [*SO:23493932*]. These questions show the worthiness of devoting research efforts to the direction of identifying information types from comments, detecting inconsistent comments, and assessing and generating comments automatically to improve code comments [115, 176]. We separated the feature-related questions, *i.e.*, the different features of the tools and IDEs into two categories, *using feature* and *asking for feature* based on the user awareness. In the former category, the user is aware of the existence of a feature in the environment, but finds problems in using it as shown in Listing 8. In the latter category, users inquire about the existence of a feature, or try to locate it, as shown in Listing 9.

```
1 How to use @value tag in javadoc?
```
Listing 8: Using the @value feature in Javadoc

```
1 How can I show pictures of keyboard keys in-line with text with Sphinx?
```
Listing 9: Asking for a feature to add inline images

7.2. Results

> **Finding.** Apart from the questions related to comment syntax and features, developers ask about adopting commenting styles from other programming languages, modifying comment templates, understanding comments, and processing comments for various purposes.

In addition to the above categories, we observed that SO encourages developers, especially novice developers, to ask questions about the basics of various topics [83]. We grouped such questions into the *commenting high levels* category. Figure A.9 reports all levels of the second dimension according to each source. For instance, the questions about setting up tools, ie *tool setup*, or asking for various features , *i.e.*, *asking for features* under *IDE and editors* are not found on Quora. Similarly, the majority of the questions about documentation tools, *i.e.*, *tools* are asked on SO, whereas the general questions about comments, *i.e.*, *commenting high levels* often exist on Quora.

7.2.4 Recommended Comment Convention

We discovered that there are various syntactic and semantic commenting conventions mentioned in the style guides, and developers are often confronted with several of them. In this chapter, we discovered that developers find it difficult to locate the conventions for a specific purpose. In Table 7.5, we collected various comment conventions recommended by developers in their answers on SO and Quora. For example, a developer asked *"Should .net comments start with a capital letter and end with a period?"* [*SO:2909241*], concerning grammar rules in the comments. The accepted answer affirmed the convention and described how it helps to improve readability. We, therefore, constructed the recommendation *"Long inline comments should start with a capital letter and end with a period"* under *".NET"* in the column *DE*, *i.e.*, Development Environment. In some answers, developers describe the limitation of a convention, we included *Limitation* for such answers. For instance, a developer asked if an API documentation can be generated for different target audience using the Doxygen tool, *e.g.*, developer and users. The accepted answer indicated that it is a currently not supported in the tool. For each recommendation, we indicated whether it is specific to a programming language, a tool, an IDE, or is instead a general recommendation, using tags such as "[Java], [Doxygen], [General]" respectively. It is important to note that we did not verify how widely these recommendations are adopted in the commenting style guidelines or projects, or how well they are supported by current documentation checker tools or style checkers. This is a future direction for this work. On the positive side, it represents an initial starting point to collect various comment conventions confirmed by developers. We argue that it can also help researchers in conducting the studies to assess the relative importance of comment conventions or help tool developers in deciding which recommendation they should include in their tools to address frequent concerns of developers.

7.3 Implications and Discussion

Coding Style Guidelines. Although various coding style guidelines provide conventions to write comments, our results showed that SO developers seek help in writing correct syntax of various comment types, *i.e.*, class, function, or package comments highlighted in Figure 7.4. They also seek help in adding specific information in comments, or formatting comments. Typical types of questions are *"What is the preferred way of notating methods in comments?"* [SO:982307], and *"Indentation of inline comments in Python"* [SO:56076686], or *"Indentation of commented code"* [SO:19275316].

Organizing the information in the comments is another concern highlighted in the study, for example, *"How to differentiate the variables within a comment"* [SO:2989522], *"Where to put class implementation details"* (in a class comment or in an inline comment) [SO:35957906], and *"Which tag to use for a particular type of information"* [SO:21823716]. We also found developer concerns regarding grammar rules and word usage in all the sources we analyzed, *i.e.*, SO [SO:2909241] and Quora [124]. Although various style guidelines propose comment conventions, there are still many aspects of comments for which either the conventions are not proposed, or developers are unable to locate them. Developers commonly ask questions, such as *"Any coding/commenting standards you use when modifying code?"* [SO:779025] on SO and *"Why is there no standard for coding style in GNU R?"* on Quora. This indicates a need to cover detailed aspects of comments in the coding style guidelines and assure their discoverability to developers to help them write high-quality comments.

Tools to Assess Comment Quality. Our results showed that developers are interested in various automated strategies, such as automatic generation of comments, detection of bad comments, identification of information embedded in comments, and the quality assessment of comments. However, they lack tools that can be integrated into their IDE, especially to automatically verify commenting style [SO:14384136]. Moreover, a limited set of documentation tools supports the comment quality assessment or the adherence of comments to their commenting conventions. For example, current style checker tools, such as Checkstyle, RuboCop, and pydocstyle provide support for format conventions, but lack support for comprehensive checks for grammar rules and content.[8,9,10] Additionally, some languages with advanced style checkers do not support comment checkers at all, such as

---

[8] https://checkstyle.org/checks.html
[9] https://rubocop.org/
[10] http://www.pydocstyle.org/

7.3. Implications and Discussion

Table 7.5: Comment conventions recommended by developers on SO and Quora

Topic	DE	Recommendation
Grammar	.NET	Long inline comments should start with a capital letter and end with a period.
	.NET	Long inline comments should be written as a complete English sentence (with subject, verb, object).
	General	Check your coding style guidelines to verify how to write plural objects in the comments, for example, Things(s) or Things.
	General	Do not mark the code section with an inline comment to highlight the modified code section, but use the version control system to keep track of code changes.
	Python	Use backslash escape whitespace to use punctuations like apostrophe symbol in docstring.
	Python	Use 'truthy' and 'falsy' words to denote boolean values 'True' and 'False' respectively.
	General	Do not write filler words, such as 'please' and 'thank you', nor swearing words in the comments.
	General	Remove TODO comments when you finish the task.
Language	General	Comments should explain why and not how.
	General	Use correct notation to write block or multiline comments.
	General	Position your inline comments (about variable declaration) above the variable declaration to remain consistent with method comment conventions.
	General	Do not write nested comments in the code.
	General	Use different tags to categorize the information in the comments.
	General	Do not use multiple single line comments instead of multi-line comments.
	General	Do not document file specifications in the code comments but rather document them in the design specs.
	General	Use a consistent style, such as *'variable'* or *<variable>* to differentiate the code variable names in the inline comments.
	Java	Implementation notes about the class should be mentioned before the class definition rather than inside the class.
	Java	To denote a method (*someMethod() of the class ClassA*) in the comments, use the template *the <someMethod> method from the <ClassA> class* instead of *ClassA.someMethod()*.
	.NET	Document 'this' parameter of an extension method by describing the need of 'this' object and its value.
	Javascript	*Limitation:* Currently, there is no existing standard to document AJAX calls of Javascript in PHPDoc style comments.
	PHP	Use '->' symbol to reference instance/object method rather than '::' in the method comments.
	SQL	Use the same documentation style for SQL objects as you are using for other code.
	Groovy	*Limitation:* There is no standard way to document properties of a dynamic map in Javadoc like JSDoc' @typedef.
Tool	Javadoc	*Limitation:* Currently, it is not possible to generate documentation of an API in multiple languages (in addition to English) with the same source code.
	Javadoc	*Limitation:* The tag @value support fields having literal values. Javadoc and IntelliJ IDEA do not support fetching value from an external file using the @value tag in Javadocs.
	Javadoc	Write annotations after the method Javadoc, before the method definition.
	Doxygen	Use @copydoc tag to reuse the documentation from other entities.
	Doxygen	*Limitation:* Currently, it is not possible to generate documentation of an API for different readers, such as developers and users.
	Doxygen	Use @verbatim / @endverbatim to document console input and output.
	Roxygen	*Limitation:* It is not possible to override docstrings so the parent docstring is used when inheriting a class.
	PHPDoc	*Limitation:* Currently, it is not supported to document array details in the return type of a method.
	PHPDoc	*Limitation:* Currently, using the @value tag or any similar tag to refer to the value of a field is not supported in PHPDoc, so developers should use the @var tag instead.
	PHPDoc	Use class aliases in import statement to write a short name in docblock.
	PHPDoc, JSDoc	Do not put implementation details of a public API in the API documentation comments, rather put them in inline comments inside the method.
	JSDoc	Mention the class name in the description to denote the instance of the class.
	GhostDoc	Create your default comment template using c# snippets.
	Sphinx	*Limitation:* It can't create sections for each class. Add yourself the sections in the .rst file.

139

OCLint for Objective-C, Ktlint for Kotlin, and Smalltalk.[11,12] We found instances of developers asking about the existence of such tools [*SO:8834991*] in Figure 7.5 and in *asking tool existence* category in Table 7.4. Therefore, more tool support is needed to help developers in verifying the high-quality of comments.

Tomasottir *et al.* showed in their interview study that developers use linters to maintain code consistency and to learn about the programming language [164]. By configuring linters early in a project, developers can use them similarly to learn the correct syntax to write and format comments according to a particular style guideline. However, due to their support to multiple languages, assisting developers in language-specific conventions, or customizing comments to add more information would still require further effort.

7.4 Threats to Validity

Threats to construct validity. This concerns the relationship between theory and experimentation. In our study, they mainly relate to the potential imprecision in our measurements. To mitigate the potential bias in the selection of developer discussions on SO, we relied on SO tags to perform an initial filtering. However, it is possible that this tag-based filtering approach missed some relevant posts concerning comment convention practices and topics. We therefore investigated the co-appearing tags to find similar relevant tags. Aghajani *et al.* studied software documentation-related posts, including code comments on SO and other sources [4]. We extracted their documentation-related tags from the given replication package and compared them to our tags (It) to verify if we missed any. We mapped the selected SO tags as keywords on Quora and searched these keywords on the Quora search interface. To avoid eventual biases in this manual process, we also adopted LDA to investigate high-level topics emerging in the SO posts. Thus, a mix of qualitative and quantitative analysis was performed to minimize the potential bias in our investigation, providing insights and direction into the automated extraction of relevant topics.

Threats to internal validity. This concerns confounding factors, internal to the study, that can affect its results. In our study, they mainly affect the protocol used to build the taxonomies, which could directly or indirectly influence our results. To limit this threat, we used different strategies to avoid any subjectivity in our results. Specifically, all posts were validated by at least two reviewers, and in case of disagreement, a third reviewer participated in the discussion to reach a consensus. Thus, for the definition

---

[11]http://oclint.org/
[12]https://github.com/pinterest/ktlint

of the taxonomy, we applied multiple iterations involving different authors of this work.

Threats to conclusion validity. This concerns the relationship between theory and outcome. In our study, they mainly relate to the extent to which the produced taxonomy can be considered exhaustive. To limit this threat, we focused on more than one source of information (SO and Quora), so that the resulting taxonomies have a higher likelihood to be composed of an exhaustive list of elements *i.e.*, comment convention topics.

Threats to external validity. This concerns the generalizability of our findings. These are mainly due to the choice of SO and Quora as the main sources. SO and Quora are widely used for development discussions to date, although specific forums such as Reddit could be considered for future works.[13] Moreover, besides all written sources of information, we are aware that there is still a portion of the developer communication taking place about these topics that are not traceable. Thus, further studies are needed to verify the generalizability of our findings.

7.5 Summary and Conclusion

In this chapter, we investigated developer discussions regarding commenting practices occurring on SO and Quora. To understand the high-level concerns of developers, we performed an automated analysis, *i.e.*, LDA on extracted discussions, and then complemented it with a more in-depth manual analysis on the selected sampled posts. From the manual analysis, we derived a two-dimensional taxonomy. The first dimension of the taxonomy focuses on the question types, whereas the second dimension focuses on five types of first level concerns and 20 types of second level concerns developers express. The first level concerns the leading topics developers write about various development environments, such as an IDE, an editor, a documentation tool, or a programming language. The second level concerns further specify the first level concerns regarding code comments, such as writing the correct syntax, asking for a particular feature, or understanding a part of the documentation in a development environment.

We qualitatively discussed our insights, and presented implications for developers, researchers, and tool designers to satisfy developer information needs with respect to commenting practices. We provide the data used in our study including the validated data and the detailed taxonomy, in the replication package [133]. We also presented a list of recommendations given by experts on SO and Quora to help developers in verifying their comment conventions.

---

[13]https://www.reddit.com

8
Conclusion and Future Work

8.1 Conclusion

IN order to build effective comment quality assessment tools, we first need to understand the practices in evaluating and writing code comments. We proposed a multi-perspective view of the comments to gain this understanding. The first perspective explored the quality attributes and techniques that are used to assess comment quality. The second perspective focused on the analysis of developer commenting practices across programming languages, and the automated identification of the information types used in comments. The third perspective gathered developer concerns about commenting practices from major Q&A forums. This chapter revisits our research questions formulated for each introduced perspective, presents the implications. We outline possible directions and the concluding remarks to improve comment quality assessment tools for future research.

RQ_1: How do researchers measure comment quality?

To understand the researchers' perspective, we conducted a systematic literature review on the comment quality assessment studies of the past ten years *i.e.*, 2010 until 2020. We found that researchers focus mainly on code comments of Java despite the increasing trend of developers in using multi-language environments in software projects. Similarly, the trend of analyzing specific types of comments, *e.g.*, method comments, or inline comments is increasing, but the studies rarely focus on class comments. Compared to previous work by Zhi *et al.*, we could identify ten additional quality attributes (QAs) researchers use to assess code comment quality. We have identified

8. Conclusion and Future Work

21 quality attributes, but not all of them are considered equally important in academia. Researchers consider some attributes more often, such as *completeness, consistency, content relevance*, and *readability*. Whereas they rarely consider other attributes, such as *coherence, conciseness, accessibility*, and *understandability* even though numerous studies showed the benefits of coherent, concise, or understandable comments. Why some attributes hold intrinsically less importance than others requires further research.

We learned from this analysis that the studies miss a precise definition of comment QAs. This poses various challenges for other researchers and developers, *e.g.*, comprehending what a specific quality attribute means, establishing metrics and approaches to measure the attributes and adapting such approaches to different programming environments. Additionally, the majority of the attributes are still assessed manually despite the advancements in technology.

RQ_2: What kinds of information do developers write in comments across languages?

To understand the developers' perspective, we analyzed 1 066 class comments from 20 open-source projects that used three different programming languages, *i.e.*, Java, Python, and Smalltalk. We mapped the code comment taxonomies of the selected languages against each other and, as a result, proposed the CCTM taxonomy. We found that developers embed at least 16 types of information in class comments across languages. For instance, the information type categories *summary, responsibilities, collaborators, usage, warnings*, and *references to external sources* are found across all languages. In contrast, we found that language-specific categories, such as *exception* are found in Java and Python but not in Smalltalk. Class comments are typically meant to provide a high-level overview of the class from an implementation independent perspective, however, we found low level implementation details such as *usage, development notes, key implementation point, warning*, or *coding guidelines*. These information types can support developers in several SE activities, but identifying them in comments is a manual and challenging task. In our study, we observed that developers follow specific natural language patterns in writing these information types. We extracted such patterns using NLP and TA-based techniques, and utilized them to build a language-independent approach (**TESSERACT**) to automatically identify top frequent information types from class comments according to the CCTM. Our results suggest that the Random Forest algorithm fed by the combination of NLP+TA features achieves the best classification performance across different programming languages.

RQ_3: To what extent do developers follow the style guidelines in their comments?

8.1. Conclusion

To further understand developer commenting practices in terms of how they write comments, we analyzed 1 066 class comments from 20 projects, and identified 21 coding style guidelines these projects recommended. We measured whether the comments follow comment conventions extracted from the guidelines. Our results highlight the mismatch between what conventions the guidelines suggest for class comments, and how often developers adopt and follow them, and what conventions developers follow in their class comments, but the guidelines do not mention them. For instance, the Smalltalk comment template suggests seven types of information, but developers embed 16 other types of information in comments. In Java and Python comments, we found that developers follow the content and writing style conventions, but violate the *structure* and *syntax* conventions. These insights of developer commenting practices across languages can help researchers to improve comment quality assessment tools, and to evaluate comment summarization and comment generation approaches.

RQ$_4$: What do developers ask about commenting practices on Q&A forums?

For this RQ, we investigated SO and Quora forums to identify developer discussions regarding commenting practices. We manually analyzed 1 209 commenting practices-related posts, and derived a *two-dimensional* taxonomy to characterize their concerns. The first dimension *question types* focused on seven types of questions , *e.g.*, *implementation strategy*, *best practice*. The second dimension *information needs* focused on specific commenting concerns, such as asking for a syntax convention, or a particular feature to process comments in a specific development environment. Our results showed that developers often seek questions about the *implementation strategy* and *limitation and possibility* of comments on SO. In contrast, developers often seek *best practice* and *background information* questions on Quora. These results indicated that Quora can be a valuable resource to understand how developers perceive certain development aspects. At the same time, SO can be a useful resource to understand what technical challenges they face during its development. We also presented a list of recommendations given by experts on SO and Quora to help developers verify their comments conventions. The analysis of questions from Q&A forums showed that developers face several problems in locating the specific comment guidelines, verifying the adherence of their comments to the coding standards, and evaluating the overall state of the comment quality.

8.2 Future Work

8.2.1 Comment Quality Assessment Tools and Techniques

Comment quality attributes. Chapter 3 listed the QAs researchers use to assess comment quality. As mentioned, not all of them are considered equally important as some of them are rarely used. Additionally, they are not measured in mutually exclusive ways, *e.g.*, *accuracy* is measured by using the *correctness* and *completeness* of comment, such as *"the documentation is incorrect or incomplete and therefore no longer accurate documentation of an API."* (S24). Another aspect is the measurement process for the attributes. We found that there are still many attributes that are evaluated manually rather using automated approaches. This analysis indicates new opportunities (i) to find the reasoning behind why certain attributes lack support for automated approaches, (ii) to identify the dependency between various QAs measurement, and (iii) to establish automated approaches to measure them.

Comment quality assessment techniques. Our results from chapter 3 presented the techniques researchers use or propose to evaluate comment quality. However, these approaches are often based on heuristics that provide limited checks, they focus on particular programming languages, mainly Java, and they are not designed to be used for other domains and languages [81, 159, 143]. For instance, Smalltalk code comments follow a different comment structure and writing style, and do not rely on annotations, making these approaches unsuitable for this language. Hence, our study insights about comment quality assessment approaches and commenting practices of various languages, and we provide further data to help researchers design tools for evaluating comment quality across languages and domains.

8.2.2 Information Granularity in Comments

Accessing specific information from comments. Cioch *et al.* presented developers' documentation information needs based on the stages of expertise [34]. The task of accessing specific information from documentation is not just limited to expert and novice developers, or to low-level and high-level information; it also depends on the task developers are performing, the software development phase they are working in, *e.g.*, development or maintenance phase, and the target audience, *e.g.*, users or developers accessing the documentation. The tools automatically extracting specific information from comments based on these factors can reduce developer and stakeholder effort in reading comments, seeking specific information from them, or evaluating them for their quality. For instance, identifying warnings in comments can help to turn them into executable test cases, so that developers can ensure that these warnings are respected. Similarly, the automatic identification and execution of code examples in comments can ensure that they are up to date, and consequently, they can be assessed with respect to the *up-to-dateness* quality attribute. Currently, our multi-language approach can identify frequent information types from class comments, however, it needs to be improved for low frequent information types, and needs to be tested on other types of comments, documentation, and programming languages to verify its generalizability.

Designing an annotation language. Annotation languages have proven to improve the reliability of software.[1] They can help the community in labeling and organizing a specific type of information, and to convert particular information types into formal specifications, which can further help in synchronizing comments with code [111]. We identified various information types in chapter 4, but not all of them are denoted by annotations or tags. For instance, in Java and Python, the categories *Expand*, or *Usage* are not denoted by any specific annotation or tag in comments. Even though Smalltalk comments do not follow any annotation at all, they do have some explicit patterns for different information types, such as instance variables denoted by the *Instance variables* header, or main methods of a class that are indicated by *Key Messages*. Tool or language designers can utilize the identified patterns to design information headers, annotations, and default comment templates. Designing such templates based on developer commenting practices can support developers in writing high-quality comments, as our results showed that developers follow them.

Visualizing the comment information types. Once various types of information are automatically identified and their purpose for various software activities is known, the next challenge would be to find a suitable visualization to present it to developers. Cioch *et al.* proposed to use different documents for each phase, *e.g.*, interns require task-oriented documentation, such as process description, examples, and step-by-step instructions, whereas experts require low-level documentation as well as a design specification [34]. In the current state of code comments, developers who seek specific information have to skim entire comments due to a lack of annotations, the non-uniform way of placing information, and relaxed style conventions. Building visualizations to automatically highlight the required information from comments can help developers to notice the information more quickly. At the same time, such a visualization could also be used to identify the individual parts of a comment or code that lacks documentation, thus making comments adequate, consistent, and complete.

---

[1] https://docs.microsoft.com/en-us/cpp/c-runtime-library/sal-annotations?redirectedfrom=MSDN&view=vs-2019

8. Conclusion and Future Work

8.2.3 Tool Support for Comments

More accurate tools to automate the detection of comment changes. Soetens *et al.* envision that future IDEs will use the notion of changes as first-class entities, which are also known as change reification approaches. These change-based approaches can help in communicating changes between IDEs and their architectures, and to produce accurate recommendations to boost complex modular and dynamic systems [152]. Analyzing and detecting change patterns of comments can enable the vision of Soetens *et al.* of integrating code comments easily in such change-oriented IDEs. Additionally, detecting which types of information in the comments tend to change more often can help researchers generate comments automatically. For example, in Smalltalk we found a code change due to a class deprecation, which triggered a change in the class comment by adding the deprecation notice information to inform other developers. This manual effort of updating the class comment whenever a code deprecation change is introduced can be reduced by automatically generating that notice information. These comment change patterns are not only helpful for developers to reduce their commenting effort, but also for researchers to improve their bug-prediction models. For instance, Ibrahim *et al.* showed statistically significant improvements in their bug-prediction models using comment update patterns [75]. Similarly, analyzing what change in which information type triggers changes in the code or vice versa can further improve these models. This can assist in answering particular developer questions, such as *"what specific type of the code change led to this comment change?"* or *"which specific comment changes does a commit consist of?"* [44]. Wen *et al.* presented a large-scale study in this direction to highlight code-comment inconsistencies [176]. However, our results highlighted that commenting practices vary to some extent across languages. Thus, it is possible that developers show a different behavior when they change comments across languages.

Style checker support. Tomasottir *et al.* showed in their interview study that developers use linters to maintain code consistency and to learn about the programming language [164]. By configuring linters early in a project, developers can use them similarly to learn the correct syntax to write and format comments according to a particular style guideline. However, only a limited set of linters, also known as style checkers, support the adherence of comments to the commenting conventions. For example, tools such as Checkstyle,[2] RuboCop,[3] and pydocstyle[4] provide support for formatting comment conventions, but they lack support for comprehensive grammar and content rules. In chapter 6, we identified the convention types and the

---
[2] https://checkstyle.org/checks.html
[3] https://rubocop.org/
[4] http://www.pydocstyle.org/

associated rules as various style guidelines suggest. Based on this taxonomy of convention types, researchers can investigate *the extent to which various comment conventions or rules are covered in style checkers*. Some languages with advanced style checkers do not support comment checkers at all, such as OCLint for Objective-C, [5] and Ktlint for Kotlin,[6] Smalltalk. We found instances of questions where developers ask about the existence of such tools in chapter 7. Therefore, more tool support is required to help developers in verifying the high-quality of comments. However, supporting multiple languages, assisting developers in language-specific conventions, or customizing comments to add more information would still require further effort.

8.2.4 Documentation Sources

Coding style guidelines. Our results from chapter 7 indicated that developers find it difficult to locate various comment-related conventions. This can be due to the availability of multiple coding style guidelines and scattered conventions across web pages or paragraphs. This indicates the need to improve the findability of coding style guidelines related to comments. We futher found that developers embed various types of information in comments, but not all of them are suggested by the style guidelines (see Table 6.3). In fact, the majority of the information types mentioned by developers in comments are not suggested by the guidelines. Even though some information types are suggested, the syntax and style conventions to write them are not usually described in the style guidelines. Therefore, there is a need to cover more detailed comment-related aspects in the coding style guidelines to help developers in writing high-quality comments.

Project sources and online platforms. Finding the required conventions to write good comments is not just limited to the exploration of coding style guidelines. Our results in chapter 7 showed that developers also seek online sources, such as SO and Quora to gather such information. There exist other sources where developers often discuss software information, such as Wikis, GitHub, issue trackers, and mailing lists. We plan to exploit such web-based project sources. We have already started to develop such a tool, *Makar* which can conduct multi-source studies [26]. Currently, it supports the mining of SO, Apache mailing lists, and GitHub. We plan to extend this tool to conduct a follow-up study to gather more diverse developer information needs.

---

[5] http://oclint.org/
[6] https://github.com/pinterest/ktlint

8.2.5 Speculative Analysis of Comment Quality

Brun et al. presented *speculative analysis* with an analogy to *speculative execution (e.g.,* branch prediction and cache pre-fetching) [28, 105]. The speculative analysis explores and speculates possible future development states of software in the background. The analysis results can provide information about the consequences of performing various actions on software, thus guiding developers in making better decisions based on the results. Such analysis can eventually lead to increased developer productivity and software quality.

We can use *speculative analysis* to inform developers early about their comment quality. The quality of available comments can be assessed in background based on identified quality attributes (*e.g., adequacy, consistency*), or aspects (*e.g., content, syntax*). Developers interested in improving specific aspects of comments can be presented with quality indications of each aspect and informed about which aspect will bring them what amount of gain in comment quality. By speculating on various options in the background, the analysis can present context-sensitive information to developers in a proactive and live manner and help them make an informed decision. In this thesis, we provide the groundwork to build such speculative analysis-based tools to generate comments, or assess comment quality.

8.3 Concluding Remarks

Software quality is a multidimensional concept and thus require a multi-perspective view of the comments to ensure high-quality comments. This thesis primarily studied code commenting practices and their evaluation from the perspective of developers and researchers. We studied the current state of literature for assessing comment quality by conducting an SLR. Furthermore, we conducted various empirical studies mining multiple software systems and online Q&A sources to understand the nature of developer commenting practices. The resulting analysis demonstrates that developers embed different kinds of information in comments and follow the style guidelines in writing the content. However, they seek support in locating relevant commenting guidelines, reducing efforts in writing comments, verifying the adherence of their comments to the guidelines, and evaluating the overall state of comment quality.

We believe that comment quality should be given much more importance with regard to software quality. Our analysis just scratched the surface by highlighting developer concerns regarding comments, and establishing a ground truth for various comment-related tasks. We are convinced that such research is more important than before when considering the latest trends in the software industry, *e.g.,* the common use of polyglot languages in highly complex software projects. We hope more developers will accept the notion of comment quality and design tools to fill the identified gaps.

A

Appendix

A.1 Makar: A Framework for Multi-source Studies based on Unstructured Data

As a software system continues to evolve, developers need various kinds of information to perform activities, such as adding features, or performing corrective maintenance [86]. Developers typically seek information on internal sources available within IDE or external sources, such as Stack Overflow (SO), mailing lists, and GitHub to satisfy their information needs [67]. To support developers in various activities and to understand their information needs, researchers have analyzed these external sources [18]. However, extracting and preprocessing unstructured data from these sources, and maintaining the processed data due to a lack of automated techniques pose various challenges in conducting reproducible studies [31, 8, 18].

To address these concerns, we propose *Makar*, a tool that leverages popular data retrieval, processing, and handling techniques to support researchers in conducting reproducible studies. We established its requirements from the surveyed studies. We conducted a case study shown in chapter 7, in which we analyze code comment related discussions from SO and Quora to evaluate Makar.

Requirements. To gain a deeper understanding of these challenges, we surveyed the literature that focuses on studying developers information needs from different external sources [25]. Based on the gathered challenges

---

✿ This appendix is based on the paper "*P. Rani, M. Birrer, S. Panichella, and O. Nierstrasz. Makar: A Framework for Multi-source Studies based on Unstructured Data, SANER'21*" [26].

A. APPENDIX

in the survey, we identified relevant functional and non-functional requirements for Makar. The tool intends to cover the common use cases found in the survey while being extensible to support additional or more specific scenarios encountered in the case study. We identified five main *functional requirements*: data import, data management, data processing, data querying, and data export. *Data import* focuses on different possibilities to import data into the tool, *data management* on building and maintaining data, *data processing* focuses on the need to preprocess data, *e.g.*, HTML removal, stop word removal, *data Querying* on searching data, and *data export* focuses on exporting data from the tool in order to support further analyses. We also identified several *non-functional requirements* for Makar. It should be easily extensible in areas where projects have different technical requirements, such as import adapters, preprocessing steps, or export adapters. The tool should further be able to handle large amounts of data (scale of 100k records) while still offering an acceptable usage performance, *e.g.*, for search queries.

A.1.1 Makar Architecture

Makar is a web application that can be hosted on public accessible and possibly powerful servers. Thus, it allows multiple users to work concurrently on the same dataset. It is a Ruby on Rails (RoR)[1] web application with a PostgreSQL[2] database in the back end. Makar runs in a Docker container to have minimal technical requirements to run the tool, to maximize the compatibility, and to ease the installation on different platforms and operating systems.[3] The instructions to run the tool can be found in the tool repository[4] and its demonstration on YouTube.[5] We show its architecture and features in Figure A.1 and explain them in more details in the following paragraphs.

- **Data import.** A user can directly import data from diverse sources, such as *CSV* and *JSON*. The tool also supports import adapters for the following sources: *Apache Mailing List Archive*,[6] *GitHub Pull Requests* (via GitHub Archive),[7] *GitHub Issues* Via the GitHub API,[8] and *Stack Overflow* Search Excerpts.[9] The import adapters can be extended easily using the `ImportAdapter` component for other sources.

- **Data management.** Makar provides *schemas*, *collections*, *filters* and *records* to manage datasets as shown in Figure A.1. *Schemas* define

---

[1] https://rubyonrails.org/
[2] https://www.postgresql.org/
[3] https://www.docker.com/
[4] https://github.com/maethub/makar
[5] https://youtu.be/Yqj1b4Bv-58
[6] https://mail-archives.apache.org/mod_mbox/
[7] http://www.gharchive.org/
[8] https://developer.github.com/v3/search/#search-issues
[9] https://api.stackexchange.com/docs/excerpt-search

A.1. Makar: A Framework for Multi-source Studies based on Unstructured Data

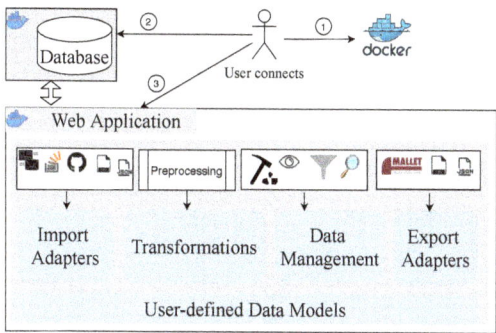

Figure A.1: Architecture overview of Makar

the structure of a dataset and its records, and *records* are rows of the dataset which are similar to schemas and records in databases. *Collections* are arbitrary selections of records, which can be used to manage various subsets of the data. A record can belong to multiple collections. *Filters* are the search queries that help one to filter data from existing collections or schemas, and can be saved to provide an efficient querying and rebuild the dataset. For example, a study analyzing SO questions first has to import the SO dataset into Makar. If the study design requires only questions with the word "javadoc" in the question title, a user could create a filter, *e.g.*, "All Questions with Javadoc in Title" filter, that searches the question titles for "javadoc" as shown in Figure A.2. The user could then create a collection that uses this filter and can use the collection as their dataset for further analyses. In the case, the user would add more data from SO to update her dataset (or collection), Makar facilitates syncing the collection using the *Auto-filter* option, which reapplies the same filter as shown in Figure A.3.

- **Data processing.** The user can preprocess the data in Makar through *transformation steps*. A *transformation step* is a single operation that is applied to all records in a collection. Currently, the tool supports operations, such as *text cleaning, natural language processing, data restructuring*, and *arithmetics and counting*.

    - In *text cleaning*, the user can strip all HTML tags, or selected HTML tags, or replace records with custom values, *e.g.*, remove HTML tags from questions in SO.

    - In *natural language processing*, the user can apply word stemming, remove all stop words, or remove all punctuation marks.

    - In *data restructuring*, the user can merge records with the same value, create new records, remove duplicates, split text on defined

A. APPENDIX

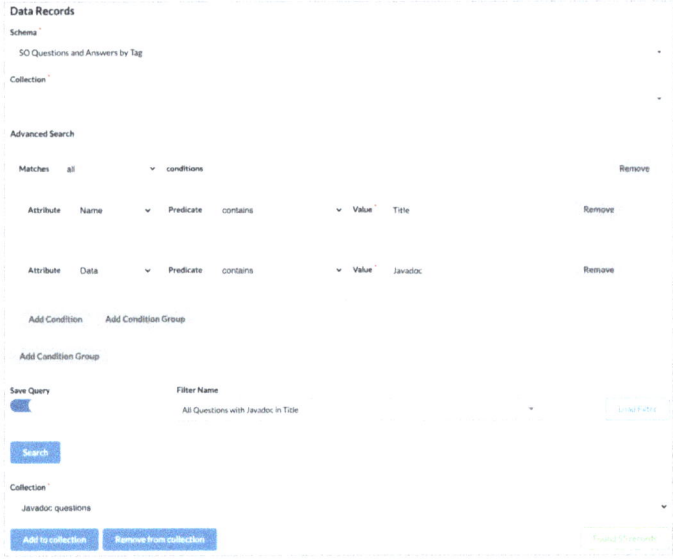

Figure A.2: Search interface of Makar

Figure A.3: Dataset preparation interface of Makar

substring, or add a static value. In addition, the user can create a new dataset with a randomized sample, which is widely performed in manual analysis studies.
- In *arithmetics and counting*, the user can also perform simple arithmetic steps, *e.g.*, counting frequent occurrences of a particular value or a word.

- **Data export**. The user can select attributes for the export and then export the data in the required format as shown in Figure A.3. Currently, the tool supports the *CSV*, *JSON*, and plain text (.txt file) formats. Makar also supports more complex export formats via the `ExportAdapter` component. To offer LDA analysis using Mallet, we added a Mallet adapter as a custom export adapter.[10]

---
[10] http://mallet.cs.umass.edu/

A.1.2 Case Study

Makar supported us in preparing the dataset suitable for the LDA analysis and the manual analyses in chapter 7.

Transformation	extract_code	strip_html	string_replace	remove_stopwords	word_stemming
	Code	HTML	Punctuation	Stop Word	Word Stemming
Attributes	- Question | Body	- Question | Body	- Question | Body - Question | Title	- Question | Body - Question | Title	- Question | Body - Question | Title

Figure A.4: Preprocessing steps in Makar with the transformations

- **Data import**: We imported the SO data using the CSV import adapter, and Quora data with the JSON adapter. The CSV files of the dataset are provided in the RP [131].

- **Data processing**: The data from SO contains HTML code, other code snippets, links, and natural language text. To get meaningful results from LDA analysis, the data needs to be cleaned, with the *text cleaning* and *language cleaning* steps. All preprocessing steps, such as removing code, HTML mark-up, punctuations, and stop words,[11] and stemming words[12] are performed by Makar using its built-in transformations as shown in Figure A.4. Further, it shows various built-in transformations of Makar and available *Attributes* of selected fields, *e.g.*, Title, Body from the sources. Each transformation is designed to produce a new attribute (a column) in the data records, that allows us to retrace the changes applied to the data. Generally it is uncertain in the beginning of a study which combination of preprocessing steps would lead to the best results, and therefore the flexible approach of Makar efficiently supported us in trying several scenarios.

- **Data export**: The dataset prepared for chapter 7 has been exported as CSV and provided in the RP [131].

Overall, Makar assisted us to process multi-source data for chapter 7 in a uniform way and allowed us to investigate various combinations of features for both LDA analysis and the manual analyses. Moreover, Makar provides an extensible framework to support custom requirements, so that further textual analysis techniques can be integrated to perform more advanced text operations.

---

[11] http://snowball.tartarus.org/algorithms/english/stop.txt
[12] https://snowballstem.org/algorithms/porter/stemmer.html

A. Appendix

A.2 Included Studies for SLR

S1. Dorsaf Haouari, Houari A. Sahraoui, and Philippe Langlais. How good is your comment? A study of comments in Java programs. In Proceedings of the 5th International Symposium on Empirical Software Engineering and Measurement, ESEM 2011, Banff, AB, Canada, September 22-23, 2011, pages 137–146. IEEE Computer Society, 2011.

S2. Daniela Steidl, Benjamin Hummel, and Elmar Juergens. Quality analysis of source code comments. In Program Comprehension (ICPC), 2013 IEEE 21st International Conference on, pages 83–92. IEEE, 2013.

S3. Golara Garousi, Vahid Garousi, Mahmood Moussavi, Günther Ruhe, and Brian Smith. Evaluating usage and quality of technical software documentation: an empirical study. In 17th International Conference on Evaluation and Assessment in Software Engineering, EASE '13, Porto de Galinhas, Brazil, April 14-16, 2013, pages 24–35. ACM, 2013.

S4. Rahul Pandita, Xusheng Xiao, Hao Zhong, Tao Xie, Stephen Oney, and Amit M. Paradkar. Inferring method specifications from natural language API descriptions. In 34th International Conference on Software Engineering, ICSE 2012, June 2-9, 2012, Zurich, Switzerland, pages 815–825. IEEE Computer Society, 2012.

S5. Barthélémy Dagenais and Martin P. Robillard. Using traceability links to recommend adaptive changes for documentation evolution. IEEE Transactions on Software Engineering, 40(11):1126–1146, 2014.

S6. Davide Fucci, Alireza Mollaalizadehbahnemiri, and Walid Maalej. On using machine learning to identify knowledge in API reference documentation. In Proceedings of the 2019 27th ACM Joint Meeting on European Software Engineering Conference and Symposium on the Foundations of Software Engineering, pages 109–119, 2019.

S7. Inderjot Kaur Ratol and Martin P Robillard. Detecting fragile comments. In Proceedings of the 32Nd IEEE/ACM International Conference on Automated Software Engineering, pages 112–122. IEEE Press, 2017.

S8. Simone Scalabrino, Gabriele Bavota, Christopher Vendome, Mario Linares Vásquez, Denys Poshyvanyk, and Rocco Oliveto. Automatically assessing code understandability: how far are we? In Proceedings of the 32nd IEEE/ACM International Conference on Automated Software Engineering, ASE 2017, Urbana, IL, USA, October 30 - November 03, 2017, pages 417–427. IEEE Computer Society, 2017.

S9. Yu Zhou, Ruihang Gu, Taolue Chen, Zhiqiu Huang, Sebastiano Panichella, and Harald Gall. Analyzing APIs documentation and code to detect directive defects. In Proceedings of the 39th International Conference on Software Engineering, pages 27–37. IEEE Press, 2017.

S10. Sarah Fakhoury, Yuzhan Ma, Venera Arnaoudova, and Olusola O. Adesope. The effect of poor source code lexicon and readability on developers' cognitive load. In Proceedings of the 26th Conference on Program Comprehension, ICPC 2018, Gothenburg, Sweden, May 27-28, 2018, pages 286–296. ACM, 2018.

A.2. Included Studies for SLR

S11. Emad Aghajani, Csaba Nagy, Gabriele Bavota, and Michele Lanza. A large-scale empirical study on linguistic antipatterns affecting APIs. In 2018 IEEE International Conference on Software Maintenance and Evolution, ICSME 2018, Madrid, Spain, September 23-29, 2018, pages 25–35. IEEE Computer Society, 2018.

S12. Hongwei Li, Sirui Li, Jiamou Sun, Zhenchang Xing, Xin Peng, Mingwei Liu, and Xuejiao Zhao. Improving API caveats accessibility by mining API caveats knowledge graph. In 2018 IEEE International Conference on Software Maintenance and Evolution, ICSME 2018, Madrid, Spain, September 23-29, 2018, pages 183–193. IEEE Computer Society, 2018.

S13. Chong Wang, Xin Peng, Mingwei Liu, Zhenchang Xing, Xuefang Bai, Bing Xie, and Tuo Wang. A learning-based approach for automatic construction of domain glossary from source code and documentation. In Proceedings of the ACM Joint Meeting on European Software Engineering Conference and Symposium on the Foundations of Software Engineering, ESEC/SIGSOFT FSE 2019, Tallinn, Estonia, August 26-30, 2019, pages 97–108. ACM, 2019.

S14. Pengyu Nie, Rishabh Rai, Junyi Jessy Li, Sarfraz Khurshid, Raymond J. Mooney, and Milos Gligoric. A framework for writing trigger-action todo comments in executable format. In Proceedings of the ACM Joint Meeting on European Software Engineering Conference and Symposium on the Foundations of Software Engineering, ESEC/SIGSOFT FSE 2019, Tallinn, Estonia, August 26-30, 2019, pages 385–396. ACM, 2019.

S15. Fengcai Wen, Csaba Nagy, Gabriele Bavota, and Michele Lanza. A large-scale empirical study on code-comment inconsistencies. In Proceedings of the 27th International Conference on Program Comprehension, pages 53–64. IEEE Press, 2019.

S16. Emad Aghajani, Csaba Nagy, Olga Lucero Vega-Márquez, Mario Linares-Vásquez, Laura Moreno, Gabriele Bavota, and Michele Lanza. Software documentation issues unveiled. In Proceedings of the 41st International Conference on Software Engineering, ICSE 2019, Montreal, QC, Canada, May 25-31, 2019, pages 1199–1210. IEEE / ACM, 2019.

S17. Tri Minh Triet Pham and Jinqiu Yang. The secret life of commented-out source code. In ICPC '20: 28th International Conference on Program Comprehension, Seoul, Republic of Korea, July 13-15, 2020, pages 308–318. ACM, 2020.

S18. Xiaobing Sun, Qiang Geng, David Lo, Yucong Duan, Xiangyue Liu, and Bin Li. Code comment quality analysis and improvement recommendation: an automated approach. International Journal of Software Engineering and Knowledge Engineering, 26(06):981–1000, 2016.

S19. Sean Stapleton, Yashmeet Gambhir, Alexander LeClair, Zachary Eberhart, Westley Weimer, Kevin Leach, and Yu Huang. A human study of comprehension and code summarization. In ICPC '20: 28th International Conference on Program Comprehension, Seoul, Republic of Korea, July 13-15, 2020, pages 2–13. ACM, 2020.

A. Appendix

S20. Juan Zhai, Xiangzhe Xu, Yu Shi, Guanhong Tao, Minxue Pan, Shiqing Ma, Lei Xu, Weifeng Zhang, Lin Tan, and Xiangyu Zhang. CPC: Automatically classifying and propagating natural language comments via program analysis. In ICSE '20: 42nd International Conference on Software Engineering, Seoul, South Korea, 27 June - 19 July, 2020, pages 1359–1371. ACM, 2020.

S21. Mohammad Masudur Rahman, Chanchal K. Roy, and Iman Keivanloo. Recommending insightful comments for source code using crowdsourced knowledge. In 15th IEEE International Working Conference on Source Code Analysis and Manipulation, SCAM 2015, Bremen, Germany, September 27-28, 2015, pages 81–90. IEEE Computer Society, 2015.

S22. Simone Scalabrino, Mario Linares-Vasquez, Denys Poshyvanyk, and Rocco Oliveto. Improving code readability models with textual features. In 2016 IEEE 24th International Conference on Program Comprehension (ICPC), pages 1–10. IEEE, 2016.

S23. Paul W. McBurney and Collin McMillan. Automatic source code summarization of context for Java methods. IEEE Transactions on Software Engineering, 42(2):103–119, 2016.

S24. Yu Zhou, Changzhi Wang, Xin Yan, Taolue Chen, Sebastiano Panichella, and Harald C. Gall. Automatic detection and repair recommendation of directive defects in Java API documentation. IEEE Transactions on Software Engineering, 46(9):1004–1023, 2020.

S25. Xin Xia, Lingfeng Bao, David Lo, Zhenchang Xing, Ahmed E. Hassan, and Shanping Li. Measuring program comprehension: A large-scale field study with professionals. IEEE Transactions on Software Engineering, 44(10):951–976, 2018.

S26. Golara Garousi, Vahid Garousi-Yusifoğlu, Guenther Ruhe, Junji Zhi, Mahmoud Moussavi, and Brian Smith. Usage and usefulness of technical software documentation: An industrial case study. Information and Software Technology, 57:664–682, 2015.

S27. Martin Monperrus, Michael Eichberg, Elif Tekes, and Mira Mezini. What should developers be aware of? an empirical study on the directives of API documentation. Empirical Software Engineering, 17(6):703–737, 2012.

S28. Yuhao Wu, Yuki Manabe, Tetsuya Kanda, Daniel M. Germán, and Katsuro Inoue. Analysis of license inconsistency in large collections of open source projects. Empirical Software Engineering, 22(3):1194–1222, 2017.

S29. Luca Pascarella, Magiel Bruntink, and Alberto Bacchelli. Classifying code comments in Java software systems. Empirical Software Engineering, 24(3):1499–1537, 2019.

S30. Yu Zhou, Xin Yan, Wenhua Yang, Taolue Chen, and Zhiqiu Huang. Augmenting Java method comments generation with context information based on neural networks. Journal of Systems and Software, 156:328–340, 2019.

S31. Andrea De Lucia, Massimiliano Di Penta, and Rocco Oliveto. Improving source code lexicon via traceability and information retrieval. IEEE Transactions on Software Engineering, 37(2):205–227, 2011.

A.2. Included Studies for SLR

S32. Hao Zhong and Zhendong Su. Detecting API documentation errors. In Proceedings of the 2013 ACM SIGPLAN International Conference on Object Oriented Programming Systems Languages & Applications, OOPSLA 2013, part of SPLASH 2013, Indianapolis, IN, USA, October 26-31, 2013, pages 803–816. ACM, 2013.

S33. Yuhao Wu, Yuki Manabe, Tetsuya Kanda, Daniel M. Germán, and Katsuro Inoue. A method to detect license inconsistencies in large-scale open source projects. In 12th IEEE/ACM Working Conference on Mining Software Repositories, MSR 2015, Florence, Italy, May 16-17, 2015, pages 324–333. IEEE Computer Society, 2015.

S34. Martin P. Robillard and Yam B. Chhetri. Recommending reference API documentation. Empirical Software Engineering, 20(6):1558–1586, 2015.

S35. Girish Maskeri Rama and Avinash C. Kak. Some structural measures of API usability. Software Practice and Experience, 45(1):75–110, 2015.

S36. Paul W. McBurney and Collin McMillan. An empirical study of the textual similarity between source code and source code summaries. Empirical Software Engineering, 21(1):17–42, 2016.

S37. Venera Arnaoudova, Massimiliano Di Penta, and Giuliano Antoniol. Linguistic antipatterns: what they are and how developers perceive them. Empirical Software Engineering, 21(1):104–158, 2016.

S38. Anna Corazza, Valerio Maggio, and Giuseppe Scanniello. Coherence of comments and method implementations: A dataset and an empirical investigation. Software Quality Journal, 26(2):751–777, 2018.

S39. Simone Scalabrino, Mario Linares-Vásquez, Rocco Oliveto, and Denys Poshyvanyk. A comprehensive model for code readability. Journal of Software: Evolution and Process, 30(6):e1958, 2018.

S40. Zhiyong Liu, Huanchao Chen, Xiangping Chen, Xiaonan Luo, and Fan Zhou. Automatic detection of outdated comments during code changes. In 2018 IEEE 42nd Annual Computer Software and Applications Conference, COMPSAC 2018, Tokyo, Japan, 23-27 July 2018, Volume 1, pages 154–163. IEEE Computer Society, 2018.

S41. Jingyi Zhang, Lei Xu, and Yanhui Li. Classifying Python code comments based on supervised learning. In Web Information Systems and Applications - 15th International Conference, WISA 2018, Taiyuan, China, September 14-15, 2018, Proceedings, volume 11242 of Lecture Notes in Computer Science, pages 39–47. Springer, 2018.

S42. Luca Pascarella, Achyudh Ram, Azqa Nadeem, Dinesh Bisesser, Norman Knyazev, and Alberto Bacchelli. Investigating type declaration mismatches in Python. In 2018 IEEE Workshop on Machine Learning Techniques for Software Quality Evaluation, MaLTeSQuE, SANER 2018, Campobasso, Italy, March 20, 2018, pages 43–48. IEEE Computer Society, 2018.

S43. Maria Kechagia, Marios Fragkoulis, Panos Louridas, and Diomidis Spinellis. The exception handling riddle: An empirical study on the Android API. Journal of Systems and Software, 142:248–270, 2018.

S44. Hideaki Hata, Christoph Treude, Raula Gaikovina Kula, and Takashi Ishio. 9.6 million links in source code comments: Purpose, evolution, and decay. In Proceedings of the 41st International Conference on Software Engineering, pages 1211–1221. IEEE Press, 2019.

S45. Yaoguo Xi, Liwei Shen, Yukun Gui, and Wenyun Zhao. Migrating deprecated API to documented replacement: Patterns and tool. In Proceedings of the 11th Asia-Pacific Symposium on Internetware, pages 1–10, 2019.

S46. Martina Iammarino, Lerina Aversano, Mario Luca Bernardi, and Marta Cimitile. A topic modeling approach to evaluate the comments consistency to source code. In 2020 International Joint Conference on Neural Networks, IJCNN 2020, Glasgow, United Kingdom, July 19-24, 2020, pages 1–8. IEEE, 2020.

S47. Otávio Augusto Lazzarini Lemos, Marcelo Suzuki, Adriano Carvalho de Paula, and Claire Le Goes. Comparing identifiers and comments in engineered and non-engineered code: a large-scale empirical study. In SAC '20: The 35th ACM/SIGAPP Symposium on Applied Computing, online event, Brno, Czech Republic, March 30 - April 3, 2020, pages 100–109. ACM, 2020.

S48. Yusuke Shinyama, Yoshitaka Arahori, and Katsuhiko Gondow. Analyzing code comments to boost program comprehension. In 2018 25th Asia-Pacific Software Engineering Conference (APSEC), pages 325–334. IEEE, 2018.

A.3 Pharo Template Models

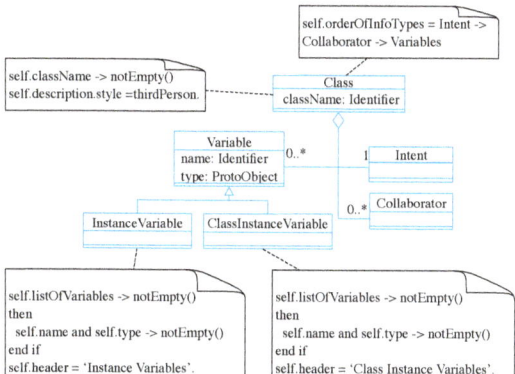

Figure A.5: Writing style constraints formulated from the Pharo 1 template

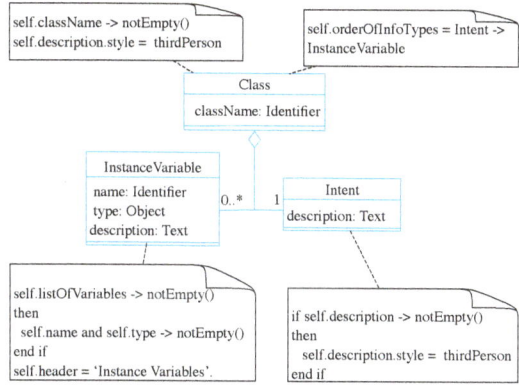

Figure A.6: Writing style constraints formulated from the templates of Pharo 2 and 3

A. Appendix

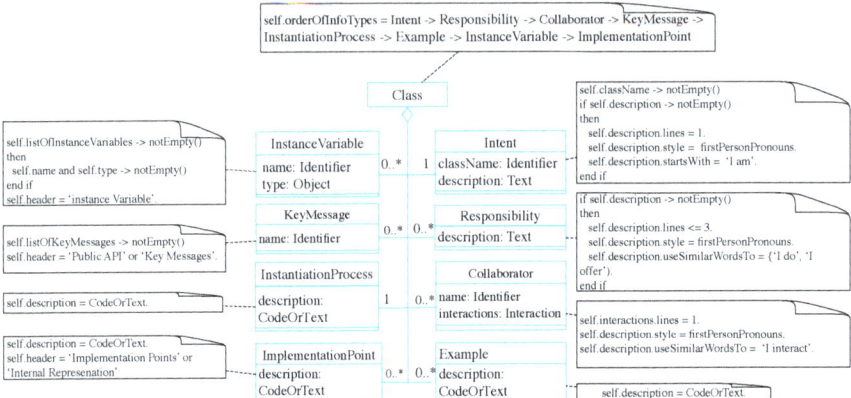

Figure A.7: Writing style constraints formulated from the Pharo 4 template

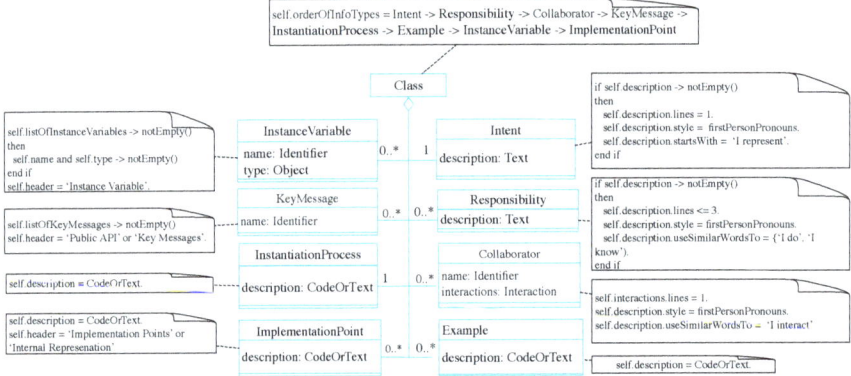

Figure A.8: Writing style constraints formulated from the templates of Pharo 5, 6, and 7

A.4 Developer Information Needs

A.4. Developer Information Needs

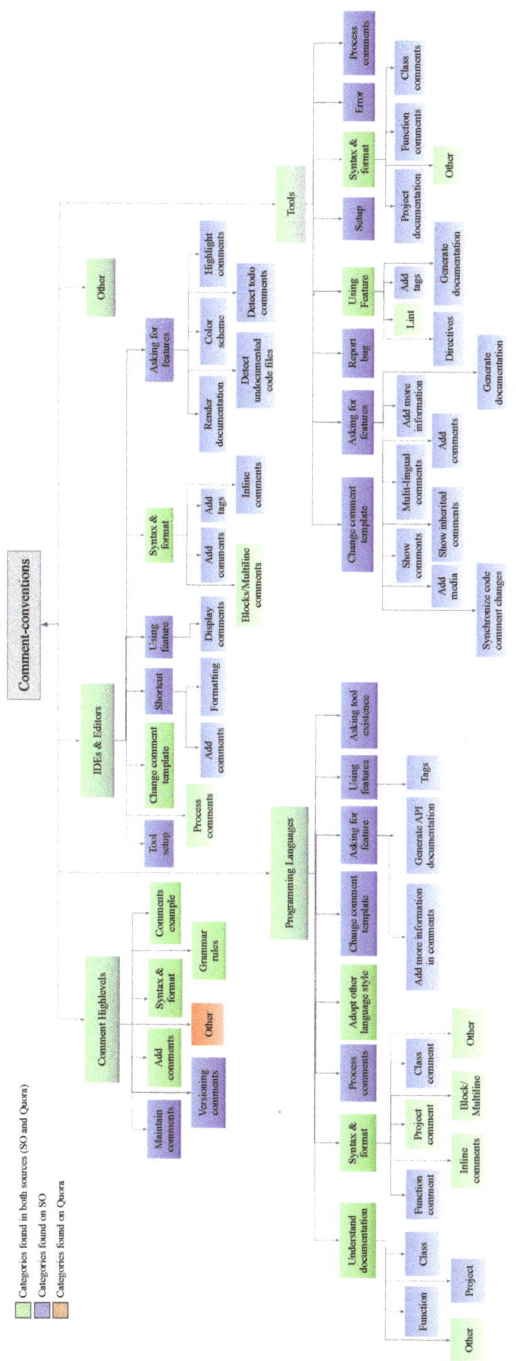

Figure A.9: Taxonomy of information needs on SO and Quora

Bibliography

[1] Mouna Abidi and Foutse Khomh. Towards the definition of patterns and code smells for multi-language systems. In *EuroPLoP '20: European Conference on Pattern Languages of Programs 2020, Virtual Event, Germany, 1-4 July, 2020*, pages 37:1–37:13. ACM, 2020.

[2] Emad Aghajani, Csaba Nagy, Gabriele Bavota, and Michele Lanza. A large-scale empirical study on linguistic antipatterns affecting APIs. In *2018 IEEE International Conference on Software Maintenance and Evolution, ICSME 2018, Madrid, Spain, September 23-29, 2018*, pages 25–35. IEEE Computer Society, 2018.

[3] Emad Aghajani, Csaba Nagy, Mario Linares-Vásquez, Laura Moreno, Gabriele Bavota, Michele Lanza, and David C Shepherd. Software documentation: the practitioners' perspective. In *2020 IEEE/ACM 42nd International Conference on Software Engineering (ICSE)*, pages 590–601. IEEE, 2020.

[4] Emad Aghajani, Csaba Nagy, Olga Lucero Vega-Márquez, Mario Linares-Vásquez, Laura Moreno, Gabriele Bavota, and Michele Lanza. Software documentation issues unveiled. In Joanne M. Atlee, Tevfik Bultan, and Jon Whittle, editors, *Proceedings of the 41st International Conference on Software Engineering, ICSE 2019, Montreal, QC, Canada, May 25-31, 2019*, pages 1199–1210. IEEE / ACM, 2019.

[5] Luís A Alexandre, Aurélio C Campilho, and Mohamed Kamel. On combining classifiers using sum and product rules. *Pattern Recognition Letters*, 22(12):1283–1289, 2001.

[6] Miltiadis Allamanis, Earl T. Barr, Christian Bird, and Charles Sutton. Learning natural coding conventions. In *Proceedings of the 22nd ACM SIGSOFT International Symposium on Foundations of Software Engineering*, FSE 2014, pages 281–293, New York, NY, USA, 2014. ACM.

[7] Miltiadis Allamanis and Charles Sutton. Why, when, and what: Analyzing Stack Overflow questions by topic, type, and code. In *Proceedings of the 10th Working Conference on Mining Software Repositories*, MSR '13, pages 53–56, Piscataway, NJ, USA, 2013. IEEE Press.

[8] Sven Amann, Stefanie Beyer, Katja Kevic, and Harald Gall. *Software Mining Studies: Goals, Approaches, Artifacts, and Replicability*, pages 121–158. Springer International Publishing, 2015.

[9] Scott W Ambler. Agile/lean documentation: strategies for agile software development. *Retrieved June*, 20:2007, 2007.

[10] Apache Spark, 2021. https://github.com/apache/spark.

[11] Masayuki Arai. Development and evaluation of eclipse plugin tool for learning programming style of java. In *2014 9th International Conference on Computer Science & Education*, pages 495–499. IEEE, 2014.

[12] Venera Arnaoudova, Massimiliano Di Penta, and Giuliano Antoniol. Linguistic antipatterns: what they are and how developers perceive them. *Empir. Softw. Eng.*, 21(1):104–158, 2016.

[13] James D Arthur and K Todd Stevens. Assessing the adequacy of documentation through document quality indicators. In *Proceedings. Conference on Software Maintenance-1989*, pages 40–49. IEEE, 1989.

[14] Ricardo Baeza-Yates and Berthier Ribeiro-Neto. *Modern Information Retrieval*. Addison-Wesley, 1999.

[15] Nikolaos Bafatakis, Niels Boecker, Wenjie Boon, Martin Cabello Salazar, Jens Krinke, Gazi Oznacar, and Robert White. Python coding style compliance on stack overflow. In *2019 IEEE/ACM 16th International Conference on Mining Software Repositories (MSR)*, pages 210–214. IEEE, 2019.

[16] Jagdish Bansiya and Carl Davis. A hierarchical model for object-oriented design quality assessment. *IEEE Transactions on Software Engineering*, 28(1):4–17, January 2002.

[17] Anton Barua, Stephen W. Thomas, and Ahmed E. Hassan. What are developers talking about? An analysis of topics and trends in Stack Overflow. *Empirical Software Engineering*, 19(3):619–654, 2014.

[18] Gabriele Bavota. Mining unstructured data in software repositories: Current and future trends. In *2016 IEEE 23rd International Conference on Software Analysis, Evolution, and Reengineering (SANER)*, volume 5, pages 1–12. IEEE, 2016.

[19] Beautifulsoup, Aug, 2021. https://pypi.org/project/beautifulsoup4/.

[20] Stefanie Beyer, Christian Macho, Massimiliano Di Penta, and Martin Pinzger. What kind of questions do developers ask on stack overflow? a comparison of automated approaches to classify posts into question categories. *Empirical Software Engineering*, pages 1–44, 2019.

[21] Stefanie Beyer and Martin Pinzger. A manual categorization of Android app development issues on Stack Overflow. In *Proceedings of the 2014 IEEE International Conference on Software Maintenance and Evolution*, ICSME '14, pages 531–535, Washington, DC, USA, 2014. IEEE Computer Society.

[22] Lauren R Biggers, Cecylia Bocovich, Riley Capshaw, Brian P Eddy, Letha H Etzkorn, and Nicholas A Kraft. Configuring latent dirichlet allocation based feature location. *Empirical Software Engineering*, 19(3):465–500, 2014.

[23] Dave Binkley, Marcia Davis, Dawn Lawrie, Jonathan I Maletic, Christopher Morrell, and Bonita Sharif. The impact of identifier style on effort and comprehension. *Empirical Software Engineering*, 18(2):219–276, 2013.

[24] Dave Binkley, Dawn Lawrie, Emily Hill, Janet Burge, Ian Harris, Regina Hebig, Oliver Keszocze, Karl Reed, and John Slankas. Task-driven software summarization. In *2013 IEEE International Conference on Software Maintenance*, pages 432–435. IEEE, 2013.

[25] Mathias Birrer. Analysis of developer information needs on collaborative platforms. Masters thesis, University of Bern, July 2020.

[26] Mathias Birrer, Pooja Rani, Sebastiano Panichella, and Oscar Nierstrasz. Makar: A framework for multi-source studies based on unstructured data. In *2021 IEEE International Conference on Software Analysis, Evolution and Reengineering (SANER)*, pages 577–581, 2021.

[27] David M Blei, Andrew Y Ng, and Michael I Jordan. Latent Dirichlet Allocation. *Journal of machine Learning research*, 3(Jan):993–1022, 2003.

[28] Yuriy Brun, Reid Holmes, Michael D. Ernst, and David Notkin. Speculative analysis: Exploring future development states of software. In *Proceedings of the FSE/SDP Workshop on Future of Software Engineering Research*, FoSER '10, pages 59–64, New York, NY, USA, 2010. ACM.

[29] Jonathan Chang, Sean Gerrish, Chong Wang, Jordan L Boyd-Graber, and David M Blei. Reading tea leaves: How humans interpret topic

models. In *Advances in neural information processing systems*, pages 288–296, 2009.

[30] Jie-Cherng Chen and Sun-Jen Huang. An empirical analysis of the impact of software development problem factors on software maintainability. *Journal of Systems and Software*, 82(6):981–992, 2009.

[31] Tse-Hsun Chen, Stephen W. Thomas, and Ahmed E. Hassan. A survey on the use of topic models when mining software repositories. *Empirical Softw. Engg.*, 21(5):1843–1919, oct 2016.

[32] S. R. Chidamber and C. F. Kemerer. A metrics suite for object oriented design. *IEEE Transactions on Software Engineering*, 20(6):476–493, June 1994.

[33] Namyoun Choi, Il-Yeol Song, and Hyoil Han. A survey on ontology mapping. *ACM Sigmod Record*, 35(3):34–41, 2006.

[34] Frank A. Cioch, Michael Palazzolo, and Scott Lohrer. A documentation suite for maintenance programmers. In *Proceedings of the 1996 International Conference on Software Maintenance*, ICSM '96, pages 286–295, Washington, DC, USA, 1996. IEEE Computer Society.

[35] Alan Cline. Testing thread. In *Agile Development in the Real World*, pages 221–252. Springer, 2015.

[36] Arturo Curiel and Christophe Collet. Sign language lexical recognition with propositional dynamic logic. In *Proceedings of the 51st Annual Meeting of the Association for Computational Linguistics, ACL 2013, 4-9 August 2013, Sofia, Bulgaria, Volume 2: Short Papers*, pages 328–333. The Association for Computer Linguistics, 2013.

[37] Andreas Dautovic, Reinhold Plösch, and Matthias Saft. Automated quality defect detection in software development documents. In *First International Workshop on Model-Driven Software Migration (MDSM 2011)*, page 29, 2011.

[38] Sergio Cozzetti B. de Souza, Nicolas Anquetil, and Káthia M. de Oliveira. A study of the documentation essential to software maintenance. In *Proceedings of the 23rd annual international conference on Design of communication: documenting & designing for pervasive information*, SIGDOC '05, pages 68–75, New York, NY, USA, 2005. ACM.

[39] Uri Dekel and James D Herbsleb. Reading the documentation of invoked API functions in program comprehension. In *2009 IEEE 17th International Conference on Program Comprehension*, pages 168–177. IEEE, 2009.

[40] Janez Demšar. Statistical comparisons of classifiers over multiple data sets. *The Journal of Machine Learning Research*, 7:1–30, 2006.

[41] Andrea Di Sorbo, Sebastiano Panichella, Corrado A Visaggio, Massimiliano Di Penta, Gerardo Canfora, and Harald Gall. Deca: development emails content analyzer. In *2016 IEEE/ACM 38th International Conference on Software Engineering Companion (ICSE-C)*, pages 641–644. IEEE, 2016.

[42] Andrea Di Sorbo, Sebastiano Panichella, Corrado A Visaggio, Massimiliano Di Penta, Gerardo Canfora, and Harald C Gall. Development emails content analyzer: Intention mining in developer discussions (T). In *2015 30th IEEE/ACM International Conference on Automated Software Engineering (ASE)*, pages 12–23. IEEE, 2015.

[43] Andrea Di Sorbo, Sebastiano Panichella, Corrado Aaron Visaggio, Massimiliano Di Penta, Gerardo Canfora, and Harald C Gall. Exploiting natural language structures in software informal documentation. *IEEE Transactions on Software Engineering*, 2019.

[44] Martín Dias, Mariano Martinez Peck, Stéphane Ducasse, and Gabriela Arévalo. Fuel: a fast general purpose object graph serializer. *Software: Practice and Experience*, 44(4):433–453, 2014.

[45] Wei Ding, Peng Liang, Antony Tang, and Hans Van Vliet. Knowledge-based approaches in software documentation: A systematic literature review. *Information and Software Technology*, 56(6):545–567, 2014.

[46] Rodrigo Magalhães dos Santos and Marco Aurélio Gerosa. Impacts of coding practices on readability. In *Proceedings of the 26th Conference on Program Comprehension*, pages 277–285, 2018.

[47] Natalia Dragan, Michael L. Collard, and Jonathan I. Maletic. Automatic identification of class stereotypes. In *Proceedings of the 2010 IEEE International Conference on Software Maintenance*, ICSM '10, page 1–10, USA, 2010. IEEE Computer Society.

[48] Mahmoud Omar Elish and Jeff Offutt. The adherence of open source Java programmers to standard coding practices. In *Proceedings of the 6th IASTED International Conference on Software Engineering and Applications (SEA'02)*, pages 193–198. MIT, 2002.

[49] Jonathan Scott Enderle, Arun Balagopalan, Xiaojing Li, and David Newman. Senderle/topic-modeling-tool: First stable release, April 2017.

[50] Jérôme Euzenat. Towards a principled approach to semantic interoperability. In *Proc. IJCAI 2001 workshop on ontology and information*

sharing, Proc. IJCAI 2001 workshop on ontology and information sharing, pages 19–25, Seattle, United States, August 2001. No commercial editor. euzenat2001b.

[51] Sarah Fakhoury, Yuzhan Ma, Venera Arnaoudova, and Olusola O. Adesope. The effect of poor source code lexicon and readability on developers' cognitive load. In Foutse Khomh, Chanchal K. Roy, and Janet Siegmund, editors, *Proceedings of the 26th Conference on Program Comprehension, ICPC 2018, Gothenburg, Sweden, May 27-28, 2018*, pages 286–296. ACM, 2018.

[52] M.S. Farooq, S.A. Khan, K. Abid, F. Ahmad, M.A. Naeem, M. Shafiq, and A. Abid. Taxonomy and design considerations for comments in programming languages: A quality perspective. *Journal of Quality and Technology Management*, 10(2), 2015.

[53] R. K. Fjeldstad and W. T. Hamlen. Application Program Maintenance Study: Report to Our Respondents. In *Proceedings GUIDE 48*, April 1983.

[54] Beat Fluri, Michael Wursch, and Harald C Gall. Do code and comments co-evolve? On the Relation between Source Code and Comment Changes. In *Reverse Engineering, 2007. WCRE 2007. 14th Working Conference on*, pages 70–79. IEEE, 2007.

[55] Beat Fluri, Michael Würsch, Emanuel Giger, and Harald C Gall. Analyzing the co-evolution of comments and source code. *Software Quality Journal*, 17(4):367–394, 2009.

[56] Andrew Forward and Timothy C. Lethbridge. The relevance of software documentation, tools and technologies: a survey. In *Proceedings of the 2002 ACM symposium on Document engineering*, DocEng '02, pages 26–33, New York, NY, USA, 2002. ACM.

[57] Golara Garousi, Vahid Garousi-Yusifoğlu, Guenther Ruhe, Junji Zhi, Mahmoud Moussavi, and Brian Smith. Usage and usefulness of technical software documentation: An industrial case study. *Information and Software Technology*, 57:664–682, 2015.

[58] Vahid Garousi, Michael Felderer, and Mika V. Mäntylä. The need for multivocal literature reviews in software engineering: complementing systematic literature reviews with grey literature. In Sarah Beecham, Barbara A. Kitchenham, and Stephen G. MacDonell, editors, *Proceedings of the 20th International Conference on Evaluation and Assessment in Software Engineering, EASE 2016, Limerick, Ireland, June 01 - 03, 2016*, pages 26:1–26:6. ACM, 2016.

[59] S Geerthik, K Rajiv Gandhi, and S Venkatraman. Domain expert ranking for finding domain authoritative users on community question answering sites. In *2016 IEEE International Conference on Computational Intelligence and Computing Research (ICCIC)*, pages 1–5. IEEE, 2016.

[60] Verena Geist, Michael Moser, Josef Pichler, Stefanie Beyer, and Martin Pinzger. Leveraging machine learning for software redocumentation. In *2020 IEEE 27th International Conference on Software Analysis, Evolution and Reengineering (SANER)*, pages 622–626. IEEE, 2020.

[61] Michael W Godfrey, Ahmed E Hassan, James Herbsleb, Gail C Murphy, Martin Robillard, Prem Devanbu, Audris Mockus, Dewayne E Perry, and David Notkin. Future of mining software archives: A roundtable. *IEEE Software*, 26(1):67–70, 2008.

[62] Adele Goldberg and David Robson. *Smalltalk 80: the Language and its Implementation*. Addison Wesley, Reading, Mass., May 1983.

[63] Ira P. Goldstein and Daniel G. Bobrow. Extending object-oriented programming in Smalltalk. In *Proceedings of the Lisp Conference*, pages 75–81, August 1980.

[64] Jesús M. González-Barahona and Gregorio Robles. On the reproducibility of empirical software engineering studies based on data retrieved from development repositories. *Empirical Software Engineering*, 17(1):75–89, 2012.

[65] Google style guidelines, 2021. https://google.github.io/styleguide/.

[66] Google trend popularity index, 2021. https://pypl.github.io/PYPL.html.

[67] Harshit Gujral, Abhinav Sharma, Sangeeta Lal, Amanpreet Kaur, A Kumar, and Ashish Sureka. Empirical analysis of the logging questions on the Stack Overflow website. In *2018 Conference On Software Engineering & Data Sciences (CoSEDS)(in-press)*, 2018.

[68] Anja Guzzi, Alberto Bacchelli, Michele Lanza, Martin Pinzger, and Arie van Deursen. Communication in open source software development mailing lists. In *Proceedings of the 10th Working Conference on Mining Software Repositories*, pages 277–286. IEEE Press, 2013.

[69] Sonia Haiduc, Jairo Aponte, Laura Moreno, and Andrian Marcus. On the use of automated text summarization techniques for summarizing source code. In *2010 17th Working Conference on Reverse Engineering*, pages 35–44. IEEE, 2010.

[70] Dorsaf Haouari, Houari A. Sahraoui, and Philippe Langlais. How good is your comment? A study of comments in java programs. In *Proceedings of the 5th International Symposium on Empirical Software Engineering and Measurement, ESEM 2011, Banff, AB, Canada, September 22-23, 2011*, pages 137–146. IEEE Computer Society, 2011.

[71] Hans J. Happel and Walid Maalej. Potentials and challenges of recommendation systems for software development. In *RSSE '08: Proceedings of the 2008 international workshop on Recommendation systems for software engineering*, pages 11–15, New York, NY, USA, 2008. ACM.

[72] Hideaki Hata, Christoph Treude, Raula Gaikovina Kula, and Takashi Ishio. 9.6 million links in source code comments: Purpose, evolution, and decay. In *Proceedings of the 41st International Conference on Software Engineering*, pages 1211–1221. IEEE Press, 2019.

[73] Matthew Hoffman, Francis Bach, and David Blei. Online learning for latent dirichlet allocation. *advances in neural information processing systems*, 23:856–864, 2010.

[74] Daqing Hou, Kenny Wong, and H. James Hoover. What can programmer questions tell us about frameworks? In *Proceedings of the 13th International Workshop on Program Comprehension*, IWPC '05, pages 87–96, Washington, DC, USA, 2005. IEEE Computer Society.

[75] Walid M Ibrahim, Nicolas Bettenburg, Bram Adams, and Ahmed E Hassan. On the relationship between comment update practices and software bugs. *Journal of Systems and Software*, 85(10):2293–2304, 2012.

[76] Oracle documentation guideline, 2021. https://www.oracle.com/technetwork/java/javase/documentation.

[77] Zhen Ming Jiang and Ahmed E Hassan. Examining the evolution of code comments in PostgreSQL. In *Proceedings of the 2006 international workshop on Mining software repositories*, pages 179–180. ACM, 2006.

[78] Rafael Kallis, Andrea Di Sorbo, Gerardo Canfora, and Sebastiano Panichella. Predicting issue types on GitHub. *Science of Computer Programming*, 205:102598, 2021.

[79] Staffs Keele. Guidelines for performing systematic literature reviews in software engineering. Technical report, Technical report, EBSE Technical Report EBSE-2007-01, 2007.

[80] Brian W. Kernighan and Rob Pike. *The Practice of Programming (Addison-Wesley Professional Computing Series)*. Addison-Wesley, 1 edition, February 1999.

[81] Ninus Khamis, René Witte, and Juergen Rilling. Automatic quality assessment of source code comments: the JavadocMiner. In *International Conference on Application of Natural Language to Information Systems*, pages 68–79. Springer, 2010.

[82] Barbara Kitchenham and Stuart Charters. Guidelines for performing systematic literature reviews in software engineering, 2007.

[83] Pavneet Singh Kochhar. Mining testing questions on Stack Overflow. In *Proceedings of the 5th International Workshop on Software Mining*, SoftwareMining 2016, pages 32–38, New York, NY, USA, 2016. ACM.

[84] Jacob Krüger. Are you talking about software product lines? An analysis of developer communities. In *Proceedings of the 13th International Workshop on Variability Modelling of Software-Intensive Systems*, pages 1–9, 2019.

[85] Taek Lee and Jung-Been Lee. Effect analysis of coding convention violations on readability of post-delivered code. *IEICE Transactions on Information and Systems*, 98(7):1286–1296, 2015.

[86] Manny Lehman, Dewayne Perry, Juan Ramil, Wladyslaw Turski, and Paul Wernick. Metrics and laws of software evolution–the nineties view. In *Proceedings IEEE International Software Metrics Symposium (METRICS'97)*, pages 20–32, Los Alamitos CA, 1997. IEEE Computer Society Press.

[87] Mario Linares-Vásquez, Bogdan Dit, and Denys Poshyvanyk. An exploratory analysis of mobile development issues using Stack Overflow. In *Proceedings of the 10th Working Conference on Mining Software Repositories*, MSR '13, pages 93–96, Piscataway, NJ, USA, 2013. IEEE Press.

[88] Yangchao Liu, Xiaobing Sun, and Yucong Duan. Analyzing program readability based on WordNet. In *Proceedings of the 19th International Conference on Evaluation and Assessment in Software Engineering*, page 27. ACM, 2015.

[89] Zhiyong Liu, Huanchao Chen, Xiangping Chen, Xiaonan Luo, and Fan Zhou. Automatic detection of outdated comments during code changes. In Sorel Reisman, Sheikh Iqbal Ahamed, Claudio Demartini, Thomas M. Conte, Ling Liu, William R. Claycomb, Motonori Nakamura, Edmundo Tovar, Stelvio Cimato, Chung-Horng Lung, Hiroki Takakura, Ji-Jiang Yang, Toyokazu Akiyama, Zhiyong Zhang, and

Kamrul Hasan, editors, *2018 IEEE 42nd Annual Computer Software and Applications Conference, COMPSAC 2018, Tokyo, Japan, 23-27 July 2018, Volume 1*, pages 154–163. IEEE Computer Society, 2018.

[90] Julie Beth Lovins. Development of a stemming algorithm. *Mech. Transl. Comput. Linguistics*, 11(1-2):22–31, 1968.

[91] Walid Maalej, Rebecca Tiarks, Tobias Roehm, and Rainer Koschke. On the comprehension of program comprehension. *ACM TOSEM*, 23(4):31:1–31:37, September 2014.

[92] Suman Kalyan Maity, Aman Kharb, and Animesh Mukherjee. Language use matters: Analysis of the linguistic structure of question texts can characterize answerability in quora. In *Eleventh International AAAI Conference on Web and Social Media*, 2017.

[93] Rabee Sohail Malik, Jibesh Patra, and Michael Pradel. Nl2type: inferring JavaScript function types from natural language information. In Joanne M. Atlee, Tevfik Bultan, and Jon Whittle, editors, *Proceedings of the 41st International Conference on Software Engineering, ICSE 2019*, pages 304–315. IEEE / ACM, 2019.

[94] David Patrick Marin. What motivates programmers to comment? *Technical Report No. UCB/EECS-2005018, University of California at Berkeley*, 2005.

[95] Robert Martin. What killed Smalltalk could kill Ruby, too. (RailsConf 09 – http://blip.tv/file/2089545).

[96] Binny Mathew, Ritam Dutt, Suman Kalyan Maity, Pawan Goyal, and Animesh Mukherjee. Deep dive into anonymity: Large scale analysis of quora questions. In *International Conference on Social Informatics*, pages 35–49. Springer, 2019.

[97] Andrew Kachites McCallum. Mallet: A machine learning for language toolkit, 2002.

[98] Collin McMillan, Denys Poshyvanyk, and Mark Grechanik. Recommending source code examples via API call usages and documentation. In *Proceedings of the 2nd International Workshop on Recommendation Systems for Software Engineering*, pages 21–25, 2010.

[99] Qing Mi, Jacky Keung, and Yang Yu. Measuring the stylistic inconsistency in software projects using hierarchical agglomerative clustering. In *Proceedings of the The 12th International Conference on Predictive Models and Data Analytics in Software Engineering*, pages 1–10, 2016.

[100] Elisa Miller. Universal Methods of Design: 100 ways to research complex problems, develop innovative ideas, and design effective solutions, 2012.

[101] Shervin Minaee, Nal Kalchbrenner, Erik Cambria, Narjes Nikzad, Meysam Chenaghlu, and Jianfeng Gao. Deep learning–based text classification: A comprehensive review. *ACM Computing Surveys (CSUR)*, 54(3):1–40, 2021.

[102] Vishal Misra, Jakku Sai Krupa Reddy, and Sridhar Chimalakonda. Is there a correlation between code comments and issues?: an exploratory study. In *SAC '20: The 35th ACM/SIGAPP Symposium on Applied Computing, online event, [Brno, Czech Republic], March 30 - April 3, 2020*, pages 110–117, 2020.

[103] Laura Moreno, Jairo Aponte, Giriprasad Sridhara, Andrian Marcus, Lori L. Pollock, and K. Vijay-Shanker. Automatic generation of natural language summaries for Java classes. In *IEEE 21st International Conference on Program Comprehension, ICPC 2013, San Francisco, CA, USA, 20-21 May, 2013*, pages 23–32, 2013.

[104] Manish Motwani and Yuriy Brun. Automatically generating precise oracles from structured natural language specifications. In Joanne M. Atlee, Tevfik Bultan, and Jon Whittle, editors, *Proceedings of the 41st International Conference on Software Engineering, ICSE 2019*, pages 188–199. IEEE / ACM, 2019.

[105] Kıvanç Muşlu, Yuriy Brun, Michael D Ernst, and David Notkin. Making offline analyses continuous. In *Proceedings of the 2013 9th Joint Meeting on Foundations of Software Engineering*, pages 323–333, 2013.

[106] Najam Nazar, Yan Hu, and He Jiang. Summarizing software artifacts: A literature review. *Journal of Computer Science and Technology*, 31(5):883–909, 2016.

[107] Mahmood Neshati, Zohreh Fallahnejad, and Hamid Beigy. On dynamicity of expert finding in community question answering. *Information Processing & Management*, 53(5):1026–1042, 2017.

[108] Sebastian Nielebock, Dariusz Krolikowski, Jacob Krüger, Thomas Leich, and Frank Ortmeier. Commenting source code: Is it worth it for small programming tasks? *Empirical Software Engineering*, 24(3):1418–1457, 2019.

[109] Eriko Nurvitadhi, Wing Wah Leung, and Curtis Cook. Do class comments aid Java program understanding? In *33rd Annual Frontiers in Education, 2003. FIE 2003.*, volume 1, pages T3C–T3C. IEEE, 2003.

[110] Paul W Oman and Curtis R Cook. A taxonomy for programming style. In *Proceedings of the 1990 ACM annual conference on Cooperation*, pages 244–250, 1990.

[111] Yoann Padioleau, Lin Tan, and Yuanyuan Zhou. Listening to programmers — taxonomies and characteristics of comments in operating system code. In *Proceedings of the 31st International Conference on Software Engineering*, pages 331–341. IEEE Computer Society, 2009.

[112] S. Panichella, A. Panichella, M. Beller, A. Zaidman, and H. C. Gall. The impact of test case summaries on bug fixing performance: An empirical investigation. In *2016 IEEE/ACM 38th International Conference on Software Engineering (ICSE)*, pages 547–558, May 2016.

[113] Sebastiano Panichella, Jairo Aponte, Massimiliano Di Penta, Andrian Marcus, and Gerardo Canfora. Mining source code descriptions from developer communications. In Dirk Beyer, Arie van Deursen, and Michael W. Godfrey, editors, *IEEE 20th International Conference on Program Comprehension, ICPC 2012, Passau, Germany, June 11-13, 2012*, pages 63–72. IEEE Computer Society, 2012.

[114] Sebastiano Panichella, Andrea Di Sorbo, Emitza Guzman, Corrado A Visaggio, Gerardo Canfora, and Harald C Gall. How can I improve my app? Classifying user reviews for software maintenance and evolution. In *2015 IEEE International Conference on Software Maintenance and Evolution (ICSME)*, pages 281–290. IEEE, 2015.

[115] Luca Pascarella and Alberto Bacchelli. Classifying code comments in Java open-source software systems. In *Proceedings of the 14th International Conference on Mining Software Repositories*, MSR '17, pages 227–237. IEEE Press, 2017.

[116] Sumanth Patil and Kyumin Lee. Detecting experts on quora: by their activity, quality of answers, linguistic characteristics and temporal behaviors. *Social network analysis and mining*, 6(1):5, 2016.

[117] Pharo consortium, 2020. verified on 10 Jan 2020.

[118] Reinhold Plösch, Andreas Dautovic, and Matthias Saft. The value of software documentation quality. In *2014 14th International Conference on Quality Software, Allen, TX, USA, October 2-3, 2014*, pages 333–342. IEEE, 2014.

[119] Rashmi Pokharel, Pari Delir Haghighi, Prem Prakash Jayaraman, and Dimitrios Georgakopoulos. Analysing emerging topics across multiple social media platforms. In *Proceedings of the Australasian Computer Science Week Multiconference*, ACSW 2019, pages 16:1–16:9, New York, NY, USA, 2019. ACM.

[120] Python PEP 257 Docstring conventions, last accessed on Dec, 2021. https://www.python.org/dev/peps/pep-0257/.

[121] Python documenation guideline, last accessed on Dec, 2021. https://www.python.org/doc/.

[122] J. Ross Quinlan. Induction of decision trees. *Machine learning*, 1(1):81–106, 1986.

[123] Quora, 2021. https://www.quora.com.

[124] Should code comments be formal English or informal English, last accessed on August, 2021. Online.

[125] Václav Rajlich. Incremental redocumentation using the web. *IEEE Software*, 17(5):102–106, 2000.

[126] Pooja Rani. Replication package for "Academic support for comment quality assessment", 2021. https://github.com/s0nata/SLR-code-comments-quality-replication-package.

[127] Pooja Rani. Replication package for "Comment adherence to conventions", 2021. https://doi.org/10.5281/zenodo.5153663.

[128] Pooja Rani. Replication package for "Commenting practice concerns", 2021. https://doi.org/10.5281/zenodo.5044270.

[129] Pooja Rani. Replication package for "Automated identification of CITs", last accessed on Dec, 2021. https://github.com/poojaruhal/RP-class-comment-classification.

[130] Pooja Rani. Replication package for "Comment information types (CITs) in Smalltalk", last accessed on Dec, 2021. https://github.com/poojaruhal/CommentAnalysisInPharo.

[131] Pooja Rani. Replication package for Makar tool, last accessed on Dec, 2021. https://doi.org/10.5281/zenodo.4434822.

[132] Pooja Rani, Suada Abukar, Nataliia Stulova, Alexander Bergel, and Oscar Nierstrasz. Do comments follow commenting conventions? A case study in Java and Python. In *2021 IEEE 21st International Working Conference on Source Code Analysis and Manipulation (SCAM)*, 2021.

[133] Pooja Rani, Mathias Birrer, Sebastiano Panichella, Mohammad Ghafari, and Oscar Nierstrasz. What do developers discuss about code comments? In *2021 IEEE 21st International Working Conference on Source Code Analysis and Manipulation (SCAM)*, 2021.

[134] Pooja Rani, Arianna Blasi, Nataliia Stulova, Sebastiano Panichella, Alessandra Gorla, and Oscar Nierstrasz. A decade of code comment quality assessment: A systematic literature review. *Journal of Systems and Software*, 2021.

[135] Pooja Rani, Sebastiano Panichella, Manuel Leuenberger, Andrea Di Sorbo, and Oscar Nierstrasz. How to identify class comment types? A multi-language approach for class comment classification. *Journal of Systems and Software*, 181:111047, 2021.

[136] Pooja Rani, Sebastiano Panichella, Manuel Leuenberger, Mohammad Ghafari, and Oscar Nierstrasz. What do class comments tell us? An investigation of comment evolution and practices in Pharo Smalltalk. *Empirical Software Engineering*, 26(6):1–49, 2021.

[137] Inderjot Kaur Ratol and Martin P Robillard. Detecting fragile comments. In *Proceedings of the 32Nd IEEE/ACM International Conference on Automated Software Engineering*, pages 112–122. IEEE Press, 2017.

[138] Martin P. Robillard. What makes apis hard to learn? answers from developers. *IEEE Softw.*, 26(6):27–34, November 2009.

[139] Martin P Robillard, Andrian Marcus, Christoph Treude, Gabriele Bavota, Oscar Chaparro, Neil Ernst, Marco Aurélio Gerosa, Michael Godfrey, Michele Lanza, Mario Linares-Vásquez, et al. On-demand developer documentation. In *2017 IEEE International conference on software maintenance and evolution (ICSME)*, pages 479–483. IEEE, 2017.

[140] Michael Röder, Andreas Both, and Alexander Hinneburg. Exploring the space of topic coherence measures. In *Proceedings of the eighth ACM international conference on Web search and data mining*, pages 399–408, 2015.

[141] Christoffer Rosen and Emad Shihab. What are mobile developers asking about? A large scale study using stack overflow. *Empirical Software Engineering*, 21(3):1192–1223, 2016.

[142] Simone Scalabrino, Mario Linares-Vásquez, Rocco Oliveto, and Denys Poshyvanyk. A comprehensive model for code readability. *Journal of Software: Evolution and Process*, 30(6):e1958, 2018.

[143] Simone Scalabrino, Mario Linares-Vasquez, Denys Poshyvanyk, and Rocco Oliveto. Improving code readability models with textual features. In *2016 IEEE 24th International Conference on Program Comprehension (ICPC)*, pages 1–10. IEEE, 2016.

[144] Daniel Schreck, Valentin Dallmeier, and Thomas Zimmermann. How documentation evolves over time. In *IWPSE '07: Ninth international workshop on Principles of software evolution*, pages 4–10, New York, NY, USA, 2007. ACM.

[145] Selenium, Aug, 2021. https://www.selenium.dev/.

[146] Khaironi Yatim Sharif and Jim Buckley. Developing schema for open source programmers' information-seeking. In *Information Technology, 2008. ITSim 2008. International Symposium on*, volume 1, pages 1–9. IEEE, 2008.

[147] Khaironi Yatim Sharif, Mohd Rosmadi Mokhtar, and Jim Buckley. Open source programmers' information seeking during software maintenance. *Journal of Computer Science*, 7(7):1060–1071, 2011.

[148] Yusuke Shinyama, Yoshitaka Arahori, and Katsuhiko Gondow. Analyzing code comments to boost program comprehension. In *2018 25th Asia-Pacific Software Engineering Conference (APSEC)*, pages 325–334. IEEE, 2018.

[149] Andrew J Simmons, Scott Barnett, Jessica Rivera-Villicana, Akshat Bajaj, and Rajesh Vasa. A large-scale comparative analysis of coding standard conformance in open-source data science projects. In *Proceedings of the 14th ACM/IEEE International Symposium on Empirical Software Engineering and Measurement (ESEM)*, pages 1–11, 2020.

[150] Michael Smit, Barry Gergel, and H James Hoover. Code convention adherence in evolving software. In *2011 27th IEEE International Conference on Software Maintenance (ICSM)*, pages 504–507. IEEE, 2011.

[151] Michael Smit, Barry Gergel, H James Hoover, and Eleni Stroulia. Maintainability and source code conventions: An analysis of open source projects. *University of Alberta, Department of Computing Science, Tech. Rep. TR11*, 6, 2011.

[152] Quinten David Soetens, Romain Robbes, and Serge Demeyer. Changes as first-class citizens: A research perspective on modern software tooling. *ACM Comput. Surv.*, 50(2):18:1–18:38, April 2017.

[153] SM Sohan, Frank Maurer, Craig Anslow, and Martin P Robillard. A study of the effectiveness of usage examples in rest api documentation. In *2017 IEEE Symposium on Visual Languages and Human-Centric Computing (VL/HCC)*, pages 53–61. IEEE, 2017.

[154] Xiaotao Song, Hailong Sun, Xu Wang, and Jiafei Yan. A survey of automatic generation of source code comments: Algorithms and techniques. *IEEE Access*, 7:111411–111428, 2019.

[155] Diomidis Spinellis. Code documentation. *IEEE software*, 27(4):18–19, 2010.

[156] Stack Exchange, 2021. https://data.stackexchange.com/.

[157] Stack Overflow, Aug, 2021. https://www.stackoverflow.com.

[158] Sean Stapleton, Yashmeet Gambhir, Alexander LeClair, Zachary Eberhart, Westley Weimer, Kevin Leach, and Yu Huang. A human study of comprehension and code summarization. In *ICPC '20: 28th International Conference on Program Comprehension, Seoul, Republic of Korea, July 13-15, 2020*, pages 2–13. ACM, 2020.

[159] Daniela Steidl, Benjamin Hummel, and Elmar Juergens. Quality analysis of source code comments. In *Program Comprehension (ICPC), 2013 IEEE 21st International Conference on*, pages 83–92. IEEE, 2013.

[160] Margaret-Anne Storey, Jody Ryall, R Ian Bull, Del Myers, and Janice Singer. Todo or to bug. In *2008 ACM/IEEE 30th International Conference on Software Engineering*, pages 251–260. IEEE, 2008.

[161] Lin Tan, Ding Yuan, Gopal Krishna, and Yuanyuan Zhou. /* iComment: Bugs or bad comments?*/. In *Proceedings of twenty-first ACM SIGOPS symposium on Operating systems principles*, pages 145–158, 2007.

[162] Shin Hwei Tan, Darko Marinov, Lin Tan, and Gary T Leavens. @tcomment: Testing Javadoc Comments to Detect Comment-Code Inconsistencies. In *2012 IEEE Fifth International Conference on Software Testing, Verification and Validation*, pages 260–269. IEEE, 2012.

[163] TIOBE Index, last accessed on Dec, 2021. https://www.tiobe.com/tiobe-index/.

[164] Kristín Fjóla Tómasdóttir, Mauricio Aniche, and Arie van Deursen. Why and how JavaScript developers use linters. In *2017 32nd IEEE/ACM International Conference on Automated Software Engineering (ASE)*, pages 578–589. IEEE, 2017.

[165] Federico Tomassetti and Marco Torchiano. An empirical assessment of polyglot-ism in GitHub. In *Proceedings of the 18th International Conference on Evaluation and Assessment in Software Engineering*, pages 1–4, 2014.

[166] Martin Törngren and Ulf Sellgren. *Complexity Challenges in Development of Cyber-Physical Systems*, pages 478–503. Springer International Publishing, Cham, 2018.

[167] Mario Triola. *Elementary Statistics*. Addison-Wesley, 2006.

[168] Gias Uddin and Foutse Khomh. Automatic mining of opinions expressed about APIs in Stack Overflow. *IEEE Transactions on Software Engineering*, 2019.

[169] Marcello Visconti and Curtis R Cook. Assessing the state of software documentation practices. In *International Conference on Product Focused Software Process Improvement*, pages 485–496. Springer, 2004.

[170] Hanna M Wallach, David M Mimno, and Andrew McCallum. Rethinking lda: Why priors matter. In *Advances in neural information processing systems*, pages 1973–1981, 2009.

[171] Yao Wan, Zhou Zhao, Min Yang, Guandong Xu, Haochao Ying, Jian Wu, and Philip S. Yu. Improving automatic source code summarization via deep reinforcement learning. In *Proceedings of the 33rd ACM/IEEE International Conference on Automated Software Engineering*, ASE 2018, pages 397–407, New York, NY, USA, 2018. Association for Computing Machinery.

[172] Gang Wang, Konark Gill, Manish Mohanlal, Haitao Zheng, and Ben Y Zhao. Wisdom in the social crowd: an analysis of quora. In *Proceedings of the 22nd international conference on World Wide Web*, pages 1341–1352, 2013.

[173] Shaowei Wang, David Lo, and Lingxiao Jiang. An empirical study on developer interactions in Stack Overflow. In *Proceedings of the 28th Annual ACM Symposium on Applied Computing*, SAC '13, pages 1019–1024, New York, NY, USA, 2013. ACM.

[174] Zhiyi Wang and Jungpil Hahn. The effects of programming style on open source collaboration. In Yong Jin Kim, Ritu Agarwal, and Jae Kyu Lee, editors, *Proceedings of the International Conference on Information Systems- Transforming Society with Digital Innovation, ICIS 2017, Seoul,South Korea, December 10-13, 2017*. Association for Information Systems, 2017.

[175] Weka, 2021. http://waikato.github.io/weka/.

[176] Fengcai Wen, Csaba Nagy, Gabriele Bavota, and Michele Lanza. A large-scale empirical study on code-comment inconsistencies. In *Proceedings of the 27th International Conference on Program Comprehension*, pages 53–64. IEEE Press, 2019.

[177] Claes Wohlin. Guidelines for snowballing in systematic literature studies and a replication in software engineering. In *18th International Conference on Evaluation and Assessment in Software Engineering, EASE 2014*, pages 38:1–38:10. ACM, 2014.

[178] Scott N Woodfield, Hubert E Dunsmore, and Vincent Yun Shen. The effect of modularization and comments on program comprehension. In *Proceedings of the 5th international conference on Software engineering*, pages 215–223. IEEE Press, 1981.

[179] Xin-Li Yang, David Lo, Xin Xia, Zhi-Yuan Wan, and Jian-Ling Sun. What security questions do developers ask? A large-scale study of Stack Overflow posts. *Journal of Computer Science and Technology*, 31(5):910–924, 2016.

[180] Annie T. T. Ying, James L. Wright, and Steven Abrams. Source code that talks: An exploration of Eclipse task comments and Their Implication to repository mining. *SIGSOFT Softw. Eng. Notes*, 30(4):1–5, May 2005.

[181] Annie TT Ying and Martin P Robillard. Selection and presentation practices for code example summarization. In *Proceedings of the 22nd ACM SIGSOFT International Symposium on Foundations of Software Engineering*, pages 460–471, 2014.

[182] Jingyi Zhang, Lei Xu, and Yanhui Li. Classifying python code comments based on supervised learning. In Xiaofeng Meng, Ruixuan Li, Kanliang Wang, Baoning Niu, Xin Wang, and Gansen Zhao, editors, *Web Information Systems and Applications - 15th International Conference, WISA 2018, Taiyuan, China, September 14-15, 2018, Proceedings*, volume 11242 of *Lecture Notes in Computer Science*, pages 39–47. Springer, 2018.

[183] Junji Zhi, Vahid Garousi-Yusifoğlu, Bo Sun, Golara Garousi, Shawn Shahnewaz, and Guenther Ruhe. Cost, benefits and quality of software development documentation: A systematic mapping. *Journal of Systems and Software*, 99:175–198, 2015.

[184] Hao Zhong, Tao Xie, Lu Zhang, Jian Pei, and Hong Mei. MAPO: Mining and recommending API usage patterns. In Sophia Drossopoulou, editor, *ECOOP 2009 - Object-Oriented Programming*, volume 5653 of *Lecture Notes in Computer Science*, pages 318–343. Springer Berlin Heidelberg, 2009.

[185] Yu Zhou, Ruihang Gu, Taolue Chen, Zhiqiu Huang, Sebastiano Panichella, and Harald Gall. Analyzing APIs documentation and code to detect directive defects. In *Proceedings of the 39th International Conference on Software Engineering*, pages 27–37. IEEE Press, 2017.

Bibliography

www.ingramcontent.com/pod-product-compliance
Lightning Source LLC
Chambersburg PA
CBHW040520220526
45473CB00013B/2932